W9-BLX-240

SUCCESSFUL FIRST DEPOSITIONS

Fourth Edition

■ ■ ■

Bradley G. Clary
Clinical Professor
University of Minnesota Law School
Minneapolis, Minnesota

Sharon Reich Paulsen
Chief of Staff and Senior Counsel to the President
University of Vermont
Burlington, Vermont

Michael J. Vanselow
Adjunct Professor
University of Minnesota Law School
Minneapolis, Minnesota

AMERICAN CASEBOOK SERIES®

444 Cedar Street, Suite 700
St. Paul, MN 55101
1-877-888-1330

Printed in the United States of America

ISBN: 978-1-68328-234-1

DEDICATIONS

To Rich, a fine lawyer and
an even better brother.
B.G.C.

To my father.
S.R.P.

To my mother.
M.J.V.

ACKNOWLEDGMENTS

The authors gratefully acknowledge the contributions of numerous individuals and organizations to the publication of this book.

The West Group (now West Academic), including Douglas Powell and Pamela Siege Chandler in particular, graciously decided in a burst of enthusiasm following the publication of a previous book, to permit us to write and publish this book. (By the way, in case you and others are interested, our previous book is entitled *Advocacy on Appeal*. It deals with appeals.)

Susan Miller and Michelle Jacobs Tillman provided invaluable typing assistance and management of the manuscript. University of Minnesota Law School students Janelle Ibeling (first edition), Joshua Heggem (second edition), and Mark Thomson (third edition) offered critical research assistance dealing with our many and sometimes wacky research requests. Erin Hendel provided additional formatting assistance for the first edition, as did University of Minnesota Law School student Michael Wilson.

Mark Olson of the Oppenheimer Wolff & Donnelly (now merged into Fox Rothschild) law firm and Professor Maury Landsman of the University of Minnesota Law School were most generous with their helpful reviews of our book and their kind discretion to be gentle, even as they freely offered suggestions from their many years of practice and teaching experience. Mark Olson provided special assistance with the chapter on expert depositions.

Arthur H. Cobb, Dr. George Logan, Michael Logan, and Craig Roen provided generous and insightful help in preparing parts of one of the case problems used in the book.

We also wish to acknowledge the many lawyers, judges, and professors who taught us what we know about depositions that we did not learn ourselves through some of our own good and not so good deposition experiences. In particular, Mitchell Hamline School of Law Professors Peter Knapp and Roger Haydock taught us much about teaching deposition practice and that one can retain a sense of humor even after one acquires a license to practice law.

Special thanks for the loving patience of our families, who maintained their good humor throughout this project, even as we may have, at times, lost ours.

Finally, we would be remiss if we did not thank Pierre Depose, the French inventor of the deposition, without whom this book would not have been possible.

The views we express are our own and we take responsibility for any failings that others may perceive in this book except, of course, if those others are wrong (which we hereby reserve the sole discretion to decide).

SUMMARY OF CONTENTS

TABLE OF CONTENTS

CHAPTER 3

CHAPTER 8

CHAPTER 9

PREFACE

This is a handbook on depositions. It is intended to be a short, convenient, and ready reference for law students and new attorneys preparing to take and defend their first depositions. It also may serve as a handy refresher for more senior attorneys who take and defend depositions on a more intermittent basis. The book is based on the collective seventy-four years of practice and law school teaching experience of the authors. While we do not claim that everything you will ever want to know about depositions is in this book, we can say with confidence that if you study this book, you will be well prepared to take and defend successful first depositions. Hence, the name of the book.

Why would you want to read this book instead of, say, another Scott Turow novel? In a survey of litigators, 92 percent rated depositions as "extremely important" or "very important."[1] At the same time, 57 percent said they received no classroom training before taking their first deposition, and 60 percent had no deposition practice or rehearsal time before taking their first deposition.[2] One of us, sent off as a new attorney to take a deposition without having read about or observed any depositions, averted certain disaster only due to the kindness of a court reporter who patiently and privately answered dozens of questions about the mechanics of taking a deposition (e.g., "How do I start the deposition?", "How can I get the witness to show me the route she drove that morning?", and "By the way, what is it you do at one of these things?"). The author avoided the finals of "America's Funniest First Depositions," and the court reporter undoubtedly enjoyed a few laughs.

To help you avoid flirting with disaster, this book starts at the beginning. Chapter 1 discusses "The Big Picture," including the various purposes depositions serve. One of the keys to a successful deposition is understanding how it fits in the overall scheme of the case. Attorneys take far too many mindless and inevitably unsuccessful depositions because they lack an overall game plan. Chapter 2 contains all the basics regarding how to prepare for and take a

---

[1] Mieke Biesheuvel, The Adequacy of Deposition Training: Should Law Schools Undertake To Do What Law Firms Fail To Do? 6 (October 2003) (draft), http://www.law.ucla.edu/docs/biesheuvel-depotraining-oct2003.pdf.

[2] *Id.* at 9-10.

deposition, including logistics, mechanics, strategy, and tactical advice. Chapter 3 deals with preparing the deponent to be deposed – a crucial aspect of deposition training. Chapter 4 discusses the defense of a deposition – how to protect the deponent and the record within the confines of the rules. Chapter 5 is especially valuable for newer attorneys. It talks about how to deal with difficult witnesses and difficult attorneys, such as the forgetful witness and the belligerent opposing counsel. Chapter 6 deals with expert witness depositions and includes a model expert witness outline. Chapter 7 discusses the various ways in which depositions can be used. This important information affects strategy decisions regarding whether and how to take certain depositions. Chapter 8 discusses several miscellaneous deposition practice topics such as the ethical propriety of compensating fact witnesses to be deposed and emerging new technological advances in deposition practices, including Internet depositions. The final chapter outlines some of the important intricacies of the applicable procedural rules, including not only the mechanics, but also useful tactical advice.

We also have prepared an accompanying Teacher's Manual that can be used in connection with a law school or in-house deposition training course. The manual contains the confidential parts of three case problems that can be used to teach deposition practice. The manual is designed to provide in one place everything a law professor or law firm needs to teach an introductory depositions course, including exercises and critique forms. Most law schools historically have devoted minimal attention to teaching deposition practice. Students may hear about depositions in civil procedure class, but little or nothing is taught about the actual mechanics, the strategic decisions that need to be made, and such real world problems as how to deal with difficult witnesses and lawyers. Likewise, gone are the days when law firms teach new lawyers about deposition practice by having them tag along with senior attorneys for a couple of years. Young lawyers are expected to hit the ground running.

And thus, the genesis of this book, *Successful First Depositions*. Read it, practice with it, and be successful.

B. G. C.
S. R. P.
M. J. V.

PREFACE TO THE FOURTH EDITION

Although much of our practical advice regarding depositions has not changed over the years, some of the federal rules have. Moreover, new case law has developed, and some subjects, such as discovery related to electronic data, have become increasingly important. We have updated the materials in this Fourth Edition accordingly. Read it, practice with it, and be successful.

B. G. C.
S. R. P.
M. J. V.

SUCCESSFUL FIRST DEPOSITIONS

Fourth Edition

CHAPTER 1

The Big Picture

A. Begin at the End – Victory

Remember Always

- Depositions are a means to an end
- That end is to obtain facts to win your lawsuit

A deposition is not merely an item to cross off of a litigation preparation checklist. Properly used, a deposition can be a powerful and indispensable pretrial discovery tool. One of the biggest mistakes lawyers can make – and all too frequently do make – is to mechanically schedule depositions without a proper plan. "The rules say we can take depositions, so we better take one." Then the deposition goes into a file drawer until trial, if there is one.

You do not take depositions simply because they are available. You take them to get facts or to get leads to facts. And you want those facts to win your client's lawsuit. Everything you do in discovery, including your deposition strategy, should be aimed at an ultimate litigation victory, by trial or summary judgment. (If the facts do not support a victory, settle the case as favorably as you can, and get out!)

Let us begin our discussion of depositions, then, where any such discussion *must* begin – at the end. Before you take or defend any deposition, you should have a blueprint for your lawsuit. That blueprint will be the architectural plan for your case, and will describe the following building blocks and construction notes.

First, lawsuits are about alleged wrongs to be made right. Lawsuits have themes, either "goods" to be preserved and rewarded (such as loyalty, responsibility, and trust), or "bads" to be prevented and remedied (such as recklessness, laziness, and abuse).[3] So what are the themes in your lawsuit, on both sides of the case?

Second, all lawsuits involve stories. Somehow something happened. Events unfolded in a particular sequence. People did or did not do various things. Those things were good or bad. So what are the basic stories, on both sides of your case?[4]

Third, all lawsuits involve claims and defenses. Those in turn all involve component legal elements. In a simple breach of contract case, there must first be a contract, then a breach, and then a foreseeable injury flowing from the breach. In a simple tort negligence case, there must first be a duty of care owed by the defendant to the plaintiff, then a breach of that duty and an injury directly caused

---

[3] BRADLEY G. CLARY, SHARON REICH PAULSEN, & MICHAEL J. VANSELOW, ADVOCACY ON APPEAL 6 (3d ed. 2008); *cf.* James W. McElhaney, *Clutter*, A.B.A. J., Mar. 1991, at 73.

[4] *See, e.g.*, James W. McElhaney, *Craft a Dynamic Direct*, A.B.A. J., July 2001, at 52.

by the breach. So what are the elements of the claims and defenses on both sides of your case?

Fourth, all legal claims and defenses depend upon the existence or non-existence of certain combinations of facts. Contracts are formed when certain promissory bargains take place. Tort duties of care arise when people stand in certain relationships to each other. So what combinations of facts need to exist for the claims and defenses to prevail on both sides of your case?

Fifth, facts are proven by evidence. Evidence comes in multiple forms. There are witness recollections. There are business records. There are photographs. There are tape recordings. There are journal entries. There are models. There are letters and memoranda. There are computer graphics. There are all kinds of factual bits. So what kinds of evidentiary items will prove the facts on both sides of your case?

Sixth, and of special importance for deposition practice, if your evidence comes in the form of witness testimony, recognize that witnesses are of many types. There will be parties. There will be outside observers. There will be experts. Some will be favorable, some hostile, and some neutral. So who are all the potential witnesses in your lawsuit, on both sides of the case?

Finally, not all evidence will have equal value. Some will be helpful, some not. Some will be expressly and obviously probative of an important fact, some not. Some will be admissible in court, some not. So what is the value of each piece of evidence in your lawsuit, on both sides of the case?

LITIGATION WORKING BLUEPRINT

A. Our Theme:	A. Their Likely Theme:
______________	______________
______________	______________
B. Our Story:	B. Their Likely Story:
______________	______________
______________	______________
C. Our Legal Elements:	C. Their Legal Elements:
______________	______________
______________	______________
D. Our Key Facts:	D. Their Key Facts:
______________	______________
______________	______________
E. Our Evidence: (Including Type and Value)	E. Their Evidence: (Including Type and Value)
______________	______________
______________	______________

B. Consider Deposition Advantages and Disadvantages

Before noticing any deposition, you should assess your reasons for and the timing of the deposition to convince yourself that the advantages of taking the deposition outweigh the disadvantages. In those jurisdictions that limit the number of depositions allowed, it is especially important to assess in advance your overall deposition strategy together with the potential advantages and disadvantages of any given deposition you are considering in relation to other investigative and formal discovery options.

1. Advantages

Depositions offer many potential advantages. They provide an opportunity to observe and assess the deponent; they provide an opportunity to get the deponent's answers in the deponent's words, rather than the more carefully crafted and edited responses of an attorney; they provide the opportunity for immediate follow-up questions; and they provide the opportunity to preserve the testimony of witnesses who may be unavailable at the time or place of the trial. Depositions also may provide the opportunity to educate the other party about certain strengths of your case. When settlement appears to be the most advantageous avenue for resolving a dispute, a strong deposition can be an enormously persuasive means of enhancing your settlement posture.

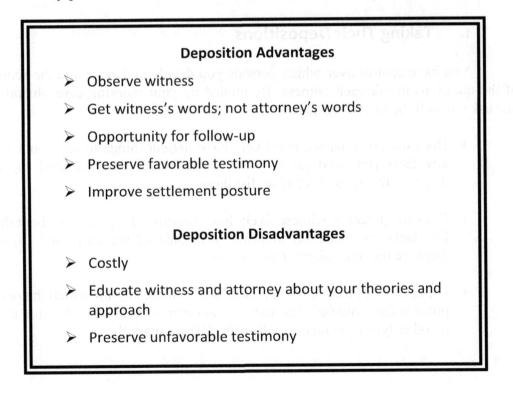

Deposition Advantages

- Observe witness
- Get witness's words; not attorney's words
- Opportunity for follow-up
- Preserve favorable testimony
- Improve settlement posture

Deposition Disadvantages

- Costly
- Educate witness and attorney about your theories and approach
- Preserve unfavorable testimony

2. Disadvantages

Depositions are costly endeavors. Lawyer time, court reporter costs, and potential travel costs can be substantial. Even more critically, there may be important non-monetary costs. A deposition may educate both the witness and opposing counsel of theories, approaches, or evidence that may not be to your strategic advantage to reveal, at least at certain early stages of a case. Remember also that the very features of a deposition that make it potentially advantageous can also work to your disadvantage. A deposition is under oath, it is preserved word-for-word, and the words are those of the witness rather than the attorney. If the testimony elicited during a deposition is unfavorable, you have now preserved it in a readily-accessible and highly persuasive form. It is especially critical to be cautious about depositions if you plan to file a dispositive motion. Unless you are confident the deposition will provide necessary fuel for your position, it may be best to wait until your motion is filed and ruled upon, if your pretrial schedule allows for such timing.

C. Consider the Specific Witnesses in Your Case

1. Taking Their Depositions

You have control over which persons you decide to depose and the scope of the questions to ask each witness. Be guided by your working case blueprint and ask yourself the following questions:

- Does the potential witness likely have *helpful* things to say about the key facts you need (a) to prove your side of the case, and (b) to disprove the other side? If so, list those.

- Does the potential witness likely have *negative* things to say about the key facts you need (a) to prove your side of the case, and (b) to disprove the other side? If so, list those.

- For each fact listed, either good or bad, is there any for which the *only* proof is that witness's testimony – no other witness's recollection and no other type of evidence will suffice? If so, mark those.

- For each fact listed, either good or bad, is there any for which the *most persuasive* proof is that witness's testimony – no other witness's recollection and no other type of evidence will do as well? If so, mark those.

- How likely is it that the potential witness will be available to testify by affidavit (for summary judgment purposes) or live (for trial purposes) if you forego a deposition? Consider the witness's health status, travel plans, potential job relocations, retirement status, and the like.

- How likely is it that the potential witness will be more or less friendly over time? For example, a witness who is happy to testify favorably today may be distinctly unhappy to do so six months from now when your client downsizes, and fires the witness and three of her closest friends.

- Does the potential witness likely have information you do not possess but that may be important to the development or assessment of your case?

- As to any given witness, is a deposition the only lawful or ethical way to talk to that person? Recall, for example, Rule 4.2 of the Model Rules of Professional Conduct and the comments to that Rule, which state that *ex parte* contact with certain kinds of employees of an adversary organization is unethical. A deposition may be your only option.

As you work through the above questions for each potential witness, it may be helpful to record your notes on a chart similar to the one that follows:

Name of Witness

Likely helpful facts:	Only proof?	Best proof?
____________	________	________
____________	________	________
____________	________	________

Likely negative facts:	Only proof?	Best proof?
____________	________	________
____________	________	________
____________	________	________

Will the witness be available? ________
Will the witness be friendly? ________

2. Defending Their Depositions

You do not have control over the depositions the other side chooses to take (short of obtaining a protective order under appropriate, limited circumstances). But you still should be guided by your working case blueprint and the above specific deposition strategy questions in deciding your overall course of action regarding two defensive tactical issues:

First, in general, how vigorously should you seek to preclude or limit the taking of depositions by your adversary? Is there a legitimate reason for a protective order (e.g., all of the key facts known by the witness are privileged or the number of depositions sought by the adversary is burdensome and harassing)? Are the facts known by the witness generally helpful or negative? Are you going to need to rely upon the witness yourself for some facts?

Second, in general, should you plan to cross-examine the witness at the deposition? How likely is it that the witness will be available to you later? How likely is it that the witness will be friendly or unfriendly later? How vital are the facts the witness possesses? How damaging will the current testimony likely be, and does the damage require on-the-spot rehabilitation? Will cross-examination prematurely tip your hand? Will cross-examination help position you for a quick and favorable settlement? Will cross-examination likely open the door to additional direct-examination that best is avoided?

D. Put Everything Together

Once you have completed all of the preceding steps, you are ready to think about your plan for each specific deposition in the case. The deposition is going to happen. What facts do you or the other side need to get from this witness and, of the ones you need, what facts, if any, should you get by deposition? The answers should flow from the side-by-side comparison of your overall blueprint and your charts. Only when you have finished this analysis are you ready to begin actually taking and defending the depositions. Techniques for these tasks are the subject of the rest of this handbook.

CHAPTER 2

Taking A Deposition

Once you have completed your litigation blueprint and determined your discovery strategy, you are ready to begin planning, preparing for, and taking depositions. In this chapter, we start with a discussion of deposition purposes, as the purpose for which you are taking a deposition will affect how you prepare for and how you approach the actual deposition. Following discussion of deposition purposes, we provide detail regarding how best to prepare for a deposition. Finally, we launch into information about the logistics of the deposition itself, along with much detail regarding questioning techniques.

A. Deposition Purposes and Styles

The purpose of your deposition will affect your style and approach. This is one of many reasons why you always need to determine in advance *why* you are taking any given deposition. Following are some of the common reasons for taking a deposition, along with a brief explanation regarding how your approach should vary in order to best meet your needs in any given situation. You also should be mindful that depositions may serve multiple purposes and that you may have to vary your style at different points in the deposition to best meet your goals.

1. Discover Information

The most common type of deposition is a discovery deposition. In a discovery deposition, the examining lawyer attempts to elicit as much information as possible from the deponent. The purpose primarily is investigatory. You want to discover everything the deponent knows that is related to your case. This information should include sources of proof, such as the identities of potential witnesses, documents, and physical evidence. The key thing to remember in a discovery deposition is that you are trying to obtain information of which you otherwise may be unaware.[5]

---

[5] The Federal Rules of Civil Procedure allow discovery regarding any nonprivileged matter "relevant to any party's claim or defense and proportional to the needs of the case." FED. R. CIV. P. 26(b)(1). The proportionality requirement invites consideration of "the importance of the issues at stake in the action, the amount in controversy, the parties' relative access to relevant information, the parties' resources, the importance of the discovery in resolving the issues, and whether the burden or expense of the proposed discovery outweighs its likely benefit." *Id.* The proportionality concept originally appeared as part of Rule 26(b)(1) in 1983, but proportionality factors were subsequently moved to other rule subparts until 2015, when proportionality language was reinserted in 26(b)(1). The reinsertion of proportionality factors replaced language that broadly allowed the discovery of any information that was "reasonably calculated to lead to the discovery of admissible evidence." While the re-emergence of the proportionality language in Rule 26(b)(1) may impact the allowable scope of and objections to demands made through other discovery methods, it is unlikely to have much effect on a typical discovery deposition being conducted in good faith, particularly given that other rules already limit the number and length of depositions. *See* FED. R. CIV. P. 30(a)(2)(A)(i), (d)(1).

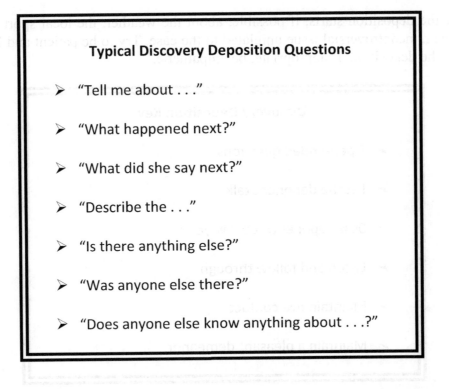

Typical Discovery Deposition Questions

- "Tell me about . . ."
- "What happened next?"
- "What did she say next?"
- "Describe the . . ."
- "Is there anything else?"
- "Was anyone else there?"
- "Does anyone else know anything about . . .?"

When your purpose is to elicit information, it is especially important to ask broad, open-ended questions. You want the deponent to talk and direct you to the paths you should pursue. Your questions should be short and open-ended; it is the deponent who should be talking in paragraphs. In the end, the transcript should be at least 90 percent the deponent and no more than 10 percent you. Be especially cautious about cutting off the deponent during a discovery deposition. If you are uncertain whether the deponent has completely finished answering, pause for a few seconds before posing your next question. Such a pause sometimes will cause the deponent to continue talking. If it does not, you may want to ask whether the witness has any more to add.

Your demeanor may be especially critical to the success of a discovery deposition. This type of deposition is most suited to a friendly, relaxed style. The saying, "you can catch more flies with honey than you can with vinegar," applies even to sophisticated deponents. You want the witness to like you and want to help you; at a minimum, you want the witness to trust you and let his or her guard down. To achieve this, smile and be pleasant when you introduce yourself. Chat before the deposition starts, if possible, about the weather, the local sports team, or some noncontroversial issue unrelated to the case. Try to be patient and helpful during the deposition. If appropriate, be empathetic.[6]

Discovery Deposition Key

- Open-ended questions
- Let the deponent talk
- 90% deponent/10% lawyer
- Listen and follow through
- Maintain eye contact
- Maintain a pleasant demeanor

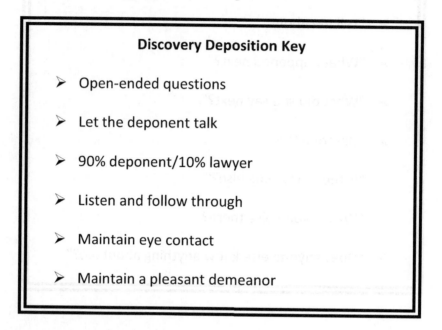

Listening, as always, is critical. So is maintaining eye contact. While the deponent is answering a question, jot down very brief notes (a word or two) regarding areas to pursue in more detail. Do not let note taking interfere with maintaining eye contact. Once you break eye contact the witness may stop talking. Similarly, maintaining eye contact without interruption may encourage the witness to continue providing information.

Once you are certain there is nothing else to elicit on a given question, then it is time for follow-up. It generally is least confusing and most effective to exhaust all follow-through questions in one area before going on to the next. Each follow-up question on a particular subject should get progressively narrower.

[6] One commentator who ascribes to this view of taking depositions advises that you, as the deposing attorney, treat the witness as you would a guest in your home, that you develop a genuine interest in the witness, that you be self-effacing to let the witness see you as a "regular" person, that you periodically compliment the witness, and that you ask the witness for help in understanding the events at issue. Edward G. Connette, *How to Take Better Depositions and Perhaps Improve Your Marriage*, LITIG., Spring 2005, at 3, 7-8.

What you should end up with is an answer tree. For example, one answer, like the trunk of a tree, may lead to four different large branches to follow. It is best to follow through completely to the end of one major branch, including all the twigs sprouting along the way, before you return to the trunk and proceed down another major branch. What you will end up with is a transcript that will be packed full of information that will be useful to you, but it will not be a narrative that you would want to read to a jury.

2. Pin the Deponent Down

Frequently, you not only will want to discover information from the deponent, but you also will want to pin the deponent down and to commit the deponent unequivocally to a particular position, theory, or version of the facts. Sometimes you already will have the information you need and your sole purpose may be to commit the deponent. One reason to do this is for use in a dispositive motion. Another reason is to commit a witness or party to their testimony before they hear or become aware of testimony, information, or theories you intend to propound through other witnesses and other sources.

When you want to pin down your deponent, your questioning style must change. Rather than broad, brief, open-ended questions, you will want to ask narrow and more directed questions. The idea is to commit the deponent and to foreclose any possibility of the deponent testifying at a later date to something new or different without obviously contradicting the earlier deposition testimony.

Key to Pinning Down the Deponent

- Use progressively narrower questions
- Foreclose all possible escape routes
- Use leading questions before concluding
- Be serious and more assertive

The style best suited to pinning down a deponent generally is a serious, formal, and more assertive style, similar to the style you might use during cross-examination. Maintain a serious tone and demeanor, be especially vigilant about maintaining steady eye contact, even to the extent that you do not look at your pad to write notes, and consider picking up the pace of your questions. You do not necessarily need to be hostile or unpleasant; generally, it is best not to start out that way. If the witness is hostile or remains nonresponsive, then you may transition to a more aggressive and less patient style.[7] It is difficult, however, to move convincingly from an aggressive style to the pleasant kind of style that is more suited to general information gathering. The witness is unlikely to see you as warm and friendly after you have been stern and confrontational. Therefore, especially if you also are using your deposition for broad discovery purposes, consider deferring these cross-examination type questions until later in the deposition.

3. Get Admissions for Dispositive Motions

One productive use of a deposition is to get admissions for a dispositive motion. It frequently is easier and more effective to use a deposition for this purpose than it is to use interrogatories or requests for admissions. In a deposition, you get the witness's own words rather than brief responses crafted by a lawyer. In a deposition, you also can immediately follow through, clarify, and pin down the witness through a progressive series of questions tailored to the witness's responses.

---

[7] Sometimes, your best laid plans to invoke this style may backfire. One lawyer, in an effort to exhibit stern body language while deposing a hostile witness, leaned forward on his elbows with his hands clasped in front of his face. Unfortunately, the peanut butter on his suit sleeve from his son's breakfast ruined the effect.

Key to Getting Useful Admissions

- Research elements of claims/defenses
- Checklist admissions you need
- Design questions to elicit necessary facts/admissions
- Use precise, clear questions
- Lead, if necessary
- Do not linger once admission is obtained
- Consider timing admissions questions to catch witness off guard

To use a deposition in this way, there are a few things to keep in mind. First, you should research the legal bases for your claims or defenses in advance so you know before the deposition begins precisely what you will need from the deposition in order to support a dispositive motion. In contrast to a discovery deposition, you should know exactly where you want to take the witness, and your questions should be designed to do so in much the same way you would design them to prove points during a trial. Make a list of the precise points you need the deponent to make or confirm. Again, in contrast to a discovery deposition, you do not want to linger; once the witness makes the desired statement clearly on the record, move on to something else. The longer you linger, the more likely it is that the clarity of your record will be spoiled.

You will want to use a demeanor similar to that recommended for pinning down the deponent, including using cross-examination type questions. Frequently, it is useful to disguise some of the questions seeking admissions by asking them at unexpected times during the deposition. By varying your approach, you may avoid more guarded and qualified responses from the deponent as well as an avalanche of objections from opposing counsel.

4. Preserve Trial Testimony

There are several circumstances under which you may need to take a deposition to preserve trial testimony. These situations include when you have a witness who is expected to be unavailable for trial, a witness who is beyond the reach of a trial subpoena, or a witness who is ill and may become unavailable.

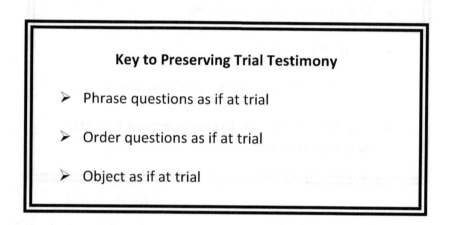

Key to Preserving Trial Testimony

- Phrase questions as if at trial
- Order questions as if at trial
- Object as if at trial

When taking a deposition to preserve trial testimony, you must craft your questions as you would for trial, and you should maintain a trial-like style. Remember that if you ask an objectionable question and fail to rephrase it upon receiving an objection, the testimony that you elicit may be excluded at trial and you will have no opportunity at that point to correct your error. Similarly, if you are defending such a deposition, you must be especially vigilant about objections during the deposition in order to preserve your right to object at trial.

5. Assess the Witness

Although assessing the witness rarely is the exclusive purpose of a deposition, it always should be one of your goals. What is the witness's general demeanor? Nervous, calm, arrogant, confident, suspicious, aggressive, meek, emotional, dispassionate, phony, genuine? How does the witness react to and answer questions? Is the witness direct? Is the witness evasive? Does the witness try to obfuscate the truth? Does the witness ramble? Does the witness need to be drawn out? Does the witness answer your question?

This opportunity to assess witnesses can be invaluable. It will give you a sense of how a jury or judge may react to a witness. It will give you a sense in advance of how you may need to alter your style at trial for a particular witness. It will help inform your assessment of your case and where the appropriate settlement line lies.

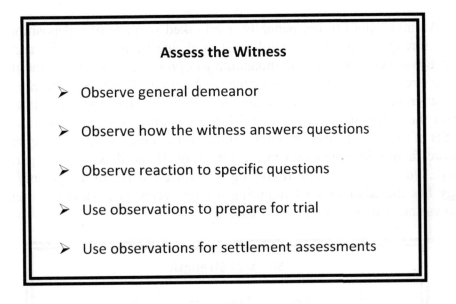

Assess the Witness

- Observe general demeanor
- Observe how the witness answers questions
- Observe reaction to specific questions
- Use observations to prepare for trial
- Use observations for settlement assessments

In addition to assessing a witness's general reaction to questions, it is important to observe reactions to individual questions during the course of the deposition. Does a particular question have a different effect on a witness? Does the witness's body language change? Is a chatty witness suddenly giving short or abrupt answers? Is the witness evasive? These reactions provide important indications of areas that may need additional follow-through.

It is equally important to assess your own witness when you are defending a deposition. You can use this information for the same purposes described above, but additionally to help prepare the witness for trial. An important witness's demeanor can have an enormous effect on the outcome of a trial, and it can have an especially material effect if the witness is a party or related to a party (for example, an officer of a corporate defendant). Even when the facts are with you, the unlikeable demeanor of an important witness can affect not only the measure of damages, but also the question of liability itself. Keep in mind that some people appear to have a completely different personality when answering questions posed by an opposing attorney. Defending a deposition may be your only opportunity to observe how your own witnesses react to such questioning.

6. Show of Strength

An important but occasionally overlooked purpose of a deposition is as a show of strength. Through carefully selected questions or exhibits and strong, favorable witnesses, you can demonstrate to opposing counsel and the opposing party the strength of your position or the weakness of their own. You can then use this as leverage in your settlement discussions. Given the costs associated with a trial and the inherent risks that a trial brings, it may be best to preview certain strengths of your case through a deposition in the hope of encouraging an earlier and more favorable conclusion to the litigation. If the deposition is particularly effective, you may consider following it with an offer of judgment.[8] Such a strategy has the advantage of requiring a quick response, while the memory of your devastating deposition is still fresh.

Show of Strength

- Use questions to show your strength
- Use questions to show the witness's weaknesses
- Use exhibits to reveal favorable evidence
- Consider following the deposition with an offer of judgment

[8] *See* FED. R. CIV. P. 68.

B. Preparation

Lawyers preparing to take a deposition should review the case file and formulate an outline.[9]

1. File Review

Review your file, including your overall litigation blueprint. What is each party's case theory? What are the elements of the claims and defenses? What is each party's story? What proof is already in hand? What will this witness add or subtract?

2. Question Outline

Once you have reviewed your file and blueprint, you should prepare a fairly detailed outline of questions for the particular witness. This outline may take a number of different forms. Some lawyers write out specific questions. This is particularly desirable in two instances. The first involves hypotheticals directed to expert witnesses. The second involves questions that will set up dispositive motions. In both cases, you want to ensure that the questions do not omit key facts that later give the other side room to disavow deposition answers.

Other lawyers simply prepare lists of topics to cover. They fear the loss of spontaneity and the risk of inadequate follow through that comes from having questions fully written out. Deposition outlines are not television scripts.

Either approach can be made to work most of the time. Pick the one that suits your comfort level. Generally, we prefer the outline approach, *except* when setting up an expert or a claim or defense for a dispositive motion, because it tends to better enable the questioning lawyer to listen carefully to the deponent and re-order questions or depart temporarily from the prepared outline entirely. Some attorneys use a separate page or set of notecards for each topic of their outline. This can be a useful technique to reorder the topics during the deposition. If, for example, the witness gets into another topic the questioning attorney was not intending to address until later, the attorney can consider turning directly and

---

[9] There is a helpful four-page summary of what lawyers should do in preparing to take a deposition in James W. McElhaney, *The Deposition Notebook*, LITIG., Summer 2001, at 55.

immediately to the separate part of the attorney's outline dealing with that topic rather than circling back to the witness's response and that topic later in the deposition.

To free yourself to listen and follow through, you need to have a way of recording answers. One device is to leave space in your outline underneath each question or topic to record an answer in shorthand. Another device is to write each question or topic on the left half of a page, and then leave space on the right half for the associated response. Yet another device is to count on a colleague to sit through the deposition and keep careful notes to help ensure that you have adequately exhausted each line of inquiry.

Again, any of these approaches can work. You just need to ensure that, if you have predetermined that you need to get five key pieces of testimony from the particular deponent, you have a way to check that you have actually obtained those five pieces before you adjourn the deposition.

3. Notices and Subpoenas

Your deposition will not take place unless you issue proper notice to obtain the attendance of the witness and to alert opposing counsel. The notice rules are described in Federal Rule of Civil Procedure 30(b) and in Chapter 9 of this book. Make sure you follow them. A notice goes to every party in the litigation.[10]

If the deponent is not a party to the lawsuit, make sure you *also* subpoena the witness. The rules for subpoenas are described in Federal Rules of Civil Procedure 45(a) and (b) and in Chapter 9. If you issue a subpoena that calls for production of documents from the witness, be sure to attach a copy of the document production description to the notice that you have served on the parties, under Federal Rule of Civil Procedure 30(b).

---

10 Throughout this handbook, we will be referring to the Federal Rules of Civil Procedure. Be aware that not all states use the same rules, and even states that use the federal rules as a model may adopt their own unique variations of the federal rules. Moreover, even federal courts have various local rules and practices. Find out what they are or risk serious consequences.

4. Miscellaneous Logistics

There are a number of logistical details you need to arrange when you take a deposition:

- Arrange for the court reporter. The deposition cannot proceed if you neglect to arrange for the attendance of a court reporter.[11]

- Reserve the conference room. You need a distraction-free space in which to take the deposition. The space needs to be big enough to accommodate all of the people who will be attending. In some cases, that will be you, one opposing lawyer, the witness, and the court reporter. In others, it will be you, an army of other lawyers, the witness, the witness's boss, party representatives, and the court reporter. In still others, it will be you, one opposing lawyer, the witness, the court reporter, and a videographer whose equipment takes up more room than the people do. Be especially cautious about reserving an appropriately sized and configured room if the deposition is taking place out of town and consequently out of your office.

- Arrange for the videographer. If you are going to videotape the deposition, you need to reserve a videographer. This person may be employed by an entirely different company than the court reporter, and requires his or her own separate reservation.

- Arrange for sufficient copies of deposition exhibits. Select in advance a universe of documents that you may show the witness as possible exhibits. You need copies for the court reporter to mark as the official exhibits. You need duplicate clean copies for the other lawyers (at least one set for each party). You need annotated copies for yourself to use in questioning the witness. Organize these copies so they are readily at hand.

- Arrange for refreshments. It is customary and helpful to have at least water, coffee, and soft drinks at depositions. Mouths get dry. Energy levels fail.

---

[11] *See* FED. R. CIV. P. 28(a), 30(b)(3).

- Arrange for lunches. Time tables may be tight. You and the other attendees may want to have lunch brought in to the deposition, take a short break, and resume. Think about that in advance.

- Arrange for travel. If a deposition is out of town, this may mean air tickets, hotel reservations, and rental cars. It also may mean advance shipment to the deposition site of all of those duplicate copies of exhibits that you otherwise will be hauling on the airplane. Think about all of this in advance. Double check everything to make sure people and documents arrive in the right place at the right time.

- Arrange for supplies: legal pads, pens, highlighters, stickers to tab documents or notes.

These are all obvious, you say. Yes and no. In calm, quiet moments they are obvious. In the press of day-to-day legal practice, they can be easy to forget. Here is a checklist. Use it for each deposition.

Deposition Logistics Checklist

Item	Arranged	Details
1. Court Reporter	___	___
2. Conference Room	___	___
3. Videographer	___	___
4. Exhibits	___	___
5. Refreshments	___	___
6. Lunch	___	___
7. Travel		
Air tickets	___	___
Hotel	___	___
Rental Car	___	___
8. Supplies	___	___

C. The Deposition

1. Introductory Remarks and Instructions

When you start a deposition, you should do at least the following:

First, have the court reporter swear in the witness. This will typically occur off the record, and then the court reporter will type at the start of the transcript that the witness has been duly sworn.

Example: *Ms. Court Reporter, would you please swear in the witness?*

Second, introduce who you are, and tell the deponent the name of the party you represent.

Example: *Good morning, Ms. Jones. We are here today to take your deposition in the Pardon v. ABC Railroad case. I am John McGreedy, the lawyer for Sam Pardon, who is the person bringing the suit.*

Third, ask if the witness has been deposed before. This helps you evaluate how much the deponent knows about the ground rules. If the witness has been deposed many times, then ask for the number. You may be dealing with a professional testifier, which is something you would want to know.

Example: *Q:* *Have you ever been deposed, Ms. Jones?*
A: *Once. [If the witness identifies multiple depositions then ask who, what, where, when, why questions to find out details.]*

Fourth, give the deponent some basic instructions.

Example: *[1] I am going to be asking you questions today about some of the matters involved in the case. The* *court reporter will take down everything we say and prepare a complete transcript of the deposition.*

[2] The transcript may be used at trial. So although there is no judge or jury sitting here today, you should testify with the same seriousness as if they were. You understand that you are under oath? [Get a "yes" from the deponent, so the witness has a difficult time later claiming a lack of appreciation for the solemnity of the deposition.]

[3] Because the court reporter is trying to take everything down, it will help if we each speak one at a time. I would appreciate it if you would let me finish each question before you start answering, and I will try not to talk over your answers. Okay? [Get a "yes" from the deponent.]

[4] Also, because the court reporter is trying to take everything down, it will help if you try to answer each question out loud with a oral response. It is hard for the court reporter to record nods of the head, and uh-huhs and uh-hums may be ambiguous. Okay? [Get a "yes" out loud from the deponent. It is not unusual for a witness to nod his or her head in response to your question, which presents you with a good opportunity to point out what you mean.]

[5] If you do not understand a question, please let me know that, and I will try to rephrase it. Will you do that? [Get a "yes" from the deponent.] If you do not ask me to rephrase a question, I will assume that you understand it. Okay? [Get a "yes" from the deponent, so the witness has a hard time later claiming confusion as to any particular question.]

> *[6] If you need to take a break at any time, please let me know. I may ask you to finish answering a particular question or series of questions before we break, but we can certainly pause from time to time. [This humanizes the process a bit, but add the admonition about finishing answers. You do not want the witness to take a break while a question is pending, and then cite your own opening invitation as a basis for doing so.]*
>
> *[7] Are you taking any medications that might affect your ability to recall events or to testify? [Not all lawyers use this question, because it is extremely personal and can negatively affect your rapport with the witness from the outset. On the other hand, if you expect no rapport with the witness anyway, or you have specific reason to wonder about witness competency, then go ahead and ask. The question is legitimate.]*
>
> *[8] Lawyers may state objections to questions at a deposition under the relevant court rules. Unless your lawyer expressly instructs you not to answer one of my questions, you must still answer it. A court will later decide whether the objection was well-taken.*[12]

2. General Questioning Techniques

a. Type of Witness

Now you are ready to move on to substantive questioning. When you do, think back to your case blueprint and witness charts. What kind of witness are you

[12] Reasonable lawyers may omit one or more of these introductory steps (except swearing in the witness) from time to time and instead launch immediately into substantive questions to catch the witness cold. Even then, these lawyers may go through this list with the witness a little later in the deposition.

facing? Is this a friendly witness – one who generally is aligned with your client's position in the case? Is this a neutral witness – for example, a bystander who happened to witness some event? Or is this a hostile witness – one who generally is aligned with your adversary's position in the case?

Deposition Question Categories

- Competency/Foundation
- Credibility/Bias
- Substance

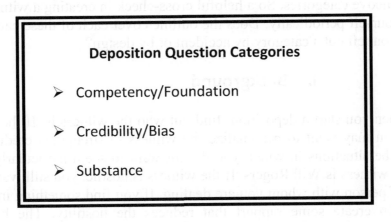

The type of witness you are facing affects your technique and approach to the deposition. Do you want the witness on a long leash or a short one? Do you want a conversation or a cross-examination? Will your own demeanor be relaxed or confrontational? Will you be content with general answers, or will you want to explore details extensively? Are you taking this deposition primarily to discover all kinds of facts, both good and bad, or primarily to preserve good facts in admissible form for trial?

In all likelihood, you will need to use some combination of techniques. For example, even though the deposition may be for fact exploration, you may want to use techniques that give you greater control over where the deponent's answers are heading in the case of a hostile witness than in the case of a friendly one. The point is: make a conscious decision about techniques. Go in with a plan.

b. What to Ask

Basically, every question you ask a witness falls into one or more of three categories. The first category is *competency/foundation.* Does the witness know anything relevant to the lawsuit, and can the witness recall and recount that information? The second category is *credibility/bias*. Can the witness be trusted when the witness claims to know something and to recall/recount that information? Finally, what is the *substance* of what the witness knows?

All of the questions below, and any other questions you may develop, fit one of the above categories. So a helpful cross-check in creating a witness outline is to ask yourself periodically: Does the outline cover each of these categories? If not, have you left out a category by accident or by design?

i. Background

When you start a deposition, find out who the witness is. If the witness is friendly, you may want to personalize the witness to strengthen credibility. Yet there may be situations in which you do not want to seem particularly friendly, even if the witness is Will Rogers. If the witness is hostile, you still want to know the kind of person with whom you are dealing. If you find something in common, it may help create some rapport that reduces the hostility. The background examination need not be long, but find out some basics.

Example: *Q: Ms. Jones, would you tell us your full name please?*
A: Amanda Sarah Jones.
Q: Where do you live?
A: 123 Main St., Capital City, State of Moot.
Q: How long have you lived there?
A: 16 years.
Q: How many years of schooling do you have?
A: I graduated from college, and have a master's degree in counseling.
Q: What kind of work do you do?
A: I am a high school counselor.
Q: Where?
A: Central City High School.
Q: Oh, I went there, graduated in 1970. How long have you been there?
A: I have been a counselor there since getting my master's degree in 1985.
Q: When did you get your undergraduate degree?

A: *1983.*
Q: *From what school?*
A: *Moot State University.*
Q: *Where did you get your master's?*
A: *Moot State University.*

Even from this short exchange, you have a definite impression of this witness. She has a stable background, does not move around a lot, is well-educated, and presumably likes analyzing problems and working with teenagers.

In some situations, background information can turn out to be especially important. Do not simply ask background questions by rote. Consider how a deponent's background relates to the case. For example, if a case involves financial records, ask about the deponent's college business and accounting courses. If a case involves advertising practices, ask about the deponent's marketing training. If a case involves a real estate sale, ask about the deponent's own experience in buying and selling homes. You might find out important substantive information or you might identify a bias.

ii. Inquiries about subpoenaed documents

If your subpoena included a request for documents, that should be an early area of inquiry. Some lawyers will handle this in advance of the actual deposition by agreeing with the deponent or the deponent's lawyer, if the witness is represented by counsel, that the witness's documents will be produced for inspection a day or two before the deposition starts. Advance production of the documents will make the whole deposition more efficient, which is to everyone's advantage. (It clearly is to your advantage as the lawyer taking the deposition. It also, frankly, is to the advantage of the defending lawyer. Although the defending attorney might think that the less efficient the deposition is the less the questioning attorney will accomplish, the defender also must take into account the value of the witness's time. The vice president of the defending lawyer's client will not take kindly to hearing from the questioning lawyer that the seven hour deposition could have taken only three if the defending lawyer had simply produced subpoenaed files in advance of the deposition, as requested.)

If advance production of documents cannot be arranged, an alternative is to bring a second lawyer or a legal assistant familiar with the lawsuit to the deposition to inspect the witness's document production and to cull out possible deposition exhibits, while the lead questioner proceeds on matters to which the documents do not necessarily relate. If attendance of a second lawyer or a legal assistant is not feasible, yet another alternative is to inspect the documents over a break or lunch.

In any event, always question the deponent near the outset of the deposition about the scope of the witness's search for documents:

Example: *Q:* *Ms. Jones, you are testifying today in response to a subpoena?*
A: *Yes.*
Q: *Is Exhibit 1 a copy of the subpoena?*
A: *Yes.*
Q: *The subpoena asked you to bring with you to the deposition all of your telephone bills for the year 1999?*
A: *Yes.*
Q: *Did you do that?*
A: *Yes.*
Q: *Are these all of the bills?*
A: *Yes.*
Q: *Are any missing?*
A: *No.*
Q: *How do you know that?*
A: *I did a search of my accounts payable file, and found the invoice for each month in 1999.*
Q: *Is each page a separate bill?*
A: *Yes.*
Q: *There are twelve pages in total?*
A: *Yes.*
Q: *Let's mark these pages collectively as Exhibit 2. [The court reporter affixes an Exhibit 2 sticker to the stapled document.] Showing you Exhibit 2, do you recognize it?*
A: *Yes.*
Q: *What is it?*

A: *It's a collection of my telephone bills for 1999.*
[Note: If the deponent gives you a troubling no or yes answer in the sequence, then pause and explore that answer.]

iii. Inquiries about deposition preparation

It is advisable to ask a deponent what he or she did to prepare for the deposition. In general, the one area of preparation that is off-limits is the substance of conversations between the deponent and his or her counsel. A line of questioning might proceed as follows:

Example:
Q: *Ms. Grandma, did you do anything to prepare for your deposition?*
A: *Yes.*
Q: *What did you do?*
A: *I searched for documents in response to your subpoena.*
Q: *Did you find some?*
A: *Yes.*
Q: *And those are the documents we marked as Exhibit 2?*
A: *Yes.*
Q: *Did you do anything else?*
A: *I told Little Red Riding Hood I was coming here today.*
Q: *What did you say?*
A: *I said I was being deposed, and asked her if she had any advice.*
Q: *What did she say?*
A: *She said I should just tell you everything that happened.*
Q: *Anything else?*
A: *No.*
Q: *Did you talk to anyone else?*
A: *Yes.*

> *Q:* *Who?*
> *A:* *My lawyer.*
> *Q:* *Is that Ms. Anderson, who is here with you today?*
> *A:* *Yes.*
> *Q:* *What did you say to Ms. Anderson?*
> *A:* *[By Ms. Anderson:] Objection, privileged and work product. I instruct the witness not to answer.*
> *Q:* *Did you talk to anyone else?*
> *A:* *No.*
> *Q:* *Did you review any documents in preparation for the deposition?*
> *A:* *No.*

This last question raises a potential legal issue. Suppose the deponent had said yes, and you had then asked to see the documents. Is such a request similar to a request for the substance of conversations between a deponent and her counsel, and thus an invasion of attorney-client privilege or work product protections? Alternatively, is the request perfectly fair because presumably the documents refreshed the witness's recollection of prior events? The answer requires attention to both Federal Rule of Civil Procedure 26(b)(3) and Federal Rule of Evidence 612.

Under Federal Rule of Civil Procedure 26(b)(3), a party may obtain documents prepared in anticipation of litigation only upon a showing of substantial need. Many attorneys would argue that an attorney's selection of documents to show a witness in preparation for a deposition implicitly reveals what the attorney thinks about the lawsuit or the approach the attorney plans to take. Rule 26, the argument goes, protects against the required disclosure of particular documents used by the defending lawyer to prepare the deponent for the deposition. An attorney propounding this view will instruct a witness not to answer any questions identifying which documents the attorney showed to the witness in preparation for the deposition.[13]

---

[13] Note, however, there is a threshold question as whether Federal Rule of Civil Procedure 26(b)(3) even applies. Unless the documents reviewed by the witness were themselves prepared in anticipation of the litigation, the questioning lawyer might argue that Rule 26(b)(3) is not applicable.

Rule 26 logic, however, should be balanced against Federal Rule of Evidence 612. This rule of evidence provides that an adverse party is entitled to inspect any "writing" that a witness uses to "refresh memory for the purpose of testifying" in a civil case. Many attorneys would say that Rule 612 trumps Rule 26 if a witness concedes that a document reviewed for a deposition helped refresh the witness's memory about a particular event.[14]

One way for you as the questioning attorney to improve your chances of seeing the documents is to use the following series of questions:

Example: *Q:* *Ms. Grandma, did you review any documents in preparation for this deposition?*
A: *Yes.*
Q: *Have those documents refreshed your memory about subjects we are discussing?*
A: *Yes.*
Q: *Have you used those documents to help you testify?*

---

[14] *See e.g.*, Sporck v. Peil, 759 F.2d 312, 318 (3d Cir. 1985) (detailing discussion on this debate and ultimately holding that counsel's selection of documents in preparation for a deposition is protected by the work-product doctrine in a case where "deposing counsel failed to lay a proper foundation under Rule 612 for production of the documents selected by counsel"); *cf.* F.D.I.C. v. Wachovia Ins. Servs., Inc., 241 F.R.D. 104, 107 (D. Conn. 2007) (interpreting the "*Sporck* exception" narrowly). Some courts have been openly critical of *Sporck* and have declined to apply it or have distinguished it. *See, e.g.*, In re San Juan Dupont Plaza Hotel Fire Litig., 859 F.2d 1007, 1018 (1st Cir. 1988); In re Pradaxa Prods. Liab. Litig., MDL No. 2385, 2013 WL 1776433, at *1 (S.D. Ill. Apr. 25, 2013) (attorney entitled to know which documents a witness reviewed prior to a deposition, but not entitled to know which of those documents were selected by counsel; counsel may not, however, "manufacture a zone of privacy by gratuitously disclosing" that all documents have been selected by counsel); *but see* Stevens v. Corelogic, Inc., No. 14cv1158, 2016 WL 397936, at *9-10 (S.D. Cal. Feb. 1, 2016) (declining to follow *In re Pradaxa*; attorney selection of documents in preparation for deposition is protected work product, although a witness's independent selection of documents is not protected). For a helpful and fairly comprehensive discussion of the intersection of the work-product doctrine and Federal Rule of Evidence 612, see In re Xarelto Prods. Liab. Litig., 314 F.R.D. 397 (E.D. La. 2016) (ultimately holding in a case involving over three million documents that "a list of documents reviewed by a witness in preparation for a deposition is discoverable under Rule 26(b), because the list is relevant, proportional to the needs of the case, and not privileged").

A: *Yes.*
Q: *May I see them, please?*

The two middle questions that set up memory refreshment for the purpose of testifying should help you trump an attorney work product objection. If the witness will not give you yes answers to the middle questions as to all the documents, then just ask about document review in connection with each deposition subject as you get to it. You might get the necessary concessions as to some documents, even if you cannot get the concessions as to the entire document preparation universe.

iv. Pleadings, discovery responses, affidavits

If the deponent is a party to the lawsuit, he or she has authorized pleadings and discovery responses and may have signed them. Even a deponent who is not a party may have participated in preparing the company's documents, or may have signed an affidavit or statement. It is appropriate to ask a deponent about information presented in documents in which the deponent has participated. "What did you mean by . . . ?" is a very useful question.

v. Who, what, where, when, why and how

In virtually all depositions, you will want to ask the journalist's classic five "w" questions: who, what, where, when, and why? We add: how? These six words will be useful in many different settings.

Example: *Q:* *All right, Mr. Wolf. Where did you go on the morning of the fifth?*
A: *To Grandma's house.*
Q: *When did you go there?*
A: *About 10:00 in the morning.*
Q: *How did you get there?*
A: *I walked.*
Q: *What route did you take?*
A: *The high road through the woods.*
Q: *What were you planning to do when you arrived?*

A: *Eat someone.*
Q: *Who?*
A: *Little Red Riding Hood.*
Q: *Why?*
A: *Because I am a wolf, and that's what wolves do.*

The series of six "w/h" questions should be a fixture in your repertoire. Every time you encounter a document, a meeting, a conversation, or an event, you should ask these questions automatically, unless you have a special reason not to do so.

Examples:

Q: *Ms. Jones, let me show you Exhibit 2. What is it?*
A: *A letter.*
Q: *Who wrote it?*
A: *I did.*
Q: *When?*
A: *July 12, 2004.*
Q: *To whom?*
A: *My boss.*
Q: *Where were you when you wrote it?*
A: *My office.*
Q: *Why did you write it?*
A: *I wanted the boss to know the facts in the middle paragraph.*

* * *

Q: *Ms. Jones, you say you had a conversation with Mr. Williams.*
A: *Yes.*
Q: *Who is Mr. Williams?*
A: *My boss.*
Q: *When did you have the conversation?*
A: *July 12, 2004.*
Q: *Where did you have the conversation?*
A: *His office.*

Q: *Was anyone else present?*
A: *No.*
Q: *How long was the conversation?*
A: *5 minutes.*
Q: *What did you say?*
A: *I said the harassment had to stop.*
Q: *What did he say?*
A: *He said, "You are fired."*

* * *

Q: *Ms. Jones, you say you were fired after a series of meetings with Mr. Williams?*
A: *Yes.*
Q: *How many meetings were there?*
A: *Three.*
Q: *Let's take each one. When did you have the first?*
A: *July 12, 2004.*
Q: *Where was it?*
A: *My office.*
Q: *Who was there?*
A: *Mr. Williams and I.*
Q: *How long was the meeting?*
A: *Five minutes.*
Q: *Did either of you take notes?*
A: *No.*
Q: *Who called the meeting?*
A: *He did.*
Q: *What did Mr. Williams say at this meeting?*
A: *He said I needed to do better work.*
Q: *What did you say?*
A: *I said my last review said I was doing great work.*
Q: *What else did he say?*
A: *I don't remember.*
Q: *What else did you say?*
A: *Nothing.*

[Repeat as to second and third meeting.]

The who, what, where, when, why, and how questions accomplish at least three purposes. First, remember that you ultimately will be telling a story. Good story tellers always weave in some details; in the end, the details make the story more interesting and colorful for the audience. Second, the six questions help test the deponent's credibility. Do the details of the story hang together? Third, the questions help establish an evidentiary foundation for the admissibility (in the case of helpful facts) or the inadmissibility (in the case of unhelpful facts) of the witness's testimony.

Examples: *Q:* *Tell me about the meeting, Ms. Jones. Who participated?*
A: *All the conspirators.*
Q: *Who are they?*
A: *Mr. Smith, Ms. Crawler, and me.*
Q: *Where did the meeting take place?*
A: *In a smoke-filled room in my house.*
Q: *When?*
A: *The night of April 6.*
Q: *What time?*
A: *1:00 a.m.*
Q: *What did you say at the meeting?*
A: *I said, "Let's rob the bank."*
Q: *Did Ms. Crawler say anything in response?*
A: *Yes.*
Q: *What did Ms. Crawler say?*
A: *She said, "Good idea."*
Q: *Did Mr. Smith say anything?*
A: *Yes.*
Q: *What did he say?*
A: *He said, "I agree."*
Q: *Why did you want to rob the bank?*
A: *I just lost a lot of money in technology stocks.*

* * *

Q: *Now, Ms. Jones, you say you had a conversation about robbing a bank?*
A: *Yes.*
Q: *Let's explore that in more detail. Who participated?*
A: *I don't know their names.*
Q: *Where was it?*
A: *Some hotel.*
Q: *Do you know the name?*
A: *No.*
Q: *When was the meeting?*
A: *I don't remember.*
Q: *What did you say at it?*
A: *I don't recall.*
Q: *Did any of these nameless people say anything?*
A: *They must have, but I can't think what that was.*
Q: *Why did you meet these people?*
A: *No particular reason.*[15]

vi. The good, the bad, and sometimes even the ugly

Should you limit yourself to questions that are likely to elicit only helpful answers? Or should you ask questions that may elicit good *or* bad information?

The answer depends on the purpose for your deposition. Sometimes you are deposing a friendly witness to preserve favorable testimony for use at summary judgment or trial, when you know that the witness likely will be unavailable later. In that event, you are concerned with eliciting favorable facts. If the witness also has bad things to say, let the other side ask the questions to get those bad facts in cross-examination, unless you are engaged in inoculating the

[15] Even if you are getting "I don't know answers," do not abort the "who, what, where, when, why, and how" sequence. The sequence might spark a memory. If not, you have effectively disqualified a witness from testifying later about the same subject.

judge and jury against the damaging information by bringing some of it out yourself with the best possible spin.

More often, you are deposing a witness who is likely to testify for the adversary. Your main purpose in the deposition is to avoid unpleasant later surprises. You want to know everything the witness is likely to say, so that you can defuse the testimony, either on the spot through immediate impeachment or cross-examination, or later through other witnesses and evidence. In this type of deposition, do not refrain from asking a question solely because you believe you will not like the answer. Just make sure to ask abundant “who, what, where, when, why, and how” questions, to test credibility and to set up possible impeachment on the spot or later.

vii. Sources of proof

You typically will want to know whether the deponent knows of other sources of proof for a particular fact. Are there other potential witnesses who know something about the same facts? Are there records, pictures, tape recordings, telephone logs, diaries, and like items that bear on a subject? Where can you find those? Make sure you ask for potential leads.

viii. Sources of answers

Another typical area of inquiry concerns the sources of proof for the deponent’s answers (e.g., eye witness observation, statements of others, documents, presumptions based on habit). What are those sources of proof? What is the extent of the witness’s reliance on them? Why does the witness rely on them? In what way does the witness rely on them? These questions all relate to the foundation and credibility of the deponent’s version of the facts. Who is really testifying – the deponent or some other source?

ix. Feelings and attitudes

Deponents are people too. They have feelings and attitudes, just as do other people. These attitudes and feelings can affect their perceptions and motives, and thus their testimony.

Example: *Q:* *Mr. Deponent, you just gave us an unusually detailed description of the car accident scene for a bystander. You must have been concentrating hard?*
A: *Yes, I made a point of that.*
Q. *Why did you do that?*
A: *I wanted to make sure Ms. Smith sued Mr. Anderson for everything he had.*
Q: *Why?*
A: *I was in a car accident two years ago, and never got a dime out of it.*
Q: *How do you feel about that?*
A: *Really angry.*

Feelings and attitudes may not always be relevant, and you may not always want to explore them for fear of looking like you are unfairly prying into the deponent's personal life. But think beyond the objective facts of the lawsuit in deciding what to ask each deponent. Bias caused by feelings and attitudes could reduce a deponent's credibility. And you want to know how strong those feelings and attitudes are, to gauge how the witness will appear to the judge and jury, and to determine whether you will be able to establish bias at trial.

Probing into feelings and attitudes also may help you establish inconsistencies when the witness talks about conduct. For example, assume that a deponent testifies that a defendant's conduct left the department an emotional wreck. Yet, when you ask the deponent later about events that occurred on the day in question, the deponent talks about partying all night with friends. The story does not fit together.

x. Hearsay, speculation and opinions

It is absolutely permissible to ask deponents for hearsay, speculation, and opinions.[16] Hearsay will not be admissible at trial, unless an evidentiary exception exists. Speculation will not be admissible. Some forms of opinion will not be

[16] The standard, remember, is that: "Parties may obtain discovery regarding any nonprivileged matter that is relevant to any party's claim or defense. . . . *Information . . . need not be admissible in evidence to be discoverable*." FED. R. CIV. P. 26(b)(1) (emphasis added).

admissible either. But that does not mean you have to avoid asking for these kinds of information at the deposition. If challenged, simply explain that the information you seek need not be admissible to be discoverable, and may in fact lead to admissible evidence later. The deponent, for example, may testify that she knows some information because Mr. X told her this. You may then want to talk to or depose Mr. X regarding the source of his knowledge.

This, by the way, is why it is flatly impermissible for lawyers to instruct witnesses during pre-deposition preparation to say, "I don't know," in response to questions merely because they call for hearsay.

Example: *Q:* *Ms. Grandma, why did Mr. Wolf come to your home on the morning of the 5th?*
A: *I don't know. [So far, this could be a truthful and permissible answer; Ms. Grandma is not Mr. Wolf, and does not know what he was truly thinking.]*
Q: *Did Mr. Wolf ever tell you why he came to your home that morning?*
A: *Yes.*
Q: *When did he tell you?*
A: *That morning.*
Q: *Where were you at the time?*
A: *In my living room at my house.*
Q: *Was the conversation face-to-face?*
A: *Yes.*
Q: *Was anyone else present besides you and Mr. Wolf?*
A: *No.*
Q: *Who started the conversation?*
A: *I did.*
Q: *What did you say?*
A: *I asked Mr. Wolf why he had come to my home.*
Q: *What did Mr. Wolf say to you?*
A: *Objection, calls for hearsay. [This is a theoretically permissible, but unnecessary substantive objection by Mr. Wolf's lawyer.*

Hearsay objections are typically preserved until trial. Moreover, the objection will eventually be overruled on the merits as Mr. Wolf is a party to the case.]

Q: *You may answer the question.*

A: *He said that he had come to eat Little Red Riding Hood.*

In the above sequence, if the lawyer for Ms. Grandma had instructed Ms. Grandma not to answer the question about what Mr. Wolf had told her, the instruction would have been inappropriate.[17] Furthermore, if Ms. Grandma, acting on instructions from her lawyer to testify only to what she knows firsthand and not to speculate, had answered all questions with "I don't know," she would have been committing perjury. The question, "why did he come?", which may call for speculation, is not the same thing as the question, "were you told?", which calls for a fact.

xi. Exhaustion/closure questions

Especially in the case of a deposition of a neutral or hostile witness whom you are deposing for discovery purposes, you need to make sure you have exhausted the witness's knowledge on any given topic. Do not assume that a witness has told you everything; a properly prepared witness will not volunteer knowledge.

There is no magic formula for closure on each subject. Different lawyers use different forms. But they all resemble the following:

Examples: *Q:* *Did anything else happen?*

Q: *Did he say anything else?*

Q: *Did you observe anything else?*[18]

Q: *Have you told me everything you remember about . . .?*

---

[17] FED. R. CIV. P. 30(c)(2).

[18] The first three of these examples appear in M. Melvin Shralow, *Cross and redirect examination,* 4 TRIAL DIPL. J. 36, 37 (Summer 1981).

Q: *Anything else?*
Q: *Is that everything?*

Keep asking the same exhaustion or closure question until you get a firm "no" to the "anything else" inquiry or a firm "yes" to the "everything" inquiry. Do not stop until that occurs. Ask similar closure questions after each break and at the end of the deposition.

Example: *Ms. Grandma, did you have a chance during the break to think about your testimony from this morning? [Yes.] Is there any answer you would like to supplement or change now that you have had a chance to think about it?*

These closure and exhaustion questions will show that you gave the deponent every opportunity to be as accurate as possible, thereby making it doubly difficult for the witness to modify or contradict answers later.

c. Organization of Questions

i. Logical/chronological

There are two basic styles of deposition question organization. The first is to put questions in a sequence that flows in a predictable manner, such as by logical subjects or by chronology.

Examples: *Q:* *Good morning, Ms. Jones. Today, we are going to be talking about the accident, the nature of your injuries, and your medical expenses. Let's start with the accident. [Discussion of accident.] Now let's talk about your injuries. [Etc.]*

Q: *Good morning, Dr. Smith. Today, we are going to talk about your operating procedures. What is the first thing you do when you walk into the operating room?*

[Discussion of first thing.] Then what do you do? [Discussion of second thing.] What next? [Etc.]

These kinds of approaches help an examination proceed in a way that is easy for a judge or jury to follow. Moreover, these approaches help the deponent stay on track with a coherent story. They are especially helpful when you are deposing a friendly or neutral witness through whom you are developing easily understood explanations of events. This approach to questioning also is advisable if you are taking the deposition to preserve testimony for trial.

ii. Unpredictable

There is a downside to the logical/chronological approach, of course. Precisely because the deponent can predict where you are going next, the deponent is less easily trapped with inconsistencies in a story. For that reason, lawyers may prefer a more unpredictable approach with hostile witnesses. With this approach, the questioning lawyer jumps around among subjects, and comes back to a given subject multiple times.

Example:

Q: Please state your name for the record.
A: Wilbur H. Wolf.
Q: What is your address?
A: 225 Carnivore Lane, Capital City.
Q: Mr. Wolf, on the morning of the fifth, you tried to eat Little Red Riding Hood, didn't you?
A: No.
Q: You were planning to eat her, true?
A: No.
Q: What did you do when you first awoke on the 5th, Mr. Wolf? [Discussion of early morning tasks]
Q: Mr. Wolf, let me show you Exhibit 6. It's an email you wrote to Mrs. Wolf on the morning of the 4th?
A: Yes.

> *Q:* *It says you are going to eat Little Red Riding Hood, doesn't it? [Etc.]*

The point of the unpredictable approach is to keep the witness off balance. Be careful, however, that the approach does not also keep you off balance and cause you to lose track of the proceedings and forget to cover key points. Being unpredictable does not mean being disorganized yourself.

Some attorneys like to save the "critical," tough questions for witnesses until near the end and late in the day when witnesses are more likely to be fatigued and just want to get the deposition completed. Witnesses are often less guarded and alert at this time and their answers are often shorter and cleaner.

d. Probing for Details/Listening to the Deponent

Always plan on asking follow up questions. You want details. If the witness is friendly, you want details because it helps the deponent tell a persuasive story. If the witness is hostile, you want details (often, but not necessarily always) to test credibility and to avoid later surprise. Think of your "who, what, where, when, why, and how" sequence.

Part of probing for details, however, is not just remembering to ask questions like "who, what, where, when, why, and how." In addition, it is developing the habit of actually listening to the witness. This is harder than it sounds. If you are prepared properly, you have gone into the deposition with a plan for what you want out of it. You have specific points you want to prove and to disprove. But you cannot always predict all of the points that may come up with a given witness, especially one who is not in your control. So a witness may tender a promising line of testimony you did not anticipate. If you are not listening to the witness, but instead concentrating solely on your own planned questions, you may miss the opportunity to probe for important detail. To ask most effectively for details or to pick up on a promising line of questioning, you have to be paying attention to the actual previous answers in a sequence.

Example: *Q:* *Mr. Wolf, what is your age?*
A: *Now, or at the time I tried to eat Little Red Riding Hood?*
Q: *Now.*

A: *26.*
Q: *How much education do you have?*

Another part of probing for details is developing the habit of watching a deponent's demeanor. Witnesses send clues about their testimony through facial expressions, posture, pauses, vocal volume, and the like. These signals are important. Watch for them.

e. Pace of Questioning

Vary your pace to fit your purpose. Try to develop a rhythm. If you are trying to pin the witness down and the questioning is going well, use short, quick questions, and try to entice the witness to keep up with you through short, quick answers. Then perhaps turn to a longer question for a mini-summary of the favorable testimony before proceeding to the next topic.

Example: *Q:* *On the night of the first, Ms. Jones, was it dark?*
A: *Yes.*
Q: *Was it raining?*
A: *Yes.*
Q: *Were there clouds?*
A: *Yes.*
Q: *Was the moon out?*
A: *No.*
Q: *Were you wearing your glasses?*
A: *No.*
Q: *Do you usually?*
A: *Yes.*
Q: *So it was a dark, rainy, cloudy, moonless, glass-less night when you were driving 40 miles per hour in a 30 mile per hour zone?*

On the other hand, if the testimony is not going well, there is no benefit to you in letting the witness go on a roll of harmful answers. Slow the questions down. Take the witness out of rhythm.

Your pace and rhythm will be different if you are trying to draw a witness out and discover all aspects of the witness's story or sources of information. In this case, you will proceed more slowly and pause between the witness's answer and your next question. The slower pace and the pauses are more likely to create an atmosphere that will cause the witness to be more talkative and provide longer answers.

Example:

Q: *Ms. Witness, you say you didn't agree with your performance appraisal?*
A: *That's right.*
Q: *Can you please explain why?*
A: *[Some explanation provided.]*
Q: *[pause]*
A: *[Additional explanation provided.]*
Q: *Is there any other reason why you didn't agree with your performance appraisal?*
A: *Not that I can think of.*
Q: *[pause] Did you make any notes anywhere about your disagreement with the appraisal?*
A: . . .
Q: *Did you talk to your supervisor about your disagreement?*
A: . . .
Q: *Did you talk to anyone else at XYZ Co. about your disagreement?*
A: . . .
Q: *Did you talk to anyone outside XYZ Co. about your disagreement?*
A: . . .
Q: *Are you confident now that you have explained fully all bases for your disagreement with the performance appraisal?*
A: *Yes.*

f. Leading Questions

Direct exams of friendly and neutral witnesses must generally proceed through non-leading questions – an essentially important point if the depositions are to preserve testimony for use at trial. This restriction does not apply to hostile witnesses, who can be examined in a deposition just as they would be cross-examined at trial.[19]

Keep this firmly in mind. One of the authors was once in a series of depositions opposite a lawyer who seemed incapable of asking a non-leading question, even of friendly witnesses. After a while, lawyers on the opposite side began objecting to virtually every question as impermissible. The questioning lawyer refused to rephrase any of the questions. If the case had gone to trial, there would have been all-out warfare over whether large portions of the transcripts were usable.

g. Prefatory Phrases

When framing your questions, be vigilant about avoiding prefatory phrases. Common prefatory phrases include: "Do you remember whether . . . ?", "Do you recall whether . . . ?", and "Do you know whether . . . ?" Prefatory phrases confuse the record and may render the answers useless. A simple "yes" or "no" response may pertain either to the prefatory phrase or to the subsequent substantive part of the question.

h. Summarizing Testimony

One useful technique for questioners at the end of a sequence is to summarize the witness's testimony, and ask him or her to agree to the summary. Then the summary and answer are introduced into evidence for summary judgment or at trial.

Example: *So Mr. Smith, your testimony is that on the night of the accident you attended a party at which you had*

[19] "The examination and cross-examination of a deponent proceed [at a deposition] as they would at trial under the provisions of the Federal Rules of Evidence, except Rules 103 and 615." FED. R. CIV. P. 30(c).

> *six beers and three vodka martinis in the space of three hours, and ate no food, is that right?*

If the witness agrees your summary is correct, then move on to the next line of questions. If the witness disagrees, then ask the witness, "Which part of my summary is not accurate?" You may use further questions to probe the alleged inaccuracy.

There are times, however, when this technique may be counterproductive. For example, if you have a potentially hostile witness whose guard is down and who consequently is giving you good information without fully realizing the impact of what he is doing, you may be better off taking the answers as they come and leaving it at that. If you restate or summarize the testimony, that may cause the witness to try to qualify those previous responses and to become more cautious and less expansive. Use your judgment.

i. Reacting to the Witness

One difficult tactical issue is whether to react to a deponent's testimony. The important consideration is whether you likely will derive any benefit from the reaction. That depends upon the circumstances. In some cases, you will not want to react in any way to a witness's testimony; for example, you would not want to send a message that the testimony has hurt your side of the case. In other circumstances, you will want to react, to encourage or to discourage further testimony of the type you are hearing. Reasonable lawyers may differ over appropriate approaches, and each witness has to be taken one by one.

If the witness is utterly hostile, the best approach is probably a non-reactive one. You are unlikely to effect a positive change in the witness's testimony through any reaction. You should push hard. You should probe sensitive areas to see if the witness reacts. But ask what you need to ask, and get out.

If a witness is friendly or neutral, react normally, as you would in conversation with someone. A smile, an approving nod, or a warm tone of voice will put the witness at ease and will encourage the witness to continue in the same vein in which the witness has been testifying. A frown, a wrinkled brow, or a puzzled tone will cause a friendly witness to pause to consider whether the testimony is confusing, incomplete, or contradictory.

A simple pause, and silence, also may affect a deponent, friendly or not. There are some witnesses who cannot bear quiet. They will finish an answer. But if you pause, and look at them as if you expect more, they will keep talking! If you want them talking, try it. This works especially well if you have developed a rhythm with the witness. If the witness answers a question and you do not ask another question immediately, the witness may resume talking.

Suppose a witness is relatively neutral, or is unfriendly but semi-controllable. Then, rather than remain stoic in the face of unfavorable testimony, you might choose to react. One approach is to use a friendly conversational style until the witness gives the first unfavorable response, at which point you may alter your style to express confusion or disapproval. If the witness retreats, then shift back to the more friendly, conversational style. The witness gets the message over time that hostile testimony provokes negative reaction. Such an inference will not and should not cause the witness to refrain from telling the truth, but it does encourage the witness not to stretch for negative spins in the witness's answers to your questions just to please the other side. Your typical lay witness (setting aside experts for the moment) does not like to be attacked.

j. Challenging/Impeaching the Witness

Reasonable lawyers may take a variety of approaches to the tactical question of whether and when to challenge a witness through overt, aggressive cross-examination or impeachment. Some would argue that it is better not to engage in extensive cross-examination or impeachment because doing so tips the questioner's hand for trial. As long as you know all of the bad things the witness will say, save your best attacks for surprise when the witness is live on the stand in front of the judge or jury.

Other lawyers would argue that waiting until trial often is a mistake. The vast majority of civil cases never go to trial. The case is won or lost at the summary judgment stage. If there is no dismissal at that time, the case likely settles. So, if you have good cross-examination or impeachment material, you may want to use it at the deposition. Depositions are the places where the case actually gets won, lost, or positioned for settlement.

We think the correct answer to the tactical question is: it depends. First, the standard for getting summary judgment is that there are no genuine issues of material fact, and a party is entitled to win the case as a matter of law.[20] So, if your cross-examination or impeachment of a deponent will definitively remove or establish a material fact, go for it!

Suppose instead that the cross-examination or the impeachment will have a lesser effect. Then the tactical question is trickier. The questioning lawyer has to balance the potential desirability of surprising the witness on the stand later at trial against the desirability of testing the witness a bit at the deposition. In that balance, the authors distinguish between impeachment and cross-examination. Cross-examination can lead to the discovery of additional information. In that regard, the questioning fits the purposes of a deposition even when the questioning does not definitively remove or establish a material fact. On the other hand, impeachment is not likely to get you new facts. It just impacts the credibility of the witness. Seldom is the impeachment so devastating that it helps much at summary judgment, when credibility determinations are inappropriate. So, except when impeachment of the particular party or witness is likely to encourage settlement, we recommend that you save true impeachment material for later use.

k. Rephrasing Questions

There will be times during the deposition when one of the other lawyers in the room will object to a question you ask. Let's say the objection is that your question is ambiguous. You are now put to a choice: do you reframe the question or insist on an answer to the one you asked?

There is no one correct approach to this choice. If it is obvious to you upon quick reflection that your original question to the witness is seriously ambiguous, then reframe it. Otherwise, we advise in most circumstances that you insist on an answer to your question as asked. *After* you get an answer to your original question, you may want to rephrase and restate it to make sure the record is clear. The logic behind this approach is that you do not want to encourage the other lawyers in the room to believe they can dictate the content of your questions

[20] FED. R. CIV. P. 56.

merely by routinely objecting to form and causing you automatically to withdraw your initial inquiry.

On the other hand, do not be so proud as to refuse ever to reframe a question, and then watch a valuable answer be excluded from evidence because an objection to the question is sustained. This leads to an important exception to our general advice: if the primary purpose of the deposition is to preserve testimony, you need to be cautious about objections. In the deposition, you can require the witness to answer your question as framed; at trial, that answer may be excluded if the objection was well-founded.

Occasionally, it will be the *witness* who challenges your question: "What do you mean by . . . ?" If you sense that the witness truly is confused, rephrase the question. If, on the other hand, the witness seems to be attempting to assert some control over the deposition, you may try responding with a couple of different approaches. One is: "What do you not understand?" The other is: "What did you mean by [X] when you said it yourself ten minutes ago?"

3. Handling Exhibits

Handling an exhibit during a deposition is much like handling an exhibit at trial. Here are the basic steps:

- First, pre-mark the document, by handing it to the court reporter for identification. The court reporter will affix the proper number sticker to the document. If you know in advance of the deposition that you will be running through a series of exhibits, give the whole batch to the court reporter to mark before the deposition starts.[21]

[21] The authors are proponents of marking any one unique document only once as an exhibit. Then the document carries that single marking all the way through every deposition in the case and the trial. Re-marking a single document with new numbers every time it is used in new depositions is confusing and unnecessary. (E.g., Jones Exh. 2 = Smith Exh. 64 = Anderson Exh. 26 = Pl. Tr. Exh. 200 = Def. Tr. Exh. 82.) Just mark the document once the first time it appears as an exhibit, and forever after refer to the document by that number, no matter when it is used and no matter who uses it. If local rules of practice in your court normally require a different approach, then seek permission from the court to use a single number method.

Example: *Ms. Court Reporter, would you please mark this as Exhibit 36? [Court reporter marks exhibit with correct number and hands the document back to questioning counsel.]*

- Second, show the document to the witness, and hand a copy to counsel.

Example: *Ms. Jones, I am handing you a two-page document, dated April 16, 2000, marked as Exhibit 36. [Questioning lawyer gives the marked document to the witness and hands a copy to the witness's lawyer and to opposing counsel.]*

- Third, find out whether the witness recognizes the document. If the answer is yes, ask the witness to identify the document in sufficient detail to establish a foundation for the witness's substantive testimony about the exhibit. Alternatively, describe the document and then ask the witness to agree with your description.

Example: *Q: Please take a moment to review Exhibit 36, and tell me if you recognize it.*
A: Yes.
Q: What is it?
A: It's a letter I wrote on April 16, 2000, to my boss.
Q: Is that your signature at the bottom of page 2?
A: Yes.[22]

- Fourth, ask the witness applicable substantive questions.[23]

---

[22] At this point in a trial, you would offer the exhibit into evidence. That is unnecessary during a deposition. You will wait to make the offer at trial.

[23] One commentator suggests that you may want to consider having the witness highlight on a clean copy of the exhibit those key sections that are important, then have the witness explain the importance of each. Lisa C. Wood, *Better Discovery Through Discovery Management*, 31 LITIG., Summer 2005, at 4, 43, 46.

Examples: *What did you mean at the bottom of page one of Exhibit 36, when you said . . .?*

Did you read Exhibit 36 when you received it?

How does your company use reports like Exhibit 36?

Is it important that reports like Exhibit 36 be accurate?

How long does your company retain reports like Exhibit 36?

- Fifth, when you have finished discussing the document with the witness, make sure the original marked exhibit goes back to the court reporter to include with the official transcript of the deposition.

Example: *At the end of the discussion, the questioning lawyer hands the marked version of Exhibit 36 back to the court reporter for safekeeping.*

4. Demonstrations, Reenactments and Diagrams

There may be occasions in which you want the deponent not only to provide oral responses to your questions but also to perform some physical act. For example, you may want the deponent to demonstrate some action (e.g., the range of motion in the deponent's injured shoulder) or to reenact some incident at issue in the suit (e.g., how the deponent was using a product at the time of the accident). Alternatively, you may want the deponent to draw a diagram (e.g., an accident scene) or to provide a handwriting sample (e.g., to try to determine if the deponent was the source of some marginalia on a document). As a threshold matter, there is the issue of whether you can compel the deponent to do any of these things. The courts that have considered this issue are divided. Some courts hold that a deponent is required only to provide oral responses to questions and that the deponent cannot be required to perform some action in the deposition.[24] Other courts disagree and hold that a deponent can be compelled to perform the types of acts described above.[25] These courts reason in part that a demonstration or reenactment may provide a more direct and accurate account of an event than a verbal description.

Assuming that the courts in your jurisdiction allow you to compel a deponent to perform nonverbal acts in a deposition, or that the deponent agrees to perform such acts, you need to consider the mechanics of recording these actions for the record. Obviously, if you videotape the deposition, you will have a visual record. Even if you videotape the deposition, however, you also may want to make a verbal record of what the deponent does so that you have a written record of the deponent's action. You may find it considerably easier to attach such a written record to a motion or to impeach the witness at trial with the written transcript.

You certainly need to make such a verbal record of any actions if the deposition is not videotaped. Otherwise, your written transcript will look something like this:

Example:

Q: *Can you point to the area of your back and neck where you still have pain?*
A: *It starts right about here and goes all along here to this area.*
Q: *Where does it hurt the most?*
A: *[Witness pointing.]*
Q: *How high can you lift your left arm?*
A: *Usually only about this high. On a good day, I can sometimes raise it this much higher.*

---

[24] *See, e.g.*, Greenidge v. Ruffin, 927 F.2d 789, 793 (4th Cir. 1991) (finding no abuse in discretion for refusing to allow a videotaped deposition of a murder reenactment); Howard v. Michalek, 249 F.R.D. 288, 290 (N.D. Ill. 2008); *see also* Jones v. Covington, No. 1:15-cv-396, 2015 WL 7721835, at *2 (N.D. Ga. Nov. 30, 2015) (plaintiff may question doctor about his previous examination of a pathology slide, but may not compel doctor to re-read the slide as that would compel the creation of new facts). Keep in mind, however, that a deponent may agree to perform some act in a deposition even if the deponent cannot be compelled to do so.

[25] *See, e.g.*, Kiraly v. Berkel, Inc., 122 F.R.D. 186, 187 (E.D. Pa. 1988); Emerson Elec. Co. v. Superior Court, 946 P.2d 841, 842, 68 Cal. Rptr. 2d 883, 884 (Cal. 1997).

There are different ways to make a verbal record of the deponent's acts. You can observe and orally describe the deponent's action, and then ask the deponent to confirm the accuracy of your description. While opposing counsel can object to your description, you can ask the deponent to correct any inaccuracies.

Example: *Q:* *You are pointing to an area about the size of a baseball directly under your left shoulder blade, is that correct?*
A: *Yes. It also sometimes hurts down here too.*
Q: *Now you are pointing to a smaller area just to the left of your spine and right above your belt line, is that right?*
A: *That's right.*

Alternatively, you can instruct the deponent to describe and perform the physical act simultaneously. This may not work very well if the deponent cannot accurately and clearly verbalize his or her actions. In that case, you should supplement the witness's description with your own, and then get the witness to agree with your description.

If you ask the deponent to draw a diagram or to mark on a photograph or other document, you can use multi-colored pens to help create a clear record of what the deponent did.

Example: *Q:* *I'm handing you a blank sheet of paper marked Exhibit 1. Please take this red pen and draw on Exhibit 1 the intersection where the accident occurred. . . . You have drawn two intersecting streets, Elm and Cedar. Is that correct?*
A: *Yes.*
Q: *Please now take this blue pen and indicate the point of rest of your car after the accident. . . . Have you done that?*
A: *Yes.*
Q: *Please take this green pen and draw the point of rest of the defendant's truck after*

> *the accident. . . . You have drawn the point of rest of the defendant's truck in the northbound lane of Cedar Street, is that correct?*
>
> *A:* *Yes.*

If you are defending the deposition of a witness asked to perform some physical reenactment, you may consider objecting to the request on the grounds that the requested reenactment is too difficult or dangerous, or that it is misleading and assumes facts not in evidence because the setting and/or circumstances in the deposition room are not the same as those at the time of the original incident.

Example: Too dangerous: *Let the record reflect that we have moved to the stairwell of my office building. Mr. Smith, I'd like you to show us how you somersaulted down two flights of stairs at my client's apartment building.*

Too misleading or difficult: *Dr. Jones, would you please take this Milton-Bradley game of "Operation" and show us how you performed a heart transplant on my client.*

You might alternatively object to the reenactment but allow it to occur, and then object to the introduction of a videotape of the reenactment at trial. As courts have noted, it does not automatically follow that a videotaped reenactment "taken for discovery purposes [is] admissible into evidence at trial."[26]

5. Dealing with Confidential Material

It is not unusual in commercial cases, for example, for parties to be dealing with trade secrets, business strategies, employment records, and the like. It is similarly standard in personal injury cases to be dealing with medical records. These and other items may be confidential.

[26] *See, e.g.*, Roberts v. Homelite Div. of Textron, Inc., 109 F.R.D. 664, 668 (N.D. Ind. 1986).

Generally, counsel will have entered into a confidentiality stipulation, approved by the court, at the outset of the case. This stipulation and order will spell out the procedures for treating disclosure of sensitive information. Follow the instructions in that order.

The most likely scenario in which confidentiality will become an issue at a deposition is when the witness says that some particular subject of testimony is especially sensitive. A standard approach to handling this scenario is to excuse all persons from the deposition room except the lawyers, the witness, and the court reporter. The questions and answers proceed. At the end of the topic, the court reporter is told to transcribe the sequence into a separate "confidential" volume, which is then available only to the witness and the lawyers in the case. (Other persons may be eligible to see the confidential volume as permitted by the operative stipulation/protective order.) Later, the court will determine the degree of confidentiality, if any, to ascribe at trial to the sensitive testimony. If any exhibits are especially sensitive, handle them in the same way.

6. Taking Notes During the Deposition

The most important thing to do when taking a deposition is to *listen*. You will miss critical follow through unless you pay careful attention to all aspects of each of the deponent's answers. Paying such careful attention to each word the deponent utters can be hard to do if you simultaneously are trying to take copious notes. One way to solve this problem is to ask a legal assistant or another lawyer to attend the deposition for the purpose of note-taking. This approach, however, increases the cost to the client.

An alternative is to go into the deposition with an outline of question topics on the left half of a page, leaving room on the right half, opposite the questions, for recording key notes about answers. This device will help you know that you have covered particular points, and will help you refresh your recollection of the deponent's prior testimony if you have to return to a topic during a deposition. It also will provide a device for jotting a quick word or two about areas to follow through on.

Example:

The April 16, 2000 letter:	*Deponent's answers:*
Who wrote it? [Deponent?]	
Where were you at the time?	
When did you write it?	
Why did you write it?	
What did you mean at the bottom of page one?	

7. Concluding Procedures

There are three things to remember about concluding a deposition. The first is instructing the witness, or inviting the witness's lawyer to instruct the witness, about the right to read and sign the transcript. Under the Federal Rules, a deponent has 30 days within which to review and correct a transcript once it is prepared.[27] If the witness waives the right, or asserts the right but then makes no changes, the transcript is deemed correct as reported. Have the witness state on the record whether the witness intends to exercise the right to review the transcript.

Second, if the witness declares that he or she wants to review the transcript, you should make sure following the deposition that the witness receives notice of the preparation of the transcript and receives a copy to review. Then, you need to make sure that the official transcript includes any corrections. Always review any corrections to determine if the witness has suddenly reversed

---

[27] FED. R. CIV. P. 30(e).

course on an important answer. If the witness has, you may need to notice a supplemental deposition to explore the change.

Third, in many jurisdictions, court reporters send the original of the deposition transcript to the lawyer who noticed the deposition for storage. Courts do not ordinarily store transcripts, and court reporters do not like using their own file space for this purpose. So it becomes your job.

If you get original transcripts to hold, make sure you set aside a secure space for them. You do not want to misplace the originals of depositions and exhibits that might wind up being used in court.

CHAPTER 3

Preparing the Deponent

Preparing a deponent for a deposition is like giving childbirth lessons. While you can significantly lessen the deponent's anxiety level by eliminating many uncertainties about the process, you cannot make the actual experience completely painless. Many lawyers say that preparing a person to be deposed is more difficult than taking a deposition. The lawyer taking a deposition generally is in control and can, to some extent, script out the process. When defending a deposition, on the other hand, the lawyer can, for the most part, only prepare the deponent for the experience and then sit back and hope that the deponent understood and follows the lawyer's advice and instructions.

Witnesses can become extremely nervous about their depositions. They start to imagine how horrible the experience could be and the images in their imagination usually are worse than reality turns out to be. One senior official in an organization, for example, was so nervous she literally could not remember her name at the start of the deposition. Another lawyer described the "brain lock" that occurs in severely nervous witnesses.[28] Hopefully, your preparation can ease some of that anxiety and prevent a case of brain lock.

When should you schedule a deposition preparation session with the deponent – a week before the deposition, the day before, in the car on the way to the deposition? If possible, avoid scheduling such sessions the day before or the day of the deposition. Some attorneys like to conduct such eleventh-hour preparation sessions because they believe the deponent will be more likely to remember their instructions and tips. In fact, deponents are probably more likely to internalize your instructions if they have some time to think about them before the deposition. You also will often discover information and potential problems in these preparation sessions. You may not have time to investigate and address these issues if the deposition is scheduled for the next day. Finally, scheduling the preparation session in advance gives you the opportunity to reschedule if the deponent cannot make the original scheduled time or needs an additional session.

In preparing a deponent for a deposition, you need to differentiate between clients covered by the attorney-client privilege and other deponents. With clients, your preparation session is privileged. With non-client witnesses, your preparation session is not privileged and the deponent can, and almost certainly will, be asked about what was said, done, and reviewed in the session. It is not always so obvious, however, whether the deponent is covered by the privilege, especially in the case of current and former employees or other representatives of an organization that is a party to the suit.[29] If you do not have an attorney-client

---

[28] Regina Perry noted that the "paralyzed witness" is her biggest difficulty in deposition practice: "Some witnesses get so nervous and uncomfortable with the process that they go into 'brain lock'. . . . They are sometimes unable to comprehend even the simplest of questions and are so nervous that they get confused and will say that the sky is green." J. Stratton Shartel, *Abuses in Depositions: Litigators Describe Response Strategies*, INSIDE LITIG., July 1994, at 1, 13.

[29] A detailed discussion of which current and former employees or representatives of an organization are covered by the attorney-client privilege is beyond the scope of this book. Some courts have limited the scope of the privilege to those in the organization's "control group." *See, e.g.*, Consol. Coal Co. v. Bucyrus-Erie Co., 432 N.E.2d 250, 257 (Ill. 1982). *But see, e.g.*, Upjohn Co. v. United States, 449 U.S. 383, 397 101 S. Ct. 677, 686 (1981) (holding the "control group" test to be unduly narrow). Most federal and state courts have recognized that the privilege extends to certain former employees of an organization. *See, e.g.*, *In re* Allen, 106 F.3d 582, 606 (4th Cir. 1997); Wylie v. Marley Co., 891 F.2d 1463, 1472 (10th Cir. 1989) (applying Kansas law). Some organizations agree to provide counsel for their ex-employees in order to cloak these individuals

relationship with the deponent, you might consider creating one. For example, corporations sometimes will offer to represent former employees in a litigation matter. On the other hand, you may not want to create such a relationship if you would prefer that the witness be perceived as disinterested. You also must be cautious about potential conflicts of interest if you offer to represent additional individuals.

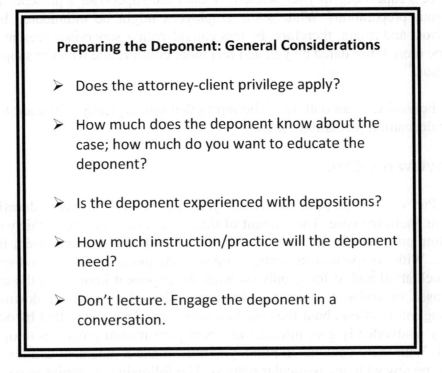

Preparing the Deponent: General Considerations

- Does the attorney-client privilege apply?
- How much does the deponent know about the case; how much do you want to educate the deponent?
- Is the deponent experienced with depositions?
- How much instruction/practice will the deponent need?
- Don't lecture. Engage the deponent in a conversation.

You also need to be careful about who attends your preparation session. If you are preparing a client covered by the privilege, you do not want to inadvertently waive the privilege by allowing someone not cloaked with the privilege to attend your session. This may mean that certain co-employees and relatives of the deponent might not be able to attend your preparation session.[30] If

with the privilege, thereby preventing *ex parte* communications between these ex-employees and the organizations' opponents.

[30] A parent or guardian usually can attend a minor's preparation session without waiving the privilege.

you are preparing a non-party witness, you need to keep in mind that everything said and done in the preparation session is discoverable.

Even in the absence of privilege waiver concerns, you need to consider whether you want to have anyone else attend your preparation session. For example, when preparing a client's employee to be deposed, do you want the employee's supervisor in your session? Would the supervisor's presence help or harm your preparation? While some employees might be intimidated by their supervisors and might, therefore, be less candid with a supervisor present, others might be more intimidated by you and feel more comfortable with the support of a supervisor.[31]

Following is an outline of the topics that you typically will want to cover in your deposition preparation session.

A. Review the Case

Part of your preparation session generally should be spent educating the deponent about the case. The amount of time you should devote to this will vary depending on what the deponent already knows and where the deponent fits into the case. With non-party deponents, attorneys sometimes decide not to discuss the case much at all and to focus only on what the deponent knows lest the attorney be accused of trying to taint the deponent. The other potential downside of providing information about the case to a non-party deponent is that by doing so you may inadvertently give information about your mental processes to opposing counsel. With these cautions in mind, you must make a judgment call about how much to review with any particular witness. The following are topics to consider.

---

[31] Some attorneys use "witness consultants" to help prepare their witnesses to be deposed. Many such consultants are members of a national organization called the American Society of Trial Consultants (ASTC) that has adopted guidelines for their member consultants. The Third Circuit Court of Appeals held that the communications between such a consultant and a witness in preparing for a deposition were protected by the work product doctrine. In re Cendant Corp. Sec. Litig., 343 F.3d 658 (3rd Cir. 2003). For a more detailed discussion about the role and function of such witness consultants, see Elaine Lewis, *Witness Preparation: What Is Ethical, and What is Not*, 36 LITIG., Winter 2010, at 41.

1. Review Applicable Claims and Defenses

Review with the deponent the basic claims and defenses in the case. With most deponents, it is not necessary for you to review every count of the complaint or to refer to "civil RICO," "Title VII," or "strict products liability" claims. It may be sufficient to refer to the case as involving "fraud," "discrimination," or "defective product" claims. An average deponent is more likely to understand the latter characterizations. It also may not be necessary for you to review certain purely legal defenses that may only confuse the deponent. Use your judgment based on your circumstances.

2. Review Theme of Case and Role of Deponent

In addition to outlining the basic claims and defenses, educate the deponent about your theme. For example, your defense theme may be that the deponent's employer is a responsible company that carefully tested its products and acted responsibly in the face of reported product injuries. In representing the plaintiff in a consumer fraud case, your theme may be one of exploitation, such as a defendant vendor taking advantage of vulnerable elderly consumers to bilk them out of their life savings. It helps if the deponent has the "big picture" in mind while testifying.

Also, try to give the deponent a sense as to the deponent's role in the case. Is the deponent a relatively minor player who is able merely to corroborate what several other witnesses said or is the deponent the individual in the company who needs to be able to explain what an exhaustive process the company had in place to detect manufacturing defects in its products? While you do not want unnecessarily to burden the deponent (e.g., "I don't want you to be nervous, but the whole case and the fate of the company rest entirely in your hands."), you may need to let the deponent know that you and the company are looking to the deponent to carry the ball on that issue and that the deponent will not be able to defer to other witnesses.

As several commentators have noted, you also may want to ask deponents what they think they will be asked in their depositions and what they think are the factual strengths and weaknesses of the case.[32] You may be surprised at the ability of deponents to accurately anticipate the likely questioning they will receive. Such questions to deponents also may elicit important factual information of which you may be unaware, including areas of vulnerability.

3. Review the Facts

It frequently is helpful to review a chronology of the facts with the deponent. Find out what the deponent knows and whether the deponent has additional information to help educate *you* about the case. Do so in question format; do not simply tell the witness what you think the facts are and ask for agreement. In the latter case, you may simply hear your own version of the case repeated back to you, as opposed to getting the deponent's real view of the facts.

4. Review Discovery Responses and Other Testimony

You may want to review prior discovery responses in the case and you *will* want to review prior discovery responses provided by the deponent. It is quite common for attorneys to ask deponents in their depositions about interrogatory answers they signed or document request responses. You also should prepare the deponent to answer a question regarding the efforts the deponent made to locate potentially responsive documents.

You may want the deponent to know what other deponents have said in their depositions. If you do not want the deponent to review the transcripts of these other depositions, you can simply summarize the other deponents' testimony in your preparation session.

5. Review Statements, Affidavits, Photos, etc.

Review other significant parts of the file, including photographs, maps, diagrams, chronologies and other physical evidence, as well as the deponent's prior statements and affidavits. Deponents are likely to be asked about their prior written or recorded statements. Even if not asked about these directly, deponents will want to refresh their recollection with such statements to minimize the

---

[32] Janeen Kerper, *Preparing a Witness for Deposition*, 24 LITIG., Summer 1998, at 11, 15 (citing trial consultant Joshua Karton).

likelihood of serious inconsistencies between the deponent's deposition testimony and previous statements.

B. Review Key Documents

Most depositions involve questioning about various documents. In preparing a deponent, you need carefully to consider which documents you will show to the deponent. The deponent may need to disclose which documents the deponent reviewed in preparation for the deposition; in turn, these documents may reveal some of your mental impressions about the case. As mentioned in Chapter 2, this disclosure risk arises out of the operation of Federal Rule of Evidence 612, which provides that documents used to refresh a witness's memory before testifying may need to be produced to the adverse party "if the court in its discretion determines it is necessary in the interests of justice." Although this is not an automatic disclosure obligation, it is best to assume that everything you show the deponent is discoverable by the other side.

The following steps will help minimize the risk of a Rule 612 waiver.[33]

- Avoid showing the deponent any privileged documents. Especially avoid showing the deponent documents containing core work product.

- If you need to show the deponent privileged documents, redact the sensitive core work product material before showing the documents to the deponent.

- Show the deponent only documents that already have been produced in the litigation. The court may be less likely to require the identification of documents the other side already has and may conclude that the other side's desire for such identification really is motivated by a desire to know which documents you thought were important.

- Show the witness a lot of documents. If you have to identify and produce a large quantity of documents, you will be less likely to reveal much about your mental impressions – the documents you believe are

[33] These steps are outlined in John S. Applegate, *Preparing for Rule 612,* 19 LITIG., Spring 1993, at 17, 21-22.

most important. Also, the deponent will be even less likely to recall the particular documents he or she reviewed.

- Ask the deponent whether the deponent remembers the event/subject before you show the deponent the documents that discuss the event/subject. A predicate to the Rule 612 disclosure obligation is that the document, in fact, refreshed the witness's recollection. If such refreshing is unnecessary, production arguably is not required.

Notwithstanding the above practice tips, you should refrain during your preparation session from showing the deponent any document you want to be sure to keep out of the hands of opposing counsel.

C. Explain Deposition Logistics and Procedures

Take some time explaining some of the basic deposition logistics and procedures. Do not assume the deponent knows what to expect. In fact, many deponents are more worried about how many people will be at the deposition and whether they can take restroom breaks than about the questions they will be asked.

Following are the principal logistics topics you should discuss with the deponent. But note: In practice, you want to keep the ground rules discussion short, say five to ten minutes. You can touch on details as needed, as they come up during the preparation. Otherwise, recitation of the ground rules starts to resemble a lecture, which you want to avoid. You want the witness to talk, early and often.

1. Definition and Uses of Depositions

It is helpful to tell deponents what a deposition is, what it is not, and how it can be used at a later date. Some deponents think that their prior written statement to an investigator was a deposition, or that testimony at trial is a deposition. Tell the witness that a deposition is an opportunity for the other side to question the deponent under oath and to get a verbatim record of the questions and answers. Explain that the other side may be taking the deponent's deposition for several different purposes, including: (1) to find out what the deponent knows about the facts; (2) to evaluate the deponent; (3) to obtain testimony for trial in lieu of the deponent's live testimony; (4) to support a motion, such as a motion for summary judgment; (5) to impeach the deponent at trial regarding trial testimony that is inconsistent with the deponent's deposition testimony; and (6) to evaluate the deponent's testimony for purposes of settlement negotiations.

2. Prior Depositions

It is a good idea to find out if the deponent has ever been deposed before. Deponents who have been deposed before often have a "been there, done that" attitude and may claim they need no preparation. In fact, their prior deposition experience may be very much unlike their next experience. Not all depositions are the same (even if it feels that way some days). Moreover, the deponent may have been poorly prepared before the last deposition or may not have been prepared at all. You may need to spend as much time and effort breaking bad habits as conveying new information.

3. Dress

What dress is appropriate for a deposition – formal, business, business-casual, casual-business, formal-business-casual? Generally speaking, professional and business deponents should wear regular business (or courtroom) attire. If your client is a laborer and has not worn a tie in eighteen years, you probably do not want your client to wear a suit. The client is only likely to feel very uncomfortable. If your deponent is a police officer, you may want the deponent dressed in uniform. Use your discretion. (Clowns may want to leave their uniforms at home.) If the deposition is to be videotaped, you may want to suggest that the deponent avoid certain patterns and wear particular colors that look better on tape.

If the witness is likely to dress casually, caution the witness to avoid wearing anything with a slogan or other message that some may find offensive.

4. Location

If you want the deponent to show up, it is usually best to tell the deponent where the deposition will occur. Otherwise, you can arrange to travel with the deponent to the deposition. It also is useful to tell deponents where they can park if they are unfamiliar with the area. You may even want to give them a map so they can find the place easier and get there on time. Tell the deponent that the deposition will take place in some sort of conference room. It is not unusual for first-time deponents to think that depositions take place in courtrooms.

5. Persons Present

You should tell the deponent that in addition to you and the deponent, there will be a court reporter at the deposition as well as the opposing attorney and possibly the opposing party. If there are multiple separately-represented parties, tell the deponent that there will be several lawyers, each of whom has the right to ask the deponent questions.

Disputes sometimes arise over who can attend a deposition. If you suspect that others beside the usual players may attend the deposition, tell the deponent ahead of time so that the deponent does not freak out on the day of the deposition. You also should explain to the deponent that you may have little or no ability to exclude the other person or persons. If the deponent is genuinely afraid of someone who might attend the deposition, you should consider moving for a protective order.

Deponents may ask if they can bring someone to the deposition, such as a spouse, a parent, or a co-worker. You should find out why the deponent wants this person or these persons to attend. Is it because the deponent is very nervous and wants someone else there for moral support? Is it because the other person is likely to be deposed at a later date and would like to hear what the deponent is asked? In the former situation, you might not object to the other person's presence if you feel it will help the deponent relax and do a better job testifying.[34] The latter scenario is a bit trickier. If it is clear that the other person is only there to hear what the deponent has to say, you and the deponent are vulnerable to the allegation that the other person plans to conform his or her testimony to that of the

---

[34] It is common, for example, for parents or guardians to attend the depositions of minors. *See* Rothenberg v. Bright Horizons Children's Ctrs., Inc., 1999 WL 959613, at *1 (Mass. Super. Sept. 23, 1999) (setting ground rules for taking the deposition of a seven-year-old child including that "[i]f necessary, minor plaintiff may have her parents and/or another adult present during the deposition"); *see also* Goodyear Dunlop Tires N. Am., Ltd. v. Gamez, 151 S.W.3d 574, 583 (Tex. App.-San Antonio 2004) ("A guardian ad litem may only attend depositions, hearings and conferences . . . when they are necessary to protect the minor's interests.").

deponent. In this situation, you are better off instructing the other person not to attend.

6. Oath

Make sure deponents know that their answers will be under oath and that they will be asked to swear to tell the truth at the start of the deposition. Occasionally, a deponent may refuse to take such an oath, usually on religious grounds. While this should not be a problem if the witness is still willing to affirm under penalty of perjury that the testimony is truthful, you would generally rather know this ahead of time. The deponent may better appreciate that a deposition is not an informal conversation if the deponent knows that the testimony given will be under oath and that everything will be recorded.

7. Deposition Record and Recording

The deponent should know that everything said during the deposition is recorded word-for-word via stenographic or other means. Warn the deponent that there really is no such thing as "off the record" in a deposition. While attorneys occasionally have "off the record" conferences during a deposition, everything said and done off the record can be put back on the record. The deponent can make a flippant remark during a break in the deposition and the questioning attorney can question the deponent about that remark when the deposition resumes. Consequently, deponents should be told not to let their guards down during breaks.

Similarly, deponents should understand that they are being evaluated the entire time. For example, opposing counsel will take note of how the personal injury plaintiff deponent walks, sits, and moves. A casual ill-advised remark in the elevator can be overheard by an employee of the opposing counsel's law firm and reported back. Likewise, you should tell the deponent to be careful about statements made to the court reporter. The deponent may assume that the court reporter is a neutral individual who is there only to transcribe the testimony. In fact, the court reporter may regularly record depositions for the opposing attorney and may readily pass along even casual remarks made by the deponent.

Be sure to tell the deponent ahead of time if the deposition will be videotaped. The most confident deponents can turn to complete mush if they find out for the first time at the deposition itself that they are to be videotaped. In fact, if you are representing deponents who are going to have their depositions taken by videotape, you may want to consider videotaping a mock partial deposition so that the deponents see what they look and sound like on tape. This will allow the deponents a chance potentially to correct distracting mannerisms, demeanor issues, and the like. A word of caution though: If you contemplate videotaping a mock practice session, be sure to review the latest decisions in your jurisdiction concerning whether the tape must be turned over to opposing counsel if requested during discovery.

8. Breaks

One of the most frequent questions deponents ask is: can I take a break when I want to? Well, can they? As a general matter, deponents can take breaks when they need to and they should be told as much. There are, however, some exceptions to this. For example, opposing counsel will not tolerate a deponent who wants to break every 20 minutes. Likewise, it may be difficult to justify a break shortly after a previous break.

What if the deponent wants to take a break to talk to you about a question or line of questioning? Most attorneys will not allow breaks while a question is pending except, perhaps, if the deponent wants to discuss whether a question calls for privileged information. Some attorneys tell deponents that if the matter is really important, they should insist on a break even if it is not time for a natural break in the deposition. These attorneys believe that avoiding a confused or otherwise inappropriate response from the deponent outweighs any adverse implications opposing counsel can infer from the deponent's decision to break and confer with counsel. Be sure to consult the rules of the jurisdiction in which the deposition is to be taken, since those rules may prohibit breaks while questions are pending.

9. What to Bring to the Deposition

Unless the deponent is compelled to bring documents or other things pursuant to a subpoena duces tecum, you should instruct the deponent to bring nothing with them to their depositions. If you do not give this instruction, you should not be surprised if the deponent brings a cribsheet with the "answers" on it or the "smoking gun" document that was in the deponent's files but that you have never before seen. It is quite natural for deponents to think they should bring documents to the deposition that might refresh their recollection. Deponents assume the documents are for their eyes only. You should explain that it is quite likely that opposing counsel will be able to view any documents the deponent brings and question the deponent about them. As counsel, it is a good idea to check with the deponent shortly before the deposition to make sure the deponent did not bring anything. It also is advisable to tell the deponent to leave all documents at home or at the office. Sometimes deponents will bring documents with them but leave them in their cars. Opposing counsel may ask the deponent to go get these documents if they are nearby.

10. Length of the Deposition

The deponent may ask how long the deposition will last. Federal Rule of Civil Procedure 30(d)(1) limits each deposition to one day of seven hours (excluding breaks) unless the parties agree or the court orders otherwise. In some cases, you can fairly estimate that a deposition will last only a few hours. If you suspect the deposition will last the entire day, you should advise the deponent to refrain from making other appointments, even for the end of the work day. Because of breaks and other circumstances, the deposition may extend into the evening. You want to avoid the need to come back for a second day to finish up an hour of testimony. And you do not want the deponent to rush and become careless at the end of the afternoon in order to get to another appointment.

11. Preliminary Instructions

You should acquaint deponents with any preliminary instructions that you expect the opposing attorney to give them at the start of their depositions.[35] You also may want to suggest how the deponent ought to respond to certain common instructions:

Example: *Q:* *If I ask you a question that you do not understand, please tell me so. If you do not tell me so, can I assume you understood my question?*

[35] *See supra* Chapter 2.

A: *No. I may respond to questions you ask without realizing that I did not really understand what you were asking.*

12. Right to Read and Sign the Deposition

You should explain to the deponent what happens at the end of the deposition. If the deponent is your client, tell the deponent whether you expect to assert the right to read and sign. If the deponent is not a client, you may want to tell the deponent what options the deponent has regarding reading and signing. You should avoid giving the non-client deponent any legal advice regarding whether to read and sign.[36]

D. Tips Regarding Answering Questions

In addition to educating deponents about deposition logistics and procedures, you should educate them about answering questions. Some attorneys use commercially-prepared videotapes or computer programs to educate deponents about answering deposition questions. There are a number of such videotapes and programs available for purchase.[37] If you use such a tape or program, you may want to watch it with the deponent so that you can answer the deponent's questions (and make sure the deponent actually watches it).[38] Generally, it is best to watch the videotape at the beginning of your preparation session.

---

[36] See Chapter 4 for a discussion of the tactical considerations involved in deciding whether to read and sign the transcript.

[37] A quick internet search will yield results, but always watch the preparation program yourself first, to make sure you agree with the advice provided, and to make sure the program is appropriate for your witness.

[38] There also are some good written materials you can give to deponents to help educate them regarding deposition procedures. *See, e.g.,* ROGER S. HAYDOCK, DAVID F. HERR & JEFFREY W. STEMPEL, FUNDAMENTALS OF PRETRIAL LITIGATION 695 (2000).

Basic Rules for Answering Questions:

- Tell the truth
- Do not guess
- Do not volunteer

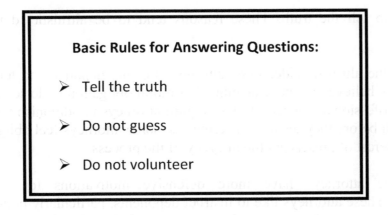

The following are general and specific tips you should pass along to the deponents you prepare. Be cautious about how you present these, however. A common mistake made by new attorneys is to overwhelm the deponent with a lengthy list of rules. It is best to boil these down to the few most important rules, and use your discussions with the deponent and any practice questions you engage in to flush out the details. As in the case of logistics and procedures, you do not want this portion of the preparation to resemble a lecture.

Note that, especially if the witness is not your own client, you may prefer not to hand out any preparation tips in writing, on the theory they are discoverable. The authors do not distribute preparation checklists to witnesses, even witnesses who are clients. Some lawyers, however, believe such lists are helpful. If you do give deponents a checklist, tell them not to bring it with them to the deposition. If they forget or disobey this instruction, however, you can minimize discoverability danger by keeping the instructions pretty innocuous (unless the deponent adds a note to the checklist reminding the deponent not to volunteer anything about certain "smoking gun" documents).

1. Tell the Truth

Some attorneys like to advise deponents to tell the truth in their depositions. Why would you want to do this? Is it really necessary? Why not assume the deponent knows this? Are you likely to insult the deponent by giving such an instruction? There are several reasons attorneys expressly instruct deponents to tell the truth. These reasons tend to be altruistic, defensive, or functional.

On the altruistic side, some attorneys instruct deponents to tell the truth because they believe they have an ethical or moral obligation to do so. The Model Rules of Professional Conduct do not require attorneys to admonish witnesses to tell the truth before they testify. Nevertheless, some attorneys feel obligated to do so in the interest of preserving the integrity of the process.

Some attorneys have more defensive motivations for giving this instruction. These attorneys like to instruct deponents, particularly non-parties, to tell the truth because they assume the deponents will be asked in their depositions what they were told in their preparation sessions with the attorneys. These attorneys believe that if the deponents testify that they were told by the attorneys to tell the truth, that testimony may help undermine any suggestion that the attorneys unduly influenced the deponents' testimony.

There also are functional reasons for telling deponents to tell the truth. Attorneys may want the deponents to understand that if they lie in their depositions, they are quite likely to hurt their chances of prevailing. The attorneys want to put to rest any preconceived notion the deponents may have that they can deceive the other side or, worse yet, that they are somehow expected to lie to help their case.

Finally, attorneys may give this instruction because they believe it enhances their own credibility with the deponent. It sends a message that the attorney is not willing to win "at all costs" and does not condone perjury. This may be very important when the attorney is preparing a non-party who may question the attorney's motives and ethics.

2. Listen to the Entire Question

Tell deponents to: (1) wait for the complete question; and (2) make sure they heard it. Some deponents tend to interrupt the attorney asking the questions because the deponents start to make assumptions about what the attorney is asking. This often happens when the pace of the questioning is fairly rapid. Tell the deponent not to assume what the question is going to be. Also, tell the deponent to make sure that he or she heard the entire question. Deponents should know they can ask for a question to be repeated if they did not hear any portion of it.

3. Make Sure You Understand the Question and Take a Moment Before Answering

Instruct deponents not only to be sure that they heard the question, but also to be sure they understand the question. A deponent should not hesitate to ask the questioning attorney to repeat or reformulate any question that is difficult to understand. Alternatively, a deponent may try to restate the question in terms that are more understandable, less inflammatory or confusing, or perhaps easier to answer.

Example: *Q:* *Why did you fire my client only one hour after learning that she reported your company's safety violations to OSHA?*

A: *I'm not sure I understand your question. Are you asking me why I fired your client after I found out that she lied about her employment history on her job application?*

The deponent also should be told that the questioning attorney may not accept the deponent's reformulation and may re-ask the same question or a revised question.

Instruct deponents to take their time in answering questions. The deponent should be comfortable pausing to think about the question and to formulate a response before starting to speak. In other words, instruct the deponent to pause and think silently, not out loud. Explain that pauses do not show up on the record, except on a videotape. Caution the deponent to be careful about getting pulled into a rapid sequence of questions and answers. Make sure the deponent knows that to a large extent, the deponent can control the pace of the deposition. Having said this, you want to make sure the deponent knows not to go overboard on this. Sitting silent for a lengthy period can look especially bad if the deposition is videotaped.

Explain also that a short delay before answering gives you an opportunity to make any objections you have to the question. Valid objections may be waived if the deponent blurts out the answer before the attorney can get the objection on the record.

4. Do Not Volunteer Information – Keep Answers Brief

Advise deponents to keep their answers as short as possible and to avoid volunteering information not requested in the question. The following exchange is typical in a deposition:

Example: *Q:* *Did you have a meeting to discuss the test results?*

A: *Oh yes. In fact, we had five or six meetings. The first meeting included me and Bill and Carol from the quality control division. Actually, my boss, Andy, stopped in for part of the meeting. We met over at Bill's office and talked about the disappointing test results. I can't remember everything we said, although I'm sure I could remember a lot more if I looked at my notes. Or better yet, I'm sure Carol's notes would jog my memory. She keeps the most meticulous notes of anyone I know. She records everything everyone says in every meeting she attends. We call her the "human tape recorder."*

The proper answer to the question in this example is a simple "yes." The rest of the information in the answer is all volunteered. You need to make sure deponents understand that a deposition is not like an examination in school in which they get a higher score for conveying more information. Tell them that this is not the time to tell their story; that time will come later. If important facts have not been elicited, you can bring them out by questioning the deponent, or you can save the information for trial. They need not worry about that. Their goal is to briefly answer the questions asked, and only the questions asked, and get out of the deposition as soon as possible.

Warn the deponent that the more information volunteered, the longer the deposition will last. Many witnesses erroneously assume that if they reveal everything they know in response to the first question or two about a topic, they can get out of the deposition sooner. More likely, long narrative responses will prompt many more questions from the examining attorney. You can give the deponent examples of a single volunteered fact that elicited a dozen more questions. Deponents especially should try to avoid gratuitous identification of documents and other records.

A good test question when practicing with the deponent is to ask, "Do you know what time it is?" The only correct answer is "yes" or "no."

5. Do Not Speculate

Always instruct a deponent not to speculate regarding information they do not know. Explain precisely what you mean by this, and then spend some time practicing. Explain that there invariably will be questions about things the deponent does not know or does not remember. The opposing attorney is entitled to find out not only what the deponent knows but also what the deponent does not know. Explain that no one expects the deponent to have total recall of events that transpired years ago, especially if those events were not particularly noteworthy to the deponent at the time. Moreover, speculation is risky business, especially when offered under oath. The deponent should not feel compelled to make up an answer because the deponent feels that he or she *should* know or remember the answer. In other words, "I don't know" and "I don't remember" are perfectly legitimate answers if they are true.[39]

The type of speculation that is relatively easy to spot and also sometimes the most dangerous is a deponent's testimony about the cause of some event, or about what other people knew or thought, or about why other people acted a certain way. It is not improper for an attorney to ask a deponent to speculate in a

---

[39] The "if they are true" qualifier is very important. Witnesses who pretend not to know or not to remember when they actually do are committing perjury. You should never counsel them or imply to them otherwise.

deposition just as it is not improper to ask for other information, such as hearsay, that would not be admissible at trial. Attorneys sometimes ask speculation questions for two purposes: (1) they might try to get the deponent's answer to the question into evidence at trial, and then argue that the deponent's suspicions comport with the attorney's version of the facts (e.g., "Even the defendant's chief engineer suspected that the cause of the fire was a broken gasket."); or (2) they might get lucky and get the deponent to identify a cause, or explanation, or culpable player they had not considered before. If the deponent has no basis to opine regarding the cause of some event, the deponent should not do so.

Likewise, you should instruct a deponent to guard against answering questions that ask for another's thought processes. You should draw the distinction between answering questions about what another individual did or said and questions about what that individual knew or why that individual acted some way. For example, if the deponent is asked about what another person *said* about why that person did something, the deponent can repeat the other person's statement. On the other hand, if the deponent is asked directly why another person did something, the best answer is to refer the questioning attorney to this other individual.

Examples: *Q:* *What did Adam say about why he fired Jane?*
A: *He told me he fired Jane because she was a poor performer.*
Q: *Why did Adam fire Jane?*
A: *I'm sorry. I don't know. You would have to ask Adam why he fired Jane.*

You should inform deponents that they may be asked to approximate an answer, and that in many situations, these requests to approximate are legitimate.

Example: *Q:* *When was the meeting that you just described?*
A: *I really can't remember.*
Q: *Was it more than three years ago?*
A: *Oh, no, it was more recent than that.*
Q: *Was it within the last year?*
A: *It had to have been longer ago than that.*

> *Q:* *So is it fair to say the meeting occurred sometime between a year ago and three years ago?*
>
> *A:* *Yes.*

This sort of approximation is legitimate, and the deponent should feel free to answer such questions. In fact, the deponent's credibility may be undermined if the deponent cannot answer or refuses to answer reasonable approximation questions (e.g., deponent is positive about having a specific conversation but cannot recall if it occurred in the last month or more than ten years ago).

6. Do Not Answer "Yes" or "No" If You Cannot Answer the Question that Way

While you want to encourage deponents to give brief answers, including "yes" and "no" answers, be sure to tell deponents that they may well be asked questions that seek a "yes" or "no" response, but that cannot be answered that way. Deponents should know that they are not forced to give a "yes" or "no" response to such questions. The best way for a deponent to handle this situation is to state that the question cannot be answered that way, to give a brief explanation for why that is the case, and then to provide the lengthier answer.

7. Be Forceful on Important Points but Do Not Exaggerate

Because of their anxiety, deponents often become tentative in almost all of their testimony. As a result, they tend to equivocate about matters they know for certain. While you should instruct deponents not to exaggerate or embellish their testimony, at the same time, you should tell them that they should be forceful regarding the matters about which they are certain. This especially applies to key parts of a deponent's testimony. For example, if the corporate supervisor is asked if an employee's disability was a factor in the supervisor's decision to fire the employee, the supervisor should not answer, "I don't really think it was" or "I don't believe so," if the true answer is "absolutely not." Deponents should know that the way in which they answer these key questions will inevitably affect the opposing attorney's evaluation of the case and may, in fact, have a substantive effect on the outcome of the case.

8. Be Wary of Agreeing to Counsel's Summary of Your Testimony

Caution the deponent that the questioning attorney may at times attempt to summarize the deponent's testimony and then get the deponent to agree that this summary is accurate.

Examples: *Q:* *Is it fair to say . . .?*

Q: *So, you would agree with me that . . .?*

Q: *So, in other words, . . .*

The deponent should be very careful in answering such summary questions. While, in some instances, the opposing counsel's summary may be an accurate characterization of a deponent's testimony, often there will be a change in tone, an omitted fact, a re-characterization, or a shift in emphasis designed to give the opposing attorney a "better" answer. If a deponent encounters such summary questions, he or she should listen very carefully to make sure that the summary is accurate in all respects. If it is, the deponent should indicate as much. If it is not, or the deponent is uncertain about its accuracy or completeness, the proper response is that the deponent's prior testimony is more accurate and complete than counsel's short summary.

9. Do Not Get Angry or Argue With Opposing Counsel

Warn the deponent not to get angry or argue with the questioning attorney. Tell the deponent that the questioning attorney may try to make the deponent angry in order to get the deponent to lose control and to say something the deponent will regret. The deponent should resist all temptation to berate the opposing counsel or party. You may want to give the deponent a few examples of angry deposition outbursts that clearly hurt the deponents' cases.[40]

[40] For a dramatic example of a witness destroying himself in an angry exchange with opposing counsel, see Jack Nicholson's character in the movie, *A Few Good Men.*

10. Avoid Humorous and Sarcastic Remarks

Caution the deponent to avoid jokes and other humorous remarks. While humorous comments may seem perfectly innocent at the time they are made, they can be made to appear more sinister later at trial when the judge or jury has only the bare transcript and cannot see the deponent's joking demeanor. Sarcasm is especially dangerous because such remarks usually are humorous not because of the words used but because of the manner in which they were said. The deposition transcript contains only the literal language uttered, which can be seriously misconstrued later at trial.

Example: *Q:* *Did you fire my client because she objected to your advances?*

A: *Oh yeah, right.*

An answer without the sarcastic tone may look like an admission on the written transcript; even if it does not, opposing counsel may later attack the deponent's levity under the circumstances (e.g., "So you didn't mean 'right,' you just thought it was funny that my client lost her job after 25 years?").

11. Feel Free to Tell the Attorney You Have Not Completed Your Answer

A deponent should feel free to speak up if the questioning attorney interrupts an answer before the deponent is finished. While sometimes these interruptions are innocent – the questioning attorney thought the deponent had finished answering – other times, the interruptions may be a deliberate ploy to distract, when the questioning attorney does not like where the deponent is going and wants to change direction to prevent a more complete response. Just as the deponent is expected not to interrupt the questioning attorney in the middle of a question, it is fair to expect that the questioning attorney not interrupt the deponent in the middle of an answer. Advise the deponent that if it appears to you that the deponent has not finished an answer, you may interject and ask the deponent if the deponent has something else to say in response to the question.

12. Do Not Testify Regarding Privileged Communications

Always instruct deponents not to testify regarding privileged communications. While you as counsel should be listening carefully and objecting to any questions that may elicit such testimony, the deponent also should know not to reveal such communications in response to questions that do not directly seek such information. Make sure that the deponent understands what a privileged communication is and is not. Do not assume that the deponent knows this. The deponent may think that the only thing privileged is what the lawyer tells the client.

Likewise, be sure to instruct the witness not to testify about any matters that are not subject to discovery pursuant to the terms of a protective order. The deponent may not even know that such an order exists.

13. Feel Free to Refer to Documents; Read Documents if Necessary Before Testifying About Them

Tell a deponent whether it is likely that the deponent will be asked about documents and other tangible evidence in the deposition. Advise the deponent to take some time before testifying about documents. If handed a document, the deponent should look it over carefully and read it if necessary before answering questions about it. Caution the deponent to carefully review documents that appear familiar but that may be an earlier version of an amended document, a signed or unsigned version of a document, or a document with handwritten notes in the text or margin.

14. Be Prepared for Closure Questions – Employ the "At This Time" Tag-On

Advise the deponent that the questioning attorney will invariably ask closure questions to try to box in the deponent's testimony. These are legitimate questions that all questioning attorneys should ask. When you are defending depositions, however, you would prefer that your deponents leave themselves a little wiggle room. Probably the best way to do this is to use a truthful "at this time" tag-on to their answers.

Example:

Q: Is that everything you remember about what was said in that conversation?

A: That is all I recall about the conversation at this time.

Q: Did you provide the customers with any other documents at the time of their purchase?

A: Not that I can recall at this time.

15. Do Not Agree to Produce Documents

Sometimes a deponent will reference a document or other thing that the opposing side has not received. In these situations, the questioning attorney likely will ask the deponent to produce the referenced item after the deposition. You should tell the deponent, if the deponent is your client, that you will deal with opposing counsel in regard to such a request. If the deponent is a non-party, this instruction does not apply, since you generally do not have the right to screen requests from opposing counsel. Having said this, you can advise non-party deponents that they may want to consult with their own attorneys before agreeing to such a production request.

16. Correct Mistakes at the Deposition

It generally is best to correct inaccuracies in a deponent's testimony at the deposition itself. Tell the deponent to let you know during a break about any mistakes or omissions from previous testimony (unless you are in a jurisdiction that strictly precludes conversations with deponents during breaks). Explain that you can give the deponent an opportunity to correct the mistake when the deponent is back on the record. You should listen carefully to the mistake or omission the deponent identifies during the break. It may turn out that something later recalled was actually never requested.

E. Discuss Your Role and the Limitations on What You May Do

It is a good idea to explain to the deponent your role and the limitations on what you can do in a deposition. Some deponents may have the preconceived notion that you will object to every other question and engage in lengthy arguments with opposing counsel. They may be surprised to see you sit through the deposition and not utter a word (especially when you then send them a bill for your seven hours of silence). In explaining your role, cover the following topics.

1. Objections

Explain your right to object to a question and the kinds of objections you may make. Advise the deponent that with few exceptions, an objection does not relieve the deponent of the obligation to answer the question. Explain also that you may choose not to object to certain questions for strategic reasons or simply to expedite the deposition, even though such questions would be objectionable at trial. Assure the deponent that you will do this only with objections that will not otherwise be waived.

Instruct the deponent to stop talking if you make an objection, and to wait until you tell the deponent to proceed. While waiting, the deponent should listen to your objection as it may indicate a problem with the question that the deponent may want to consider.

Example: *Objection. Lack of foundation. The question calls for the witness to speculate as to the cause of the accident.*

While attorneys are not permitted to make lengthy speaking objections to coach a witness, the deponent can take certain clues from a succinct statement of the grounds for an objection.

2. Instructions Not To Answer

Be sure the deponent understands that there may be circumstances in which you will instruct the deponent not to answer a question. You may instruct the deponent not to answer if the question seeks privileged information or information excluded from discovery under a protective order. You may not instruct a non-client witness, unless necessary to protect a privilege belonging to your client (e.g., former corporate employee who previously had access to privileged information). You may, however, recommend that a non-client deponent consult the deponent's own attorney if the deponent anticipates being asked or is asked a question that calls for information the deponent believes should not be disclosed.

3. Conferences With You

What do you tell deponents about their right to confer privately with you during a deposition? The answer depends on what the courts in your jurisdiction will allow. Some courts have a very restrictive view of the right to confer privately with counsel, holding that once the deposition begins, any private communication between an attorney and the deponent is either flatly prohibited or is not privileged and subject to discovery.[41] Other courts permit an attorney to

---

[41] *See, e.g.*, Hall v. Clifton Precision, 150 F.R.D. 525, 528 (E.D. Pa. 1993) (finding that there is no absolute right to confer during a client's deposition). In *Birdine v. City of Coatesville*, 225 F.R.D. 157 (E.D. Pa. 2004), however, another judge in the same jurisdiction concluded that "*Hall* goes too far in forbidding an attorney who defends a deposition . . . from making most objections and from instructing the witness not to answer an objectionable question." *Id.* at 158. The court agreed, however, that objections should be "succinct and verbally economical, stating the basis of the objection and nothing more." *Id.* (quoting *Hall*, 150 F.R.D. at 531). While *Birdine* illustrates that even though a judge in the jurisdiction that rendered the *Hall* decision is willing to retreat from that decision somewhat, there are courts that will restrict or even prohibit private communication between an attorney and the deponent once the deposition has begun. Vnuk v. Berwick Hosp. Co., No. 3:14-CV-01432, 2016 WL 907714, at *4 (M.D. Pa. Mar. 2, 2016) (counsel prohibited from speaking with client during deposition unless counsel is conferring regarding potential assertion of a privilege; if counsel and client do speak, opposing counsel may "inquire as to the contents of these conversations"); *but see* Henry v. Champlain Enters., Inc., 212 F.R.D. 73, 92 (N.D.N.Y. 2003) (privilege protects deposition break conversation between counsel and deponent). *See also, e.g.,* Plaisted v. Geisinger Med. Ctr., 210 F.R.D. 527, 532, 535 (M.D. Pa. 2002) (adopting guidelines from *Hall* and applying them to defense counsel conduct, including repeated objections, instructions to witness not to answer, and leaving deposition room with a question pending); In re Anonymous Member of South Carolina Bar, 552 S.E.2d 10, 16 (S.C. 2001) (explaining that South Carolina Rules of Civil Procedure have adopted the *Hall* approach to deposition conduct of attorneys); Calzaturficio S.C.A.R.P.A. s.p.a. v. Fabiano Shoe Co., 201 F.R.D. 33, 39-40 (D. Mass. 2001) (agreeing with *Hall* that speaking, coaching, conferring during questioning and while questions are pending, and leaving the room while questions are pending, are not permitted during depositions). For a relatively succinct summary of the *Hall* fallout, consider *AmerisourceBergen Drug Corp. v. CuraScript Inc.*, 83 Pa. D.&C. 4th 362, 368-75 (Pa. Com. Pl. 2007) (summarizing different jurisdictions' attitudes toward *Hall*). Some jurisdictions have adopted Hall through cases or amendments to local rules of civil procedure. Others have refused to implement any of the *Hall* guidelines. Moore's Federal Practice summarizes: "[*Hall*] and other similar cases are understandable and appropriate in the face of preexisting misconduct, but otherwise have the potential to interfere too greatly with legitimate attorney protection of the witness and client interests." *See* MOORE'S FEDERAL PRACTICE §§ 30.43 [6] (3d ed. 2010). *See*

confer privately with a deponent during a break in the questioning.[42] Few courts permit an attorney to confer with a deponent while a question is pending,[43] unless the conference is simply to determine whether the deponent's response is about to reveal privileged information.

Assuming that your jurisdiction permits private conferences during deposition breaks, you may want to advise deponents to request a break if they really need to talk to you. They should know, however, that they cannot overdo this. If the deposition has just recently resumed, the questioning attorney may object to another break.

4. Your Questions

Advise the deponent that you will have an opportunity to ask questions after the other attorney has finished, and that you may use this opportunity to try to correct mistakes or to allow the deponent to clarify certain answers. Also tell the deponent that you may forego this right if you feel that nothing needs to be clarified. Remind the deponent that there will be a later opportunity to tell the deponent's full story.

5. Motion for a Protective Order

Some deponents may worry that they will be harassed or embarrassed in the deposition. Reassure them by explaining that you will protect them through objections or, ultimately, by stopping the deposition and going to court if things get out of hand. Notwithstanding this right, make sure the deponent understands that this does not mean the deponent will be protected from answering difficult questions. The right to terminate the deposition is limited to the most severe situations.

---

also In re Flonase Antitrust Litig., 2010 WL 2649923 (E.D. Pa. June 30, 2010) (applying Pennsylvania state law, not *Hall*).

[42] *See, e.g.*, In re Stratosphere Corp. Sec. Litig., 182 F.R.D. 614, 621 (D. Nev. 1998).

[43] *Id.*

F. Discuss Opposing Counsel

It is useful to tell a deponent a bit about opposing counsel, including counsel's role and expected deposition style.

1. Role

Deponents should know what goals the opposing counsel is trying to accomplish in a deposition. One purpose of a deposition is to gather information. Attorneys also may use depositions to pin deponents down to a particular story. Invariably, the opposing attorney will make an assessment of the deponent – how good or bad a witness the deponent will be at trial – in order to evaluate the strength of the attorney's case. This evaluation can affect the other side's settlement posture.

2. Style

If you know the opposing attorney who will take the deposition, you may want to tell the deponent something about the opposing attorney's style: Does the attorney act like the deponent's best friend? Is the attorney disorganized? Does the attorney like to summarize a deponent's testimony? Does the attorney like to develop a rapid pace to give the deponent little time to think? In the final analysis, the deponent should know that the opposing attorney is not a friend. Some attorneys like to drive this point home by telling deponents that no matter how friendly and helpful the opposing counsel may appear, their objective is to take bread from the mouths of the deponent's children. While that may be a bit extreme, it might be worth emphasizing to the type of witness who likes to please everyone that the opposing attorney's objective, at a minimum, is to further the attorney's ultimate goal of winning the case. While that is not to suggest that the deponent should be uncivil, it is to impress upon the deponent that the other attorney's graciousness and charming demeanor may be a calculated tactic intended to lower the deponent's guard and thus to help the other side's case.

G. Discuss the Witness's Fears

Sometimes during the course of preparing a deponent, certain fears may intensify and other new ones may come to mind. Ask the deponent to identify any concerns the deponent may have. Which potential questions create the greatest anxiety? Are there particular facts or documents that cause the deponent special concern? Such questions may identify additional topics you should discuss, and may even reveal to you new facts.

H. Practice

After you have reviewed all your practice tips with the deponent, do not assume that the deponent will magically internalize these principles and be prepared and ready to testify. This is not fair to the deponent, and few deponents can do this. As with anything, practice is critical.

1. Do a Mock Examination

Take some time to conduct portions of a mock deposition to see how the deponent answers questions. This is especially crucial in regard to the tough questions the deponent is likely to face. The deponent should not hear these questions for the first time in the deposition. Do not sugarcoat the questions. If you expect the opposing attorney to ask aggressive questions and to challenge the deponent with tough follow-up questions, try to ask the same questions and to simulate the opposing attorney's style. It is far better that the deponent first experience tough questioning from you than in the deposition. If you are concerned that your aggressive mock questioning might hurt your relationship with your deponent, explain at the outset that you will be role-playing; otherwise, consider asking a colleague to play the role of opposing counsel. (You may know someone who would jump at the chance!)

While you should discuss and critique the deponent's answers in your mock deposition session, do not try to script out any answers. This will likely only back-fire. It is better for the deponent's answer to appear spontaneous than for it exactly to track a scripted response. Instead of trying to script out an answer, get the witness to remember a short list of key points or concepts to which the deponent can then testify in the deponent's own words.

Do not neglect to critique body language and eye contact. Remind the deponent that opposing counsel will be assessing the deponent's demeanor as well as the deponent's testimony. If you suspect that your deponent will be asked to draw a diagram or to perform some reenactment, you should have the deponent do these things in your preparation session. You may have some suggestions regarding this non-verbal testimony.

Example: *If you are asked to draw such a diagram of the accident scene in your deposition, I don't think you need to include such graphic detail.*

2. Consider Videotaping a Mock Deposition

In limited cases and only with clients, you may want to videotape a mock deposition of the deponent so that the deponent can watch his or her testimony. This can be especially useful if you notice that the deponent has certain distracting nonverbal mannerisms, like looking down when answering or hand-wringing. While minimizing these mannerisms obviously is more important if the deposition is to be videotaped, it also can be important in regard to the visual impression the deponent will leave with opposing counsel.

3. Get Your Deponents To Do Their Own Preparation

There is only so much you can accomplish in your face-to-face preparation session with the deponent. There are times when the deponent should engage in additional independent preparation. For example, personal injury plaintiffs should spend time inventorying their injuries and all of the ways in which the injuries have adversely affected their lives. Certain corporate employees in a commercial dispute should thoroughly familiarize themselves with the factual chronology and documents. But be careful. Except possibly in the case of a Federal Rule of Civil Procedure 30(b)(6) corporate deponent, you do not want employees to educate themselves about facts or documents that they otherwise could say honestly are not familiar.

The point is, if a lot is riding on the lawsuit, your clients should understand that they need to work hard with you to get the best result. Be sure also to tell deponents to advise you if they subsequently remember or discover additional information that you did not discuss in your review session.

I. Ethical Issues Regarding Preparation of Deponents

The preparation of deponents raises some thorny ethical issues. Some deponents show up at their depositions so shiny and smooth from their counsel's sand-papering job that their clothes practically slide off them. Where is the line between thorough preparation and ethical transgression? There are several ethical rules applicable to deposition preparation, but these rules do not always tell you precisely where the line falls. The following discussion introduces various ethical issues that arise in the preparation of deponents.[44]

1. Can You Disclose the Law Before Deponents Give Their Narrative Account of the Facts?

It is not improper *per se* for an attorney to provide an overview of the law to a deponent before asking for the deponent's recollection of the facts, but do not do so in a way that suggests how the facts ultimately should unfold. To suggest facts before you know what they are would constitute unethical coaching.

Example: *We can win this case, and you can probably keep your job, only if we can show that you did not receive the cancellation notice before December 31st. Now when did you receive that notice?*

2. Can You Challenge a Deponent's Recollection of Unfavorable Facts?

Challenging a deponent's recollection of unfavorable facts is not unethical, depending upon how it is done. Some techniques are improper:

Example: *So you think you saw your boss and the plaintiff alone in the storeroom that night. I find this rather difficult to believe since your boss denies this. Also, if you were near the storeroom, that would mean you were away from your work station without*

[44] For a good discussion of these various ethical issues, see James M. Altman, *Witness Preparation Conflicts*, 22 LITIG., Fall 1995, at 38.

> *permission. If I'm not mistaken, that would be the third time this happened in one month which is, as you know, grounds for suspension. Now, do you think your memory of that night might be mistaken?*

On the other hand, you do not have to accept as fact everything a deponent says. After the deponent discloses some fact, you can test the deponent's knowledge of that fact: Does the deponent know the fact from firsthand observation or did the deponent learn of the fact from another? Is the source of the fact reliable? Were the circumstances such that the deponent might have been mistaken about the fact (e.g., Was it dark? Was the deponent distracted?)? Is the deponent certain of the fact or only conjecturing? All of these are legitimate questions and the very kind of questions the opposing attorney will ask in regard to testimony unfavorable to the other side.

3. Can You Refresh a Deponent's Recollection of the Facts?

You can refresh a deponent's memory if the deponent's "refreshed" memory is truthful – that is, the deponent can honestly state that the facts now recalled comport with the deponent's honest, albeit refreshed, recollection and are not simply the attorney's own rendition of the facts. It is proper to help deponents remember that which they once knew. It is not proper to make them remember that which you wished they once knew.

One plaintiff personal injury law firm was accused of unethical coaching based on a memorandum the law firm gave to their class action clients. Entitled "Preparing for your Deposition," the memorandum told the clients, among other things, that it was important that they maintain that they never saw any "Danger" or "Warning" labels on asbestos products, that they should be confident that they saw just as much of one brand of asbestos product as another, and that the defense attorneys have no records to tell them what products were used on a particular job even if they act as if they do.[45] The memorandum also instructed the clients what to say when asked about injuries.[46]

---

[45] *See* Michael Higgins, *Fine Line,* A.B.A. J., May 1998, at 52, 53-54. The memorandum was inadvertently produced to the defense attorneys. While conceding that parts of the memorandum

4. Can You Instruct a Deponent Not to Discuss Some Matter?

Is it ever permissible to counsel a deponent not to discuss some matter in a deposition? For example, can you instruct a deponent not to discuss a certain meeting, document, or incident from last year's company holiday party? While you can and should counsel a witness not to volunteer information in a deposition, it is not proper to instruct a witness not to discuss some fact or matter if the deponent's truthful answer to a question would entail disclosure of the fact or matter, so long as the fact or matter is not privileged or barred from discovery under a protective order.

5. Can You Suggest That a Deponent Use Different Words While Testifying?

It is not inappropriate to suggest that a deponent describe certain matters using different words so long as the attorney's suggestion does not alter the expected testimony.

Example: *That was a pretty good response, but might I suggest that you not refer to your company's sales pitch to consumers as "our usual song and dance."*

But not:

I would suggest and prefer that you describe the color of the light using the word "green" instead of "red."

---

went too far, the law firm maintained that it did not authorize the memorandum and that it was written by a misguided paralegal. *Id.* at 55.

[46] *Id.* at 54.

6. Can You Signal a Witness?

Deponents may ask you if you will signal them if they get off track, start to ramble, or say something wrong. Short of making an on-the-record objection, the answer is an unequivocal "no."

7. What If You Discover Evidence of Your Client's Fraud or Illegal Conduct While Preparing a Deponent?

Suppose an employee of an organization that you are representing informs you in a deposition preparation session that the organization has violated the law, committed fraud, or destroyed documents. Employees sometimes spill their guts to you about such matters and consider you to be their personal attorney. They may even expect that their conversation with you is completely confidential. What do you do if this happens? Panic? Cover your ears and chant "I'm not listening"?

Before this occurs, you should make sure that the employee understands that your client is the employer, and that you cannot keep from the employer any information given to you by the employee.[47] It is advisable for attorneys to tell employee deponents at the outset of their preparation session that the attorney represents the employer, that the attorney does not have a personal attorney-client relationship with the employee, and that any privilege attached to the discussion is the employer's privilege, not the employee's. One downside of such an instruction, depending on how it is given, is that it may have the effect of scaring the employee and discouraging candor. Under no circumstances, however, should you mislead the employee about your role.

Do you talk to the employer about this incriminating information or do you pretend you did not hear it? The answer is obvious. If the information from the employee sounds like it could be credible, you must discuss the allegation

[47] The situation is more complicated and beyond the scope of a "First Depositions" book if the employee is an officer or director or otherwise also has standing as your client at the time the deponent raises allegations of illegal conduct on the part of the employer.

with the employer so you can properly address the matter in this lawsuit or a later suit.[48]

What do you do if the employer asks you to identify the source of the allegation? This is trickier. You may be concerned that the employer will retaliate against the employee or that the employee will no longer talk to you. On the other hand, the employer may need this information to respond to the allegation and to conduct its own investigation. In the final analysis, you are unlikely to be able to withhold this information from the employer. This is why it probably is best for you to advise the employee right from the start that you represent the employer and are not the employee's personal counsel.

This ethical issue is even more complicated for the government attorney who may have an obligation to reveal the government agency's or official's alleged fraud or illegal conduct to law enforcement authorities even if this results in the prosecution of one of the attorney's clients.

[48] Be mindful also of applicable ethics rules. *See, e.g.,* MODEL RULES OF PROF'L CONDUCT R. 1.13 (2002); MINN. RULES OF PROF'L CONDUCT R. 1.13 (2005).

CHAPTER 4

Representing the Deponent

There are several facets to representing deponents besides preparing them to testify. First, you should determine if you can prevent the prospective deponent from ever becoming an actual deponent. That is, can you prevent the deposition altogether? If not, should you ask the court to limit the deposition in some manner? Then you will need to defend the deponent at the deposition. The following discussion introduces each of these facets of representing deponents.

A. Preventing Depositions

You may on occasion attempt to block the deposition of a person whom you believe ought not be deposed at all by seeking a protective order.[49] The following kinds of witnesses commonly are the subject of protective order motions.

[49] *See* FED. R. CIV. P. 26(c).

1. Attorneys and Investigators

Can opposing counsel take *your* deposition? Numerous courts have addressed the right of litigants to depose opposing counsel. Some of these courts have held that an attorney is subject to a deposition like any other witness because nothing in Rule 30 exempts attorneys from this discovery device. Other courts have criticized the practice of deposing opposing counsel and have blocked such attempted depositions or have allowed them only when there were no other means of obtaining the information, and only if the information was crucial and not privileged.[50] These courts recognize the ethical dilemma that an attorney faces when acting as both counsel and witness in a case. In fact, this ethical conflict can lead to disqualification of the attorney if the attorney is compelled to testify at

---

[50] Shelton v. Am. Motors Corp., 805 F.2d 1323, 1330 (8th Cir. 1986). This case is probably the seminal case in opposition to depositions of opposing counsel. The court concluded that this practice does nothing for the administration of justice, prolongs and increases the cost of litigation, demeans the profession, and has a chilling effect on attorney-client communications. *Cf.* Phillips v. Indianapolis Life Ins. Co., 2009 WL 1564384, at *3 (S.D. Ind. June 3, 2009) ("*Shelton's* heightened burden-of-proof rule finds no support in the plain text of the Federal Rules of Civil Procedure.").

In 2002, the Eighth Circuit limited *Shelton* to depositions regarding the subject of the pending litigation. Inquiries of opposing attorneys regarding previously concluded litigation do not fall under the holding of *Shelton*, and are permissible. Pamida, Inc. v. E.S. Originals, Inc., 281 F.3d 726, 730 (8th Cir. 2002); *see also, e.g.*, aaiPharma, Inc. v. Kremers Urban Dev. Co., 361 F. Supp. 2d 770, 775 (N.D. Ill. 2005) (deposition of attorney on issues other than the underlying litigation is permitted); United States v. Philip Morris, Inc., 209 F.R.D. 13, 17-18 (D.D.C. 2002) (in-house counsel could be deposed by the government because the government only sought "testimony about non-privileged, pre-litigation factual matters," and because the attorneys being deposed were not trial counsel). *Pamida* increasingly has been distinguished or called into question. *See, e.g.*, Vazquez v. Central States Joint Bd., 2009 WL 1530709, at *3 (N.D. Ill. Jun. 1, 2009) ("In our judgment, *Pamida* does not reflect so much a limitation of *Shelton* as it does a decision, based on the facts presented in that case, that the concerns the *Shelton* rule seeks to address were not present."); FMC Techs., Inc. v. Edwards, 2007 WL 836709, at *4 (W.D. Wash. Mar. 15, 2007) (distinguishing *Pamida* on grounds that the concluded litigation into which inquiry would be made was intertwined with the case at bar); Desert Orchid Partners, L.L.C. v. Transaction Sys. Architects, Inc. 237 F.R.D. 215, 220 (D. Neb. 2006) (applying *Shelton*, rather than *Pamida*, in barring deposition of non-trial counsel).

trial.[51] Courts also have dealt with attempts to take the deposition of an investigator working with opposing counsel.[52]

Some courts draw a distinction between depositions of trial counsel and depositions of in-house attorneys, concluding that in-house attorneys may be deposed even if trial attorneys cannot. These courts reason that the concerns regarding depositions of trial attorneys are not substantially implicated in depositions of in-house attorneys.[53]

2. High Level Government/Corporate Officials

What if opposing counsel notices the deposition of the CEO of your large corporate client or the governor of a state? A number of courts have held that, absent special circumstances, a variety of grounds may protect individuals in these positions from being deposed.[54] Courts have reasoned, for example, that these individuals are simply too busy and need the freedom to perform their duties without the interference of the discovery process.[55] In instances involving high

---

[51] Some commentators have advised that a deposition of counsel may be preventable by ensuring that the opposing party has alternate sources for the same information. *See* Jerold S. Solovy & Robert L. Byman, *Opponent Deponents*, NAT'L L.J., Jan. 8, 2001, at A17.

[52] *See, e.g.*, Leyh v. Modicon, 881 F. Supp. 420, 425 (S.D. Ind. 1995) (refusing to permit deposition of E.E.O.C investigator in an employment discrimination case); *cf.* E.E.O.C. v. Cal. Psychiatric Transitions, 258 F.R.D. 391 (E.D. Cal. 2009) (allowing deposition of E.E.O.C. investigator to proceed in case where E.E.O.C. was a party, but holding subject to privilege any conclusions, interpretations, or recommendations that E.E.O.C. investigator formulated).

[53] *See, e.g.*, Luster v. Schafer, No. 08-cv-02399, 2009 WL 2219255, at *2-*4 (D. Colo. July 23, 2009); Evans v. Atwood, 1999 WL 1032811, at *3 (D.D.C. Sept. 29, 1999).

[54] *See* Walker v. NCNB Nat'l Bank, 810 F. Supp. 11, 13 (D.D.C. 1993) (applying "high government official" doctrine to block deposition of E.E.O.C. Director); Mulvey v. Chrysler Corp., 106 F.R.D. 364, 366 (D.R.I. 1985) (refusing to allow deposition of chairman of Chrysler). *But see* In re Bridgestone/Firestone, Inc., Tires Prods. Liab. Litig., 205 F.R.D. 535, 536-37 (S.D. Ind. 2002) (permitting deposition of chairman of Ford Motor Company). *See also* Apple, Inc. v. Samsung Elec. Co., 282 F.R.D. 259 (N.D. Cal. 2012) (disallowing the deposition of one officer; allowing the deposition of others, with restrictions).

[55] Warzon v. Drew, 155 F.R.D. 183, 185 (E.D. Wis. 1994); Gov't Suppliers Consol'g Servs., Inc. v. Bayh, 133 F.R.D. 531, 533 n.3 (S.D. Ind. 1990).

level government officials, courts have blocked depositions to protect the official's deliberative processes – to prevent inquiry into how government officials make policy decisions.[56] A party wishing to depose a high level corporate or government official should be prepared to show that the individual has unique, first-hand knowledge, and that the evidence sought is not available through some less burdensome means such as a deposition of a lower level official or written interrogatories.[57] Even if the high ranking official has unique, first-hand knowledge, the court may impose restrictions on the deposition in order to minimize the risk of abuse or imposition of an undue burden.[58]

---

[56] Members of Congress and legislators in certain states also are immune from discovery, including depositions, by the Speech or Debate Clause of the United States and of respective state constitutions. *See* U.S. CONST. art. I, § 6; MINN. CONST. art. IV, § 10. The elected official may, however, waive this immunity and agree to testify. For a case involving presidential aides, see Harlow v. Fitzgerald, 457 U.S. 800, 817-18 (1982) (concluding qualified immunity for certain government officials is advisable based in part on "costs of trial" and "burdens of broad-reaching discovery" that are "peculiarly disruptive of effective government"). Similarly, judicial personnel usually are immune from testifying at a deposition. *See, e.g.*, Beam v. Dep't of the Air Force, 169 F.R.D. 309, 311 (D. Md. 1996) (preventing plaintiffs from deposing federal magistrate judge); Terrazas v. Slagle, 142 F.R.D. 136, 140 (W.D. Tex. 1992) (denying depositions of judicial law clerks).

[57] In re Nat'l W. Life Ins. Deferred Annuities Litig., 2011 WL 1304587, at *1 (S.D. Cal., Apr. 6, 2011), and cases cited therein; *see also, e.g.*, Sweeney v. Bond, 669 F.2d 542, 546 (8th Cir. 1982). If you are the attorney attempting to depose a high-ranking individual, you may want to start lower in the organizational scheme, gradually working your way up. In this way, you can more likely demonstrate the need for the particular deposition. Additionally, you may better be able to show you are not fishing for information that can be obtained from others, and that the deposition can have a limited focus. *See* B. Fernandez & Hnos, Inc. v. Int'l Bhd. of Teamsters, 285 F.R.D. 185, 186 (D.P.R. 2012) (deposition of IBT president not allowed where no demonstration that deposition of lower-level executive would be insufficient).

[58] *See, e.g.*, In re Transpacific Passenger Air Trans. Antitrust Litig., No. C-07-05634, 2014 WL 939287, at *6 (N.D. Cal. Mar. 6, 2014) (CEO with unique, first-hand knowledge may be deposed, but for no more than two hours).

3. Minors and Impaired Deponents

You may on occasion be able to block the deposition of a minor or impaired witness.[59] In some instances involving very sick witnesses, the parties will take the witness's deposition at the witness's residence or in a hospital room with the witness's physician in attendance.[60] If the potential deponent is a party as opposed to a witness, the court will impose a higher burder before granting a protective order.[61]

4. Witnesses With Privileged Information

Courts have been willing to block depositions of persons who have or had access to privileged information. For example, in a case in which a party has not put his or her physical or mental condition in issue, a court may refuse to allow the deposition of the party's treating physician. Likewise, a court may block the deposition of a spouse to enforce a spousal privilege. If opposing counsel notices the deposition of someone whose relevant information is privileged, it is worth doing some research and preparing a motion for a protective order. Even if the court does not block the deposition, it may lay out some ground rules.

5. Experts

You may be able to prevent the other side from learning the identity of and later deposing experts you have informally consulted or retained who are not expected to testify at trial. As discussed in Chapter 6, courts generally refuse to require parties to disclose the identity of such experts absent some extraordinary

---

[59] *See, e.g.*, In re McCorhill Publ'g, Inc., 91 B.R. 223, 225 (Bankr. S.D.N.Y. 1988) (blocking deposition of 80-year-old man suffering from dementia); *see also* Israel v. Israel, 2014 IL App. (1st) 131707-U, at *15, (Ill. Ct. App. Sept. 18, 2014) (evidentiary hearing required to determine whether cardiac issues should preclude deposition of 94-year-old).

[60] *See, e.g.*, Haviland & Co. v. Montgomery Ward & Co., 31 F.R.D. 578, 580 (S.D.N.Y. 1962) (allowing ailing 80-year-old deponent to be deposed at his residence).

[61] *See, e.g.*, Campos v. Webb Co.Texas, 288 F.R.D. 134, 137-38 (S.D. Tex. 2012).

need (e.g., the expert was the only one who examined the product at issue before it was destroyed).[62]

B. Protective Orders Regarding the Conduct of Depositions

A court may issue a protective order not only to prevent a deposition, but also to restrict the terms and conditions under which the deposition can be taken.[63] These orders regarding the conduct of depositions may pertain to issues such as duration, location, persons present, frequency of breaks, topics to be covered, and the sealing of testimony. The court is empowered to issue such orders to protect a party or person from annoyance, embarrassment, oppression, or undue burden or expense.[64]

In instances in which an attorney or witness has been abusive or has otherwise interfered with the taking of the deposition, the court will issue a protective order requiring that the deposition resume in the presence of a magistrate judge or other court-appointed neutral who has the authority to resolve objections right on the spot. In ordering that future depositions take place in front of a court-appointed discovery master, one court remarked that the acrimony between counsel in the case "necessitates the provision of day care for counsel who, like small children, cannot get along and require adult supervision."[65]

---

[62] *See, e.g.*, Hermsdorfer v. Am. Motors Corp., 96 F.R.D. 13, 15 (W.D.N.Y. 1982) (plaintiffs not entitled to depose expert specially retained by defendants).

[63] FED. R. CIV. P. 26(c).

[64] The court in *Bucher v. Richardson Hosp. Auth.*, 160 F.R.D. 88 (N.D. Tex. 1994), required that the deposition of a sexually abused 15-year-old be taken at a treatment center, that the deposition be limited to two hours, that the deponent have a therapist present, that counsel for the defendant (and alleged abuser) ask questions from another room via closed circuit television, and that the testimony be limited to certain areas. *Id.* at 95. Be careful, though. If you want restrictions put on a deposition, you must present specific evidence supporting your request; conclusory statements, even from a doctor or psychiatrist, may not suffice. Halley v. Oklahoma, 2016 WL 4995393, No. 14-CV-562, at *2 (E.D. Okla. Sept. 19, 2016) (plaintiff granted leave to present additional evidence supporting requested restrictions on deposition of traumatized 8-year-old; doctor's conclusory statements were insufficient).

[65] Van Pilsum v. Iowa State Univ. of Sci. and Tech., 152 F.R.D. 179, 181 (S.D. Iowa 1993).

C. Defending the Deposition

Defending a deposition is all about making sure you protect your client's interests. Following are things to consider.

1. Protecting the Deponent and the Record Generally

When you defend a deposition, you are in a defensive mode. You still have your litigation blueprint. This witness presumably has information that will help establish or refute claims and defenses. You want positive testimony to come out strongly and you want negative testimony to come out with the best spin that is factually accurate. But, it is your opposing counsel who decided to take this deposition, so mostly you are striving to stay out of trouble.[66]

We recommend the following steps in that regard:

- First, do not agree to the "usual and customary stipulations" at the start of the deposition. Who knows what they are?[67] If asked to agree to such stipulations, you might respond that the federal rules should be sufficient to govern the deposition.

- Second, put on the record any limitations that apply. For example, if the court has imposed restrictions on the scope of the deposition, make sure those are stated.

Example: *Good morning, counsel. We are producing Ms. Jones today pursuant to the Court's protective order of March 6, 2001, and all of its terms are applicable.*

---

[66] The exception to this is if you represent a third-party witness, either an individual or an organization. If your individual or organization has no personal stake in the outcome of the litigation other than to try not to make either side unhappy, your main goals are to stick absolutely to the facts, to avoid speculation, and to get out of the deposition as soon as possible. You typically have no claims or defenses that you have to prove, and no special risks to avoid, other than being drawn into the litigation.

[67] *See* Diana S. Donaldson, *Deposition Essentials: New Basics for Old Masters*, 26 LITIG., Summer 2000, at 25, 26.

- Third, make sure that there is only one questioning lawyer from each party. That lawyer should ask all of his or her questions before a lawyer for another party proceeds. That way, your witness does not get whipsawed back and forth. Similarly, only that one lawyer should be allowed to state objections during the deposition.

- Fourth, demand that your witness be able to see any documents upon which the witness is questioned. Sometimes, opposing counsel will refuse to show a document because the lawyer first wants the deponent's "un-refreshed" recollection. That is not in itself objectionable if the subject of the questioning is a general topic. But an argument can be made that the refusal is objectionable when the subject of the questioning is the document itself.

Example: *Counsel, you are asking the witness questions about Exhibit 2. If you are going to do that, please allow the witness to see a copy. [I am entitled to the witness's recollection of the July 12 meeting without the document.] Then ask her about her recollection of the July 12 meeting, but do not ask her to interpret Exhibit 2.*

- Fifth, do not allow opposing counsel to stand behind your witness. Some lawyers will ask a deponent a series of questions about a document while standing behind the deponent and reading over the deponent's shoulder. This creates two problems: first, some witnesses are intimidated by people looming over them; and second, because you are sitting beside the witness, opposing counsel is now in a position to see your notes.

- Sixth, take breaks. In our experience, witnesses do not last very well except in one hour segments. After that, their concentration starts to break down. Opposing counsel is entitled to finish an immediate line of questioning before a break, but then just take one.

- Seventh, if you arrive at the deposition location in time to select your seating at the deposition table, do not place your witness where he or she is looking at a window. Windows make concentration more difficult. If you are facing a window and the sun is bright or the view is distracting, pull the shades.

- Eighth, ask the questioning lawyer to repeat a question if you missed it. Sometimes the acoustics in the deposition room make it difficult to hear. Other times, you may be concentrating on what your deponent just said, causing you to miss the next inquiry. In any event, do not let questions or answers slide by without fully hearing them.

- Ninth, never be in a hurry (even if you are!). Here is a classic example: You are at a deposition out of town. You would like to go home. You have a 4:30 p.m. flight. Opposing lawyers continue to push their questioning longer than necessary. Missing the flight will make you mad, which may cause you to start making mistakes in the deposition. The threat of missing the flight may cause you to speed up the deposition, which again may cause you to make additional mistakes. Adjourning the deposition to another day is likely a mistake, because it gives opposing counsel another shot at your witness. *["Your Honor, we could have finished in seven hours, but attorney Smith couldn't stay that long; so we need additional time."]* If you are going to be a litigator, get used to going with the flow, and do not give out a lot of specifics about your travel plans.

Example: *[So, counsel, trying to get out of here this afternoon?] If that works out, fine. There are several flights tonight and tomorrow.*

- Tenth, except for the weather and sports, do not let your deponent chit chat with opposing counsel or parties during breaks. If the conversation turns to anything substantively relevant to the case, you can be sure it will wind up on the record somehow. Witnesses forget that, and tend to let their guard down during breaks.

- Eleventh, at the conclusion of the deposition, encourage your witness to state on the record that he or she will exercise the right to read and sign the transcript after it is prepared. The deposition may be used against the witness and should be as accurate as you can make it. Of course, if there are no substantive changes to make that actually matter, the witness can always waive the signing after reviewing the transcript.[68]

- Twelfth, stay professional. Try not to panic. Try not to show emotions. Try not to rant and rave. Do not play games. Afford appropriate professional courtesies to other counsel that do not substantively damage your client's case.

Protect Deponent and Record

- No "usual and customary stipulations"
- Listen with vigilance
- Insure witness treated fairly
- Always read and sign transcript

[68] *See, e.g.*, Gerald Solovy and Robert Byman, "*Do You Sign Here?*", NAT'L L.J., Aug. 6, 2001, at B10. "So here's what we do: To keep our options open, we always invoke, before the conclusion of the deposition, the right to review and sign the deposition. Then we think very carefully about whether our witness has said anything during the deposition that absolutely requires correction. And unless he has stepped in something awful, we waive signature and let the transcript stand." *Id.* at B14.

Solovy and Byman precede this advice with some skepticism about the value of reading a transcript, making changes to it, and signing it because of the automatic impeachment possibilities that then result. But we are skeptical of the skepticism. We agree there is little point in having a witness sign a transcript with no changes. But witnesses can effectively be impeached when they try to correct transcripts at trial, even when they have not previously signed them. Moreover, waiting to correct a transcript on the fly at trial looks suspicious.

2. Objections and Instructions Not to Answer

a. The Rules

Some objections must be made immediately at the deposition or they will be waived. Other objections may safely be reserved until trial. Because you will need to decide instantly and without reflection whether to object to any given question at a deposition, you need to have the distinction between waivable and non-waivable objections down cold.

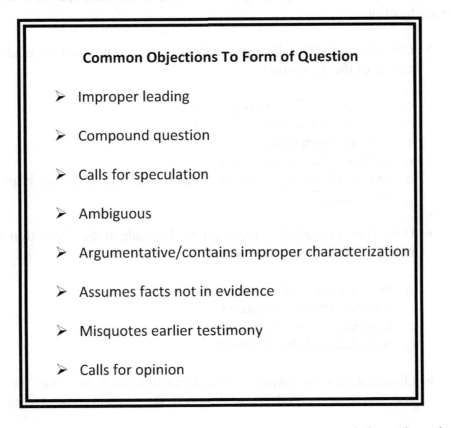

Common Objections To Form of Question

- Improper leading
- Compound question
- Calls for speculation
- Ambiguous
- Argumentative/contains improper characterization
- Assumes facts not in evidence
- Misquotes earlier testimony
- Calls for opinion

In general, objections to questions that can be cured through rephrasing and objections to procedures that can be corrected are waived unless made at the time. Other objections, like objections to questions that cannot be made proper by rephrasing, can be reserved for trial.

The idea behind this distinction is simple. If counsel asks an objectionable question at trial that can be cured through rephrasing, the court will sustain the objection and give counsel the opportunity to rephrase. If, however, the testimony is via deposition rather than live, the objectionable question and answer are excluded with no opportunity to rephrase because there is no witness available to answer a re-phrased question. Because of that, fairness dictates that objections to "correctable" questions must be made at the deposition in order to allow counsel the same opportunity to rephrase that would exist at trial.

Following are rules regarding the distinction between waivable and non-waivable objections:

- Objections to the following matters or questions *must* be made at the taking of the deposition:
    - manner of taking the deposition;
    - form of the question or answer;
    - oath or affirmation;
    - conduct of the parties; and
    - errors which might be obviated, removed, or cured if promptly presented.[69]
- Objections to the following need not be made at the deposition but can be raised for the first time at trial:
    - competency of the witness;
    - competency of the testimony;
    - relevancy of the testimony;
    - materiality of the testimony.[70]
- Objections to the notice for the deposition must be made "promptly" and must be served in writing on the notice-giving party or be

[69] FED. R. CIV. P. 32(d)(3)(B).

[70] FED. R. CIV. P. 32(d)(3)(A). Notice, though, that even these kinds of objections are not preserved if the ground of the objections is one which "might have been corrected at that time [before or during the taking of the deposition.]" *Id.*

waived.[71] Do not save these objections for trial or a hearing on a dispositive motion.

- Objections to the qualification of the court reporter must be made before the deposition, or at least as soon as the basis for disqualification could reasonably be discovered.[72] Do not save these objections for trial or a hearing on a dispositive motion.

- Objections to the following must be made promptly through a motion to suppress the deposition or some portion of it: transcription; preparation; signing; certification; sealing; indorsement; transmission; and filing.[73]

Although these rules regarding objections may appear to be fairly straightforward, not all objections fall neatly into either the "preserved" or "waived" categories. This can raise some potentially thorny technical questions. For example, a common belief is that "hearsay" objections are preserved for trial even if not made at a deposition, because the questioning lawyer cannot make the testimony non-hearsay merely by reframing the questions. But consider the following scenario:

> The questioning lawyer at a deposition is examining a witness about an exhibit. The questioner is trying obviously to qualify the exhibit as a "business record" through the deponent's testimony. Suppose, however, that the questioner leaves out one of the critical qualifying questions, and then starts examining the deponent on the substance of the document. The defender makes no objection. Now, fast forward to trial. The deposition witness is absent. The questioning lawyer offers the exhibit into evidence, based on the deposition testimony. The defending lawyer objects on hearsay grounds. The questioning lawyer says, "But if the defender had just asserted a foundation objection at the deposition, I could have

---

[71] FED. R. CIV. P. 32(d)(1).

[72] FED. R. CIV. P. 32(d)(2).

[73] FED. R. CIV. P. 32(d)(4).

cured the omitted qualification that I accidentally left out." The defending lawyer counters that, "There was nothing objectionable about any given one of the questions that were actually asked. The witness knew enough to talk about the document for discovery purposes, since the standard is not trial admissibility. It's not my job to point out omissions, and that is not what the civil procedure rules governing deposition objections require."

How should the court rule? While the defending lawyer's side of the posed scenario has a certain amount of appeal under the rules because the missing objection is not one as to form, that does not mean the deferred objection will prevail.[74] If you want to be really cautious when dealing with the "is it curable?" question, you might prefer to assert an objection rather than risk waiver. Alternatively, you might, as the defending attorney, stipulate at the outset of a deposition that all objections except as to form of question are reserved until trial. Even so, there is no guarantee that such a stipulation will change the way in which a court otherwise may rule in the above example.

Additional rules govern *how* to state objections and when you can go so far as to instruct a witness to refrain from answering.

- In general, objections must be "stated concisely," and must be "non-argumentative" and "non-suggestive."[75] It is not permissible to coach a witness through lengthy, overly-descriptive objections.

[74] *See, e.g.*, Donaldson, *supra* note 67 and accompanying text.

> An objection based on foundation is an objection to the competency of testimony. It is also an objection that might be "obviated or removed" if made at the time of the deposition. But it is not an objection as to form. Unless you stipulate that such an objection is reserved until the time of trial, you will waive it if you do not raise it.

Id. See also McElhaney, *supra* note 9 and accompanying text. "A missing foundation might have been fixed at the time. The failure to object is probably a waiver under the Federal Rules." *Id.* at 57.

[75] FED. R. CIV. P. 30(c)(2).

- If a question calls for privileged information or information outside the scope of a court-ordered limitation on discovery or on the deposition, you not only should object and state your grounds, you also should instruct the witness not to answer. If you fail to object under these circumstances, you waive your objection; if you object but allow your witness to answer anyway, then you waive your privilege.

- The other circumstance under which you may instruct a witness not to answer is when the deposition "is being conducted in bad faith or in a manner that unreasonably annoys, embarrasses, or oppresses the deponent or party." Then you can suspend the deposition in order to seek relief from the court.[76]

- Be careful, however. You may not instruct a witness to refrain from answering in a situation other than those described above, no matter how well-grounded your objection and no matter how damaging you believe the answer may be.[77]

b. Tactical Considerations

Simply having an available objection does not mean that you automatically should assert it. Objections are not like runs in baseball or goals in hockey; you do not score additional points for each one you make. As a general rule of thumb, you make an objection when: (a) you think one is valid; and (b) the objectionable question materially hurts you.

On the other hand, unlike at trial, there is no jury to wonder if all your objections mean you have a lot to hide. Even if the deposition is used at trial, the question and answer that are the subject of a sustained objection (along with the objection itself) are simply stricken from the transcript or videotape before the jury hears or sees it. If an objection is overruled, then the objection itself is stricken, and the question and answer are read or played without it. Thus, when in doubt, it is better in the deposition context to make an objection than to forego it, in order to protect the record.

---

[76] FED. R. CIV. P. 30(c)(2) and 30(d)(3)(A).

[77] *See* FED. R. CIV. P. 30(c)(2).

At the same time, even if a jury will never be counting the number of objections at a deposition, the court might. Objections are not redacted from transcripts used in connection with a bench trial or a dispositive motion. Much of the time your key audience is the judge, and you do not want to develop a reputation as an obstructionist.

In addition, it is prudent to consider the potential effect of objections on your own witness and on opposing counsel. Your witness needs to know that you are not afraid to protect him or her from a particularly aggressive questioning lawyer. That is an important message to send opposing counsel, too. Moreover, a well-placed objection to a question as "ambiguous," for example, can alert an attuned witness that there are potentially multiple meanings (and traps) that need to be addressed.

On the other hand, aggressive objections can give both your witness and opposing counsel the unfortunate impression that the witness is vulnerable. The impression is unfortunate for your witness to hold, because he or she may well respond in one of two ways: either becoming tentative and nervous ("my lawyer is scared to death of what I am going to say") or, even worse, becoming bullish ("let me take care of myself, lawyer; I can handle this just fine"). The impression is similarly unfortunate for the questioning lawyer to hold because he or she may smell blood or simply become irritated at all the interruptions, and bear down all the harder.

As you decide on your objection strategy for any given deposition, keep in mind that objections can serve as red flags to opposing counsel, especially if you suddenly interject a flurry of objections despite having let many other objectionable questions pass unchallenged. The following excerpt is from a real deposition:

Example: *During the course of a previously uneventful deposition, the examining attorney asked a specific question that suddenly elicited a simultaneous burst of objections from four opposing lawyers. The examiner's response: "I sure hit the motherlode on that one, didn't I?" The questioning continued, but now in much greater depth.*

If you are confident that your witness can handle the question and that the objection is not one that otherwise will be waived, you may choose to forego the objection and the resulting red flag.

Objecting to protect the record presents unique considerations in complex, multi-party litigation. Assume, for example, that you are counsel in a multi-district proceeding in which there are scores of lawyers and numerous depositions. You probably will pick a limited number of depositions to attend. No party wants its lawyers at every single one. But this means that each non-attending party is counting on the lawyers for attending parties to protect the record on their side of the case. It thus behooves the lawyers defending a given deposition to be more aggressive than they might otherwise personally prefer to be in objecting to questions that might affect non-attendees on the same side of the dispute.

In the end, there are some objections you *must* make at the deposition or you waive them.[78] There will be some objections that you will *want* to make at a deposition because the objectionable question goes to an important point. For everything else, you should adopt a balancing test and make your choice as best you can in light of your blueprint: Who is this witness? How crucial is the testimony? How sure are you that the witness can handle the question? What impression will be left by the objection?

3. Asserting Fifth Amendment Rights

If you believe your client faces potential criminal liability, you need to consider the advisability of having your client invoke the Fifth Amendment right against self incrimination. This right can be asserted in civil proceedings, including depositions, if the person invoking the right reasonably believes the information sought could be used in a criminal prosecution or could lead to other

[78] Even with waivable objections you need to exercise judgment before automatically objecting. For example, objections to leading are waived if not made at the deposition, but as at trial, it does not always make sense to raise the objection. This situation might arise, for example, during background questions asked of an expert witness during a deposition being taken to preserve testimony for trial.

evidence that could be used in a criminal prosecution.[79] Be cautious, however. Assertion of the privilege is not without cost. The trier of fact in a civil proceeding may, under appropriate circumstances, be allowed to draw adverse inferences from your client's invocation during a deposition of the Fifth Amendment privilege, even if your client subsequently waives the right and agrees to testify.[80] If you fail appropriately to advise your client on these issues, you could find yourself the subject of a malpractice suit.[81]

4. Seeking Court Intervention

a. Can You Get Help?

There will be times when you will need the court's assistance in controlling a deposition. If there is a material matter involved, do not be afraid to suspend the deposition and call the court for a ruling. For example, if you believe the lawyer taking the deposition is harassing the witness by inquiring about personal matters having nothing to do with the lawsuit, and the lawyer will not heed your objections and move on, you may seek the court's assistance. After warning the inquiring lawyer to stop, you may suspend the deposition to call the court to request a protective order against the offensive line of questioning.[82] Alternatively, you can have the court reporter mark the offensive questions, which you prohibit your client from answering until you can file a motion for a

---

[79] For a good discussion of the relevant legal standards and the potential issues that may arise when asserting Fifth Amendment rights in a civil context, see Doe ex rel. Rudy-Glanzer v. Glanzer, 232 F.3d 1258 (9th Cir. 2000); *see also* Harris v. City of Chicago, 266 F.3d 750 (7th Cir. 2001).

[80] Empress Casino Joliet Corp. v. Balmoral Racing Club, Inc., 831 F.3d 815, 835 (7th Cir. 2016). *Compare* Baxter v. Palmigiano, 425 U.S. 308, 318 (1976) (Fifth Amendment allows an adverse inference to be drawn against parties in non-criminal proceedings under certain circumstances, most notably when a decision-maker has independent evidence that the party engaged in misconduct), *with* Butler v. Oak Creek-Franklin School Dist., 172 F. Supp. 2d 1102, 1126 (E.D. Wis. 2001) (adverse inference may not be drawn from the invocation of a Fifth Amendment privilege alone without other evidence of misconduct).

[81] *See* Wartnick v. Moss & Barnett, 490 N.W .2d 108 (Minn. 1992).

[82] FED. R. CIV. P. 30(c)(2), 30(d)(3)(A).

protective order.[83] Be cautious, however. If you suspend a deposition and lose your motion, that loss may come with fees and costs attached to it.[84]

Another possibility is that you will foresee the need for the court's assistance in advance, and seek the court's intervention even before you begin.

Example: *The deposition of corporate in-house counsel is noticed regarding preparation of the company's affirmative action plan. Some questions likely are permissible, but others likely will implicate the attorney-client privilege. Rather than wait until what may turn into a contentious deposition with frequent instructions not to answer, it makes sense under these circumstances to seek protective ground rules from the court before the deposition ever starts. In some situations, including this one, the court may schedule the deposition in the presence of the judge or other neutral, who will rule immediately on all objections.*

In the end, be selective. Do not run to the court for help every time there is a dispute within a deposition. Go to the court when you have good grounds to be concerned about what is happening, and the matter is material.

b. From Which Court Do You Seek Help?

The Federal Rules allow you to seek assistance from either the court in which the underlying action is pending or in the jurisdiction where the deposition is taking place.[85] Which location you choose depends on the circumstances.

- If the dispute at the deposition involves a matter that requires detailed knowledge of the case to resolve properly, you are better off calling home.

---

83 FED. R. CIV. P. 30(c)(2).

84 *See* FED. R. CIV. P. 30(d)(2), 30(d)(3)(C) and 37(a)(5).

85 *See* FED. R. CIV. P. 26(c)(1), 30(d)(3)(A).

- If this is not your first discovery difficulty, if counsel's conduct is egregious, and if the judge at home has been sympathetic to you in the past, call home. The call may cost opposing counsel additional loss of good will with the court.

- If your court at home is easily aggravated by discovery disputes, call the local judge.

- If the dispute at the deposition is easy to understand, and the witness is from the local jurisdiction, you may want to be in front of a local judge.

- If the matter will involve a discretionary ruling and the two relevant districts have a propensity to treat discretionary matters differently, choose the more favorable district.

Whatever your circumstances, make a considered judgment.[86]

5. Questioning the Deponent

When should you as the defending attorney question the deponent? Some attorneys never question their own witness. You are defending the deposition. You are in a damage control posture. This is not the time for the witness to tell your side of the story in the way you would organize it. Get out of the room as soon as the other side is done! If you start asking questions, the door opens to additional inquiry from opposing counsel.

But this standard reaction is too simplistic. Think back to your blueprint. Who is this witness? Will the witness be available later? Does the witness have

[86] While motions for protective orders to stop "annoyance, embarrassment, oppression, or undue burden or expense" may be made in "the court where the action is pending—or *as an alternative* on matters relating to a deposition, in the court for the district where the deposition will be taken," FED. R. CIV. P. 26(c)(1) (emphasis added), there is not always a choice. *See, e.g.*, FED. R. CIV. P. 37(a)(2) (motions to compel discovery from a party "must" be made in the court where the action is pending, while similar motions to compel discovery from a non-party "must" be made in the court where the discovery is or will be taken); FED. R. CIV. P. 45(c)(3)(A) (motions to quash third party subpoenas on certain grounds should be made to the court that issued the subpoena).

something to say that could materially increase your chances of obtaining summary judgment if you just put that testimony on the table? Has the witness said something in a way that can be harmfully misinterpreted if not clarified at the deposition? Has the witness remembered something that makes a previous response incomplete and therefore incorrect? Will you be opening the door for more dangerous questions from the other side?

In the end, our advice is that the defending lawyer should examine the witness when necessary to correct previous testimony or when the witness can make a dispositive point sing. A series of a few short, pointed questions may be helpful for summary judgment and will guard against holes in your case created by the sudden unexpected unavailability of a person who can give important testimony.[87]

[87] One word of caution: Do not try to "wing" an impromptu examination of the witness. Often this proves disastrous. Instead of explaining away some earlier unfavorable testimony, the witness may to everyone's surprise cement the earlier bad testimony with even more bad testimony or spontaneously reveal previously unsolicited bad facts. The lesson here is that you need to be careful. If you are not confident about how the witness will respond to your questions or that the witness's answers are important, you are better off going home and regrouping.

CHAPTER 5

Problem Witnesses and Problem Attorneys

The prospect of a problem witness or a problem opposing attorney often creates the greatest anxiety for new attorneys in taking and defending depositions. While new attorneys may feel relatively confident that they can ask questions from their outlines and recognize objectionable questions of a witness, they often are most concerned about what they should do if the witness is especially difficult or the other attorney preys on their inexperience. The following discussion describes several different types of problem witnesses and problem attorneys. This discussion illustrates the difficulties that these witnesses and attorneys pose, and then explains various ways to address these problems.

A. Problem Witnesses

Following is a discussion of seven different common problem witnesses: the Forgetful Witness, the Evasive Witness, the Belligerent Witness, the

Rambling Witness, the Vulnerable or Impaired Witness, the Lying Witness, and the Wacko Witness.

1. The Forgetful Witness

The forgetful witness is either honestly forgetful or deliberately forgetful as a tactic to avoid providing useful responses to your questions. Some witnesses have selective lack of recollection – their memories fade only regarding matters that might harm their cases.

Example:

Q: Did you attend a meeting last summer with your company's marketing director to discuss the adequacy of your company's product warnings?
A: I don't remember.
Q: Did you ever attend a meeting to discuss your company's warnings?
A: Not that I recall.
Q: Did you hear of any such meeting at your company?
A: I don't recall.
Q: Did you ever communicate any recommendations to your company about its product warnings?
A: I can't remember if I ever did that.

In dealing with such a forgetful witness, you first should decide whether the witness's memory loss helps your case. You may actually prefer that the witness not remember. If so, cement the witness's inability to remember through your questioning so you can neutralize the witness later at trial, and put on the stand witnesses who do recall. The witness's inability to recall also may render the witness effectively unavailable for trial, allowing you to admit certain otherwise inadmissible hearsay, such as statements against interest.

If, on the other hand, you want to further question a forgetful witness, try one or more of the following questioning techniques.

- *Ask the witness why he or she cannot remember.* The witness may offer a very legitimate explanation for the inability to remember; for example, the incident occurred a very long time ago, the witness had no reason at the time to appreciate the later significance of the incident, or the witness was traumatized or suffered from an illness or disability at the time that affected the witness's memory. Other forgetful witnesses may not be able to offer a plausible explanation for their lost memory, which may cause you to suspect that the witness's memory loss is contrived.

- *Find out if the witness ever knew of or remembered the incident.* You may discover that the witness never remembered or knew of the incident. If the witness admits recalling the incident at an earlier time, ask if the witness discussed or likely discussed the incident with someone else at that time.

- *Ask the witness whether documents may exist that would contain information about the incident.* Forgetful witnesses can sometimes direct you to other witnesses or documents that contain the information you are seeking.

- *Ask what the witness's regular routine or practice was and if the witness has any reason to believe the witness acted differently at the time in question.* While forgetful witnesses may claim an inability to remember a specific incident, they may admit to a regular routine or practice and further admit that they cannot think of any reason they or others would have deviated from that practice or routine in regard to the incident in question. This may get you the next best thing to an outright recollection by the witness.

- *Ask the deponent if the deponent can refute the recollection of another witness.* If you know another witness who distinctly recalls the incident, you may get the deponent to admit that the deponent's inability to remember also prevents the deponent from refuting the recollection of other witnesses. When pressed on this point, some deponents find that their memories suddenly return.

- *Try to refresh the witness's recollection with documents, other testimony, or additional facts.* You sometimes successfully can refresh a witness's memory with documents or other testimony. A witness who has no recollection of an incident may quickly recall details when shown a document that the witness authored or received. You also should ask such witnesses if they know of anything else that would refresh their recollection.

- *Try to get an approximation using bracketing techniques.* While a witness may initially express no recollection regarding some event, such as the date of a meeting, further questioning using bracketing techniques (*e.g.*, "Was it more than a year ago?" "Was it less than two years ago?") sometimes can elicit an approximation that may be just as good as a precise recollection for your purposes.

- *Avoid starting your questions with phrases like "do you remember" or "do you recall."* These phrases subtly invite witnesses to respond that they do not remember or recall. Simply ask the question directly (e.g., "Who else was at the meeting?").

- *Request that the witness inform you if the witness's memory improves.* Some attorneys like to instruct forgetful witnesses that they *must* inform the attorneys if their memories improve before trial. Actually, the supplementation obligation under the Federal Rules of Civil Procedure does not apply to ordinary (non-expert) testimony.[88] Consequently, it is more appropriate to *request* that the witness inform you if the witness's memory improves before trial.[89]

One commentator suggested the following line of questions to challenge a deliberately forgetful witness's lack of recollection in a deposition:

---

[88] *See* FED. R. CIV. P. 26(e).

[89] If the matter is especially important, you may consider using interrogatories to follow through. A party does have an obligation to supplement interrogatory responses "if the party learns that in some material respect the disclosure or response is incomplete or incorrect, and if the additional or corrective information has not otherwise been made known to the other parties during the discovery process or in writing." FED. R. CIV. P. 26(e)(1)(A).

Example: *Q: You were able to explain the company's accounting procedures in 1963, true?*
Q: Then why can't you remember anything about a crucial meeting six months ago?
Q: Were you suffering from an illness at the time?
Q: Was there something about the meeting you don't want to remember?
Q: Was the meeting so distasteful for you that you put it out of your mind?
Q: Do you have trouble with amnesia in your business affairs?[90]

The last of these questions would be fun to ask. The answer would not matter. We discourage using sarcasm, however. The court may not find it amusing, and the witness likely will become even more difficult.

Every once in a while, you encounter a witness with the opposite problem – the witness's memory seems unreasonably detailed. Consider the following deposition anecdote reported to the *American Bar Association Journal*:

> The witness was describing in detail the auto accident he observed through his rearview mirror. The examining attorney asked in an incredulous tone: "You spend a great deal of time looking through your rearview mirror, don't you?" "Yes sir," the witness replied without missing a beat. "I drive a 1971 Ford Pinto."[91]

When this happens to you, probe into how it is that the witness has such a detailed memory of the incident. You may find a very plausible explanation, as in the above anecdote, or a very incredible explanation that may suggest to you that the witness is fabricating.[92]

---

[90] Christopher T. Lutz, *Fudging and Forgetting*, 19 LITIG., Spring 1993, at 10, 15.

[91] *War Stories,* A.B.A. J., Sept. 1996, at 14.

[92] A couple lawyers recounted rather interesting examples of the Forgetful Witness from their past depositions. One witness responded to a question with: "I don't know if I can't remember that right now." Another witness, after two minutes of murmuring with his attorney following a

2. The Evasive Witness

The evasive witness, also known by some as the "weasel," is almost incapable of giving a straightforward and unqualified answer to a deposition question.[93]

Example: *Q: Did you meet Clarice Starling last night?*
A: I may have.
Q: Was she still alive when you left her?
A: I don't specifically recall.
Q: Did you and Agent Starling have a disagreement?
A: I don't understand what you mean.
Q: Didn't you and Agent Starling fight over what you were going to have for dinner?
A: Not really.
Q: Where do you think Clarice Starling is right now?
A: Where do you think she is?

Deposing an evasive witness can be exhausting because you often have to ask several follow-up questions for every evasive response you get. The key to dealing with this kind of witness is not to let the witness get away with an evasive response. Do not let the witness evade your questions by claiming his or her answer depends on what "is" is. Be tenacious. In follow-up to the evasive responses in the above example, consider asking questions like the following.

Example: *Q Why do you think you may have been with her? Is there any reason to believe you were not with her?*

---

question responded: "On the advice of counsel, I don't remember." A.B.A. J. Weekly Newsletter (Sept. 1, 2010).

[93] *See, e.g.*, David R. Sonnenberg, *Eliminating Deposition Weasels*, BARRISTER, Winter 1991-92, at 41.

> Q: *What do you generally recall about her condition when you last saw her?*
> Q: *What part of my question, or what words in my question, do you not understand?*
> Q: *What do you mean, "Not really?" Did you have a fight or not?*
> Q: *It doesn't matter where I think she is. I want to know where you think she is.*

Another tactic to use with an evasive witness is to repeat your question verbatim after the evasive response. This sends a not-so-subtle signal to the witness that you know the witness is being evasive and that you do not plan to let the witness get away with it.

One commentator recommends that you deal with an evasive witness by taking the blame for your question (even if it was as clear as day), and then re-asking the question using slightly different words.[94] This can be a bit less confrontational than repeating the question verbatim with no explanation. If done correctly, this tactic can also very strongly signal your displeasure with the witness's evasiveness.

Finally, when you get a clearly evasive response, you might try something along these lines:

Example:

> Q: *Did you see my client's car before the impact?*
> A: *Well, it all happened so fast and I knew that I had the green light because I was staring at the light the whole time until your client's car smashed into my door and shoved me across the front seat breaking my right arm.*
> Q: *I believe the answer to my question is "yes" or "no." Did you see my client's car before the impact?*

[94] James W. McElhaney, *Evasive Witnesses*, 20 LITIG., Spring 1994, at 47, 48.

This response also signals to the witness that you know full well that he or she did not answer your question and that you are not going to let the witness get away with it.

3. The Belligerent Witness

Sometimes you encounter a witness who does not like being deposed and does not like you. The belligerent witness is rude and intimidating; the deposition is, to put it lightly, extremely unpleasant.

Example: *Q:* *Did you approve your company's purchase of the engines from my client?*

A: *You've got to be kidding! Why would I as CEO have time to do something like that? Have you ever run a company? Obviously not, which explains why you became a lawyer and a pretty pathetic one at that.*

Q: *Who would have approved this purchase?*

A: *This is the third time you've asked me this. It is no wonder you charge by the hour. If you wouldn't keep asking me the same thing over and over, I could get back to my business and you could get back to chasing ambulances and filing frivolous lawsuits.*

Q: *I just want to find out the truth.*

A: *Listen you ingrate, you can't handle the truth!*

Q: *[repeat initial question]*

There are several key points to keep in mind when you depose a difficult witness. First and foremost, keep your cool. Do not let the witness's rude demeanor and insulting comments get to you. Resist the temptation to fire back an insult or to argue with the witness. In most instances, this is a recipe for disaster.

Second, you might try to appeal to a value this kind of witness can appreciate. Some belligerent witnesses will respond to a crude appeal to some sense of fairness.

Example: *You were the one who brought this lawsuit. I am entitled to find out your story just as your attorney is entitled to find out my client's story in his deposition next week. I expect my client to answer your attorney's questions and I expect you to answer mine. [Repeat initial question.]*

Other belligerent witnesses sometimes can be persuaded to cooperate by appealing to their self-interest – namely, their wallets and their time. You might tell the witness that the witness's lack of cooperation is costing the witness more money by prolonging the deposition and that if the witness does not want to tell his or her story, there is no way your client will be able to consider a settlement offer. Additionally, let the witness know that you are willing to complete the deposition no matter how long it takes. Hostile witnesses sometimes will clean up their acts just to get their depositions completed.

Example: *I was expecting that I would finish this deposition in about three hours. In light of your refusal to cooperate, it is now apparent that this will take the rest of the day, at least. I am taking a five-minute break to go back to my office and cancel my other appointments for the day. You may want to call your office and do the same.*[95]

Third, if the boorish behavior continues, take a break and talk to opposing counsel. Chances are opposing counsel may agree with you that the witness is behaving very badly, even if counsel will not say so directly. You may be able to convince opposing counsel to talk to the witness and get the witness to behave.

[95] Prior to the 2000 Amendments to Rule 30, which imposed a presumptive seven hour time limit on each deposition, an examining attorney could threaten to continue the deposition of a hostile witness for multiple days. In fact, you can still probably threaten this since the Advisory Committee Notes state that if a deponent delays the examination, the court may authorize extra time. The hostile witness has to think long and hard about whether you will ask for and get this extra time.

The witness is likely to be more inclined to curtail the witness's abusive behavior at the private request of the witness's own attorney than at your direction.[96]

Fourth, consider videotaping the deposition. Some of the most belligerent witnesses quickly clean up their acts when they are being videotaped.

Finally, if none of the above measures succeed, ask the court for assistance. Before you do, however, make sure you have a good record of the witness's inappropriate conduct, especially if the offensive conduct was largely nonverbal.

4. The Rambling Witness

At some point, you will encounter the rambling witness. The witness's rambling may be a product of nervousness or it may be a deliberate ploy to muddy the record. It also may be because the witness is a genuine motor-mouth. The rambling witness may be good and bad. Such a witness is likely to spew forth a fountain of information, some of which may help your case. On the other hand, it usually is very difficult to get the kind of succinct answer from such a witness that you can use for later impeachment or that you may need to support a dispositive motion.

Example: *Q:* *Mr. Claven, did you deliver the mail to the residents on your mail route on the afternoon of December 1st of last year?*

A: *I remember that Ma's birthday was on December 2nd and that I had to get her a gift. Since Carla and Diane didn't have any good ideas, Norm and I went out shopping on the 1st before I was supposed to do my mail route. We looked all over and couldn't*

[96] Attorneys representing such hostile witnesses can be sanctioned for failing to curtail their client's behavior. A federal court severely criticized and sanctioned an attorney for failing to intervene and stop his client's abusive behavior in a deposition in which his client used the f-word no fewer than 73 times. The court concluded that by sitting idly by, and even chuckling at his client's hostile behavior, the attorney endorsed and ratified the misconduct which was the functional equivalent of advising the behavior under Rule 37(a)(5)(A). GMAC Bank v. HTFC Corp., 248 F.R.D. 182 (E.D. Pa. 2008).

> *find anything, so we went to have a cold one at "Cheers." Sammy suggested that I get her a big box of candy from the candy shop at the end of my route. Did you know that in certain African tribes, sons gave their mothers glazed insects as a token of their affection? Well, I would have remembered the candy if Norm hadn't challenged me to a game of pool against a couple of lovely ladies. After a dozen games and a dozen beers, the ladies wanted me to escort them home. Most women can't resist my U.S. Postal Service uniform. Um, now what was your question again?*

Following are several tips for dealing with a rambling witness if you are the examining attorney.

- *Let the witness get out the rambling narrative, and then go back and ask a number of narrow, leading, follow-up questions.* Rather than try to force the rambling witness to follow your pre-planned outline, you may want to ask some very open-ended questions to get the witness to ramble for awhile (e.g., "What happened next?"). After you get out the lengthy narrative, go back and ask a series of more closed-ended, cross-examination style questions that call for a simple "yes" or "no" response to pin down some specific points from the narrative.

- *Politely interrupt the witness's long narrative response.* Sometimes you need to interrupt the witness's long narrative response to ask a specific question or to prevent the witness from heading off on some long irrelevant tangent. Just be careful how you do this because you may not want to stifle the witness, who may volunteer helpful information while rambling. If you politely interrupt and then invite the witness to continue his or her answer, the witness is unlikely to be offended. One device is to simply hold up your hand. Another device is to confront the witness with a document that reins in the testimony.

- *Employ frequent summaries of the witness's testimony and get the witness to agree to your summaries.* Another technique for dealing with the rambling witness is to let the witness ramble for a time, assimilate the information that you receive, and then ask the witness to concur with several summary questions you craft.

- *Object to the witness's rambling answers as non-responsive.* At some point, you may need to object that the witness's rambling narrative is not responsive to your question and move to strike the testimony. Your failure to make this objection at the deposition may result in a waiver of the objection.

The rambling witness is usually more of a problem for the defending attorney than the examining attorney. The defending attorney often is a nervous wreck by the end of a rambling witness's deposition because the attorney never knows what the witness will say next.[97]

In defending the deposition of a rambling witness, you should remind the witness at breaks not to volunteer unrequested information (assuming that the courts in your jurisdiction do not prohibit conversations with the witness during such breaks). The best way to deal with this type of witness is by preparing well, so that the witness understands that rambling is a bad strategy that may hurt the witness's case. This preparation should include actual practice and critique.

5. The Impaired or Vulnerable Witness

You may on occasion depose a witness who is vulnerable or suffering from an illness or disability that adversely affects the witness's ability to testify but does not completely preclude the witness from testifying. A witness suffering from a nervous disorder, for example, may not be able to testify longer than about

[97] One of the authors took the deposition of a witness who could not answer a question in less than four pages of testimony. At one point, the witness unexpectedly veered off on an unrelated point and proceeded to discuss her initial conversation with her counsel, including her counsel's comments about various problems with her case. Her counsel, bored with her endless rambling, was looking at some papers and failed to notice the testimonial detour. Once he realized what his client was talking about, he nearly fell out of his chair trying to cut her off. Needless to say, the rambling witness can cause fits for the defending attorney.

two hours at a time. You should schedule such a deposition for two hour increments over several consecutive days.

If you encounter an impaired deponent, you want to make sure that the testimony you receive is reliable and not tainted by the witness's condition. You will likely want to take more frequent and longer breaks than usual and make it clear to the witness on the record that you are willing to break as needed. You also should get the witness and the witness's attorney on the record to agree to tell you if the witness is unable to continue answering your questions truthfully and accurately. While such an instruction will not necessarily win the day if the witness later claims that he or she was unable to make such a determination during the deposition, the witness's and counsel's failure to stop the questioning is at least some indication that the witness was, in fact, able to continue and that the witness's deposition testimony is reliable.

You also may need to depose a witness who is very ill and who is homebound or admitted to a hospital. In this situation, you may want to consider taking the deposition in the presence of a physician who not only can stop the questioning and attend to the witness if necessary, but who also can later verify that the witness was lucid and coherent during the examination.[98]

6. The Lying Witness

Sometimes you encounter a witness who lies, either in general or regarding selective key points. The tactical call you must make when this happens is whether you let the witness know that you are aware the witness is lying by impeaching the witness in the deposition, or whether you cement the lie and wait to impeach the witness at trial. If the witness is unlikely to provide much useful information, it may be best to save exposure of the lie for trial, where you then can discredit the witness in front of the jury or judge.

---

[98] During the deposition of an elderly woman who was the plaintiff in a product liability lawsuit, the woman, who was very ill and had to be deposed in her home, developed a spontaneous and uncontrollable nosebleed. After several minutes of a lot of blood, panic, and chaos, it was clear the deposition could not continue. Now, whenever a lawyer boasts about making a witness cry in a deposition, this lawyer curtly replies: "Big deal. Did you make the witness bleed?"

On the other hand, there may be good reasons to let the witness know in the deposition that you fully realize the witness is lying. One reason to do this is to induce a witness who has useful information to be truthful through the remainder of the deposition. If you confront the witness with an early lie, you may deter additional future lies, as the witness may suspect you will be able to identify them, too. Another reason to discredit the witness during the deposition is to improve your settlement posture. Remember, most cases never make it to trial.

7. The Wacko Witness

Sometimes you end up deposing a witness who is, well, wacko. Here are two real-world examples:

Example: *A brother and sister were fighting over the division of a large family inheritance. The brother got so angry that he refused to look at his sister during his deposition. The situation intensified to the point that the brother had to walk backwards into the deposition room so he would not have to see his sister. The court eventually had to order the brother to face the examining attorney at which point the sister put her face as close as she could to her brother's face just to make him angry.*[99]

* * *

Example: *In a case involving a claim of sexual harassment, the plaintiff returned to the deposition room the second day of her deposition, walked over to her alleged harasser, pulled out a knife, and proceeded to stab him multiple times. The defendants moved to dismiss the plaintiff's suit based on her outrageous behavior. The court denied the motion reasoning, in part, that it could not dismiss the case because the*

[99] *See* Shartel, *supra* note 28, at 15.

> *plaintiff had not previously been ordered not to stab anyone.*[100]

We really do not have any useful advice for how to deal with the wacko witness other than to be sure you put everything on the record and involve the court if things really get nuts. Generally, these witnesses just make for interesting war stories.

B. Problem Attorneys

Problem witnesses are not the only ones who can turn a deposition into an intensely unpleasant experience. Problem attorneys also create unique challenges. The following describes methods for dealing with seven common problem attorney types: the Coach, the Testifier, the Objector, the Intimidator, the Professor, the Repeater, and the Timekeeper.

1. The Coach

The coach is an attorney who skillfully tells the witness how to answer your questions. These attorneys coach witnesses by signals, direct conversations, speaking objections, instructions, and questions. Some of these methods are always improper. The rest can be.

The coach uses nonverbal or verbal signals. Nonverbal signaling to a witness can take many forms – a nod of the head, a hand on the arm, pointing at a document, tapping a pen, coughing. Regardless of its form, all nonverbal signaling is improper and unethical. Sometimes this coaching can be difficult to detect if the attorney and witness are sophisticated enough. If you happen to witness nonverbal signaling, object to the conduct on the record and admonish counsel to cease the improper conduct. Make sure to verbally describe the signaling conduct or else it will not appear on the record.

Example: *Let the record reflect that after I asked my last question, and before the witness answered, counsel*

---

[100] McKenna v. Ward, 1990 WL 71471, at *1-2 (S.D.N.Y. May 21, 1990).

> *signaled the witness by pointing to a provision on page two of the document.*

Make your objection the first time you observe the improper signaling behavior unless it is on a trivial matter. If the improper signaling continues, consider suspending the deposition and videotaping the rest of it.[101] Videotaping often puts an end to nonverbal coaching because the coach realizes his or her signals are being recorded for a judge to observe. If videotaping fails, go to court and ask for relief.[102]

The coach also may try to verbally signal the witness. This can take several forms. One of these is a direct conversation with the witness. Counsel may insist on a break in the deposition to confer with the witness. As discussed in Chapter 3, courts are split over whether counsel can privately confer with a witness during a break in the deposition. If the courts in your jurisdiction follow the ruling in *Hall v. Clifton Precision*,[103] counsel has no such right and you are entitled to know of any such discussions between counsel and the witness occurring during a break.

Even if the courts in your jurisdiction do not follow *Hall*, you should still try to prevent counsel from conferring with the witness while a question is pending, except in special circumstances, such as a potential privilege assertion. You also can insist on finishing a particular line of questioning before a break. If, however, the witness and opposing counsel get up and leave before you finish your line of questioning, there really is not much you can do about it. If your

---

[101] Riley v. Murdock, 156 F.R.D. 130 (E.D.N.C. 1994).

[102] In a recent case, counsel brought a motion for sanctions against an opposing attorney for allegedly signaling the witness by tapping her foot under the table. The lawyer taking the deposition was questioning the witness remotely by video when the lawyer's paralegal, who was at the deposition to handle the exhibits, heard some noise and looked under the table and saw the opposing attorney tapping the witness's shoe with his shoe. The paralegal snapped a photo under the table with his phone and sent it to the lawyer taking the deposition. Plaintiff's Response to Defendant's Motion for Protective Order Related to Resumption of Connie Dennis's Deposition, Motion for Sanctions, and Motion for Termination of Pro Hac Vice Status of Kenneth Engerrand at 2-3, Halmos v. Ins. Co. of N. Am., No. 08-10084 (S.D. Fla. July 30, 2010). You may consider using a cell phone camera to capture nonverbal signaling in a deposition.

[103] 150 F.R.D. 525, 531-32 (E.D. Pa. 1993).

opposing counsel insists on an inordinate number of breaks, you can stop the deposition and seek relief from the court.

To minimize the risk of damage from coaching during breaks, do not start a critical set of questions close to a logical break time. Instead, take a break right before you begin these questions. It will be more difficult for the opposing counsel to request another break right after you have returned from one. Finally, if the witness confers with his or her attorney while a question is pending, consider asking the deponent why he or she needed to confer with counsel or whether this conference refreshed the witness's recollection.

Counsel also may try to coach a witness through speaking objections, instructions, and questions. A speaking objection is an objection accompanied by a speech from counsel clearly intended to signal the witness (e.g., "Objection, calls for speculation. The witness could not possibly know the answer to this question because he did not attend any meeting in which this topic was discussed, and he did not have any conversations with anyone about this topic. He, therefore, could not know why his employer took this action."). These objections are improper. Rule 30(c)(2) expressly states that objections shall be stated concisely and in a non-argumentative and non-suggestive manner. Numerous courts have condemned such speaking objections.[104] If opposing counsel makes this kind of objection, admonish counsel that the objection is plainly improper. If the conduct persists and is compromising your ability to fairly depose the witness, go to court.

Some attorney coaches use instructions to signal a witness. One common example is a directive that counsel makes to the witness after a question is posed to answer "only if you know." This also is a clearly improper attempt to coach the

[104] *See, e.g.*, Quantachrome Corp. v. Micromeritics Instrument Corp.,189 F.R.D. 697, 700 (S.D. Fla.1999); Armstrong v. Hussmann Corp., 163 F.R.D. 299, 302-03 (E.D. Mo. 1995); O'Brien v. Amtrak, 163 F.R.D. 232, 236 (E.D. Pa. 1995) ("Defendants' counsel spoke almost as much, if not more, than the deponents did."); *see also* Howard v. Offshore Liftboats, LLC, Nos. 13-4811, 13-6407, 2015 WL 965976, at *8 (E.D. La. Mar. 4, 2015) (speaking objection is improper regardless of whether the witness is actually influenced; sanctions imposed), magistrate op. aff'd, 2015 WL 3796458 (E.D. La. June 18, 2015); Tower Mfg. Corp. v. Shanghai Elec. Mfg. Corp., 244 F.R.D. 125, 130 (D.R.I. 2007) (imposing attorney's fees and ordering second Rule 30(b)(6) deposition through written questions of defense witness when defense counsel spoke for roughly 32% of the deposition).

witness.[105] If this happens in your deposition, you can object to the coaching. Alternatively, you can remind the witness of your early instructions.

Example: *A: [Attorney: Answer only if you know.]*
Q: Do you recall at the start of this deposition that I told you to tell me if you do not know the answer to any of my questions?
A: Yes.
Q: And you agreed?
A: Yes.
Q: Fine, let me again remind you to do this. That way, your counsel won't have to try to coach you any more.

Sometimes more sophisticated coaches will assert an objection based on "lack of foundation" to signal to the witness that the witness does not know the answer to your question. While such an objection is normally legitimate, it can be used improperly as a way of signaling the witness to deny any knowledge of the answer.

Coach attorneys also may respond to your question by stating that they do not understand the question. This also constitutes improper coaching. As the court noted in *Hall*, it is immaterial whether counsel understands the question.[106] If the attorney takes this approach, turn to the witness and ask if the witness understood the question. You also can remind the witness to tell you if he or she does not understand a question and note that this should eliminate the need for counsel to try to coach the witness.

---

[105] *See* Shartel, *supra* note 28, at 12; *see also* Lund v. Matthews, No. 8:13CV144, 2014 WL 517569, at *5 (D. Neb. Feb. 7, 2014) (second deposition allowed where counsel's speaking objections impeded the fair examination of the plaintiff; counsel must refrain from commentary on his objections and may not add "if you know" or "to the best of your knowledge" after an objection); Cincinnati Ins. Co. v. Serrano, No. 11-2075, 2012 WL 28071, at *5 (D. Kan. Jan. 5, 2012) ("Instructions to a witness that they may answer a question 'if they know' or 'if they understand the question' are raw, unmitigated coaching, and are *never* appropriate.") (emphasis in original).

[106] 150 F.R.D. at 530 n.10 (condemning this "favorite objection or interjection" of lawyers).

Alternatively, coach attorneys sometimes will rephrase your question for the witness. The attorney usually does this to substitute a more desirable question. This is improper. If this happens, insist on an answer to your question and have the court reporter read it back. Tell the witness that he or she will have an opportunity to answer opposing counsel's questions after you have completed your examination.

Often the most problematic attorney coach is the one who only coaches the witness on the few really key questions in the deposition and sits back silently the rest of the time. Because this attorney does not persist in the improper conduct, it becomes almost impossible to seek any relief from the court.[107] The damage is already done after the coaching on the key questions. Unfortunately, this highly selective coaching can prevent you from getting the responses you need to support a dispositive motion or later impeachment. It is difficult to prevent this type of selective coaching. One way to prevent this is to consider mixing up the organization and sequence of your questions so that it becomes more difficult for opposing counsel to detect and to coach the witness regarding those key questions.

2. The Testifier

The testifier attorney does not need to coach the witness how to answer a question. Rather, this attorney simply answers the questions for the witness. The testifier may do this by answering the question before the witness has given any response, by supplementing the witness's answer with additional information, or even by contradicting the witness's answer.[108] Sometimes counsel defending a deposition will make a brief remark to clarify an obvious error the witness made (e.g., the witness said "1988" when she clearly meant "1998"). This sort of testimony by counsel is usually not problematic and can even help avoid a confusing record. The testifier attorney is a problem when he or she testifies to

---

[107] If, however, there are a number of depositions to be taken, and you can show some pattern on the part of opposing counsel, you may consider seeking a protective order regarding coaching conduct prior to taking additional depositions if the coaching, albeit infrequent, materially interferes with your ability to get the information you need.

[108] *See, e.g.*, Quantachrome Corp., 189 F.R.D. at 700 n.3 (there is no "better example of coaching than counsel's telling a witness, 'No, you are incorrect. The correct answer is . . . .'").

change the substance of the witness's testimony or to significantly embellish the testimony.

If you encounter the testifier, you might respond in a couple of ways. First, after the attorney has testified, you can turn to the witness and ask: "Do you agree with the testimony your attorney has just given?" Sometimes this not-so-subtle message to the attorney is enough to stop the improper conduct. If this does not work, you should admonish counsel that you are there to get the witness's testimony, that the attorney's conduct is clearly improper, and that if the attorney persists in testifying for the witness, you will stop the deposition and go to court to get a protective order.

3. The Objector

The objector has never met a question he or she did not find objectionable. While this attorney may use objections to coach the witness, as discussed above, this type of attorney often interposes numerous objections simply to rattle you and to frustrate your examination.

How do you deal with the objector? Numerous courts have held that it is improper to make an excessive number of objections in a deposition.[109] The rules clearly contemplate that counsel should usually only make those objections that would otherwise be waived if not made at the time of the deposition. The Advisory Committee Notes expressly state that counsel even can be sanctioned for making an excessive number of legitimate but unnecessary objections.[110]

---

[109] *See, e.g.*, Van Pilsum v. Iowa State Univ. of Sci. and Tech., 152 F.R.D. 179, 181 (S.D. Iowa 1993) (sanctioning counsel for, *inter alia*, groundless objections that were mere "disputatious grandstanding"); Thomas v. Hoffman-La Roche, Inc., 126 F.R.D. 522, 524-25 (N.D. Miss. 1989) (sanctioning counsel for averaging more than 45 objections each hour); *see also* Todd v. Precision Boilers, Inc. 2008 WL 4722338, *1-*4 (W.D. La. Oct. 24, 2008) (finding defense counsel's constant interruptions to have obstructed the orderly and efficient taking of meaningful depositions, and imposing costs on defense counsel for doing so); *see also* Niles v. Rodman, No. 15-cv-00296, 2016 WL 153123, at *5 (D. Colo. Jan. 13, 2016) (excessive speaking objections warranted appointment of special master to preside over depositions).

[110] *See* 1993 Advisory Committee Notes, FED. R. CIV. P. 30.

If you encounter the objector in one of your depositions, it is best to admonish him or her early in the deposition. That approach may be enough to solve the problem. If not, and if the objections become so frequent and disruptive that they effectively inhibit your ability to conduct your examination, then tell counsel that the excessive objections are improper and that you intend to stop the deposition and to go to court if the conduct persists.

When the objector cannot think of a legitimate ground for an objection, the offending attorney frequently will resort to objections "to the form of the question." If this happens, you are entitled to ask, and the objector is obligated to tell you, what about the form of the question is objectionable.[111] If you challenge the objector the first time he or she makes such a vague objection, you may be able to cut off future objections of this sort.

As a next to last resort, before going to court, you might try offering the following stipulation to the objector:

Example: *Since you apparently find all of my questions to be objectionable, I will stipulate that you objected to every question I will ask in this deposition on every ground available under the rules. That way, you need not continue interrupting my examination.*

While this may not be your first option for dealing with the objector, you might find such a stipulation worthwhile if it will allow you to complete your examination without interference and without a trip to the court.

Finally, the objector sometimes will object and improperly instruct the witness not to answer your question. As discussed in Chapters 3 and 4, there are very limited situations in which it is proper to instruct a witness not to answer a question. If opposing counsel improperly instructs a witness not to answer your question, you may want to argue with counsel about the propriety of the instruction to try to avoid the need for you to go to court. Ask counsel to recite the

---

[111] Mayor v. Theiss, 729 A.2d 965, 976-77 (Md. 1999); *see also* Security Nat'l Bank, 299 F.R.D. at 601-04 (objections as to "form" are improper and "will invite sanctions if lawyers choose to use them in the future"); *but see* Meyer Corp. v. Alfay Designs, Inc., No CV 2010 3647, 2012 WL 3536987, at *4 (E.D.N.Y. Aug. 13, 2012) (admonishing counsel to simple state "objection as to form" unless elaboration is requested by examining counsel).

basis for the instruction and make a record that the witness is refusing to answer based on counsel's instruction. You also may want to ask the witness if he or she could answer your question if allowed. You do not want to go to court, get an order compelling the witness to answer, resume the deposition, re-ask your question, and only then find out the witness could not answer it anyway. Alternatively, you may consider moving on and coming back to the same topic with a very similar question. Counsel might not instruct the witness in response to the reformulated question.

4. The Intimidator

Sometimes you have the displeasure of encountering the intimidator (a/k/a the jerk). As the following accounts demonstrate, this attorney can be the defending attorney or the examining attorney. Here are a couple of real life examples of attorneys playing this role in defending depositions.

Example: *The Delaware Supreme Court imposed sanctions against a Texas attorney for abusive conduct in defending a deposition as illustrated by the following exchange between counsel:*

Attorney A: *He's not going to answer that. Certify it. I'm going to shut it down if you don't go to your next question.*

Attorney B: *No. Joe, Joe - -*

Attorney A: *Don't "Joe" me, a--hole. You can ask some questions, but get off of that. I'm tired of you. You could gag a maggot off a meat wagon.*[112]

* * *

---

[112] Paramount Commc'ns Inc. v. QVC Network Inc., 637 A.2d 34, 53-54 (Del. 1994).

Example: *This exchange occurred at a Minnesota deposition:*

Attorney A: *If you are going to hand the complaint to him to coach him we are going to see the judge.*
Attorney B: *Just get your foul odious body on the other side.*
Attorney A: *Then don't show the witness anymore –*
Attorney B: *I'm giving the witness the complaint.*
Attorney A: *You're not entitled to coach the witness any further, you're not entitled to --*
Attorney B: *Don't use your [language omitted] tricks on me.*[113]

* * *

Example: *The Florida Supreme Court suspended and sanctioned an attorney who went on a tirade during a deposition ordering that the attorney could not attend depositions alone for two years unless the depositions were videotaped and further ordering that the attorney receive mental health counseling. When the opposing lawyer attempted to stick an exhibit sticker on the attorney's laptop, the attorney*

---

[113] Attorney B received a public reprimand from the Minnesota Supreme Court. In re Williams, 414 N.W.2d 394, 397 (Minn. 1987). In another deposition in a personal injury case, a Minnesota attorney reported that opposing counsel angrily said: "Your client doesn't have any injuries. I'll show you injuries." The lawyer then removed his shirt to show everyone a scar on his shoulder. Barbara Jones, *How to Deal With Difficult Depositions*, MINN. LAWYER, Aug. 29, 2005, at 1. Other attorneys have been sanctioned for making gender-based insults at a deposition. *See, e.g.*, Principe v. Assay Partners, 586 N.Y.S.2d 182, 184 (App. Div. 1992) (sanctioning attorney for calling opposing counsel a "little lady," "little girl," and "little mouse"). *See also* The Rottlund Co., Inc. v. Pinacle Corp., 222 F.R.D. 362, 380-81 (D. Minn. 2004) (sanctioning attorney and requiring attorney to send written apology to deponent for trying to embarrass the deponent by asking if he liked his job and planned to stay with it when the attorney knew the deponent's job was about to be eliminated).

ran around the table, forcefully leaned over and lambasted the opposing lawyer in a tirade, tore up the evidence sticker and tossed it at the opposing lawyer.[114]

Attorneys can also play the role of intimidators in taking depositions:

Example: *A federal court in Iowa noted this "great moment in legal oratory" from a deposition:*

Attorney A: *Please sit down, do not hover over the witness.*
Attorney B: *Stick it in your ear.*[115]

* * *

Example: *A friend of one of the authors was defending a very contentious deposition. The witness indicated that she wanted to take a break to use the restroom. When she returned, the examining attorney alleged that the witness did not really use the restroom and that she only wanted to break to confer with her attorney. When the witness disputed the examining attorney's allegation and the examining attorney refused to accept her account, the defending attorney noted on the record that she accompanied the witness into the women's restroom, that she occupied the stall next to the witness and that she*

---

[114] Debra Cassens Weiss, *Lawyer Suspended for Deposition Tirade: Taped Incident Is Instructive, Court Says*, A.B.A. J., Aug. 2, 2010. The out-of-control attorney's own consultant told him to take a Xanax and the court reporter protested that she could not "work like this." Calling the attorney's conduct "an embarrassment to all members of the Florida bar," the Court suggested that members of the bar and law students view the video of this incident in a course on professionalism as a glaring example of how not to conduct oneself in a legal proceeding. *Id.*

[115] Mercer v. Gerry Baby Prods. Co., 160 F.R.D. 576, 577 (S.D. Iowa 1995).

heard the distinct sound of someone using the facilities in the witness's stall.

An intimidator attorney may be a party in a case.

Example: *The plaintiff, an attorney, sued U-Haul claiming he was assaulted by a company manager at a rental office. The following example is one of the plaintiff's many angry outbursts at his deposition:*

"You're so scummy and so slimy, such a perversion of ethics and decency because you're such a scared little man, you're so insecure and so frightened and the only way you can impress your client is by being nasty, mean-spirited and ugly little man, and that's what you are. That's the kind of prostitution you are in."[116]

* * *

Example: *An attorney representing himself, with the assistance of his son, was disciplined for threatening in a deposition to take the questioning attorney's mustache off his face, to give opposing counsel the beating of his life, to slap him across the face, and to break his head.*[117]

Intimidators do not limit their outrageous behavior to verbal insults and tirades.

Example: *An attorney for a disposable lighter manufacturer was sanctioned by a federal court for flicking a lighter in the face of a woman at a deposition. The*

---

[116] Corsini v. U-Haul Int'l, Inc., 630 N.Y.S.2d 45, 46 (App. Div. 1995).

[117] Office of Disciplinary Counsel v. Levin, 517 N.E.2d 892, 895 (Ohio 1988) (per curiam).

woman brought suit against the company claiming that one of the manufacturer's lighters caused a fire that killed her two children. While the manufacturer's attorney claimed he was just testing the lighter, the judge believed the attorney was really testing the plaintiff.[118]

* * *

Example: *One of the authors once deposed a court reporter who happened to be a plaintiff in a product liability case (and no, she did not transcribe her own deposition). When the author asked the court reporter if she had ever been involved in a prior lawsuit, the reporter responded that she was supposed to be a witness in a civil battery suit that settled. The suit arose out of an incident in which an attorney at a deposition she was reporting got angry with the opposing attorney and stood up and punched the other attorney in the face.*

As these examples demonstrate, intimidators use a variety of tactics. The intimidator may insult you or your client. The intimidator may use subtler tactics to harass and intimidate by, for example, standing over the witness after handing the witness a document. The intimidator may raise his or her voice or point a finger at the witness to try to scare the witness. All of these tactics are designed to intimidate your witness and throw you off your game plan. The intimidator may hope that you will rush your questioning to get through the deposition more quickly.

How do you deal with such offensive behavior? Here are a few recommendations.

- First, and perhaps most important, keep your cool. Do not let this attorney goad you into the very kind of insulting, verbal battle the

[118] Marshall Dennehey, *Judge: Flick of a Bic Was Flip, Even Cruel*, NAT'L L.J., Mar. 25, 1996, at A5, A5.

intimidator relishes. Usually, keeping your cool is itself disarming. Moreover, remember that you might be submitting a copy of the transcript to a judge.

- Make a verbal record of the offensive conduct or tone of voice. Doing so may deter additional similar abuse, and it will help provide you with evidence in the event you need to seek a court order.

- Do not let the attorney rush your examination. Take your time, stick to your game plan, and try not to get flustered.

- Take a break. Let the intimidator calm down. If that does not work, then be more direct. Take another break, telling the intimidator: "I see you have lost your composure. Let's resume the deposition in another fifteen minutes, so you can take time to regain control of yourself and proceed in a civil manner." You are basically giving the other attorney a "timeout." This kind of response can be very effective because the intimidator does not know how to react. By refusing to take the bait and engage this kind of attorney, you often can eliminate or reduce the offensive behavior.

- Videotape the deposition. In fact, if you anticipate this kind of rude behavior, you probably should plan from the start to videotape the deposition.

- Use humor to disarm the intimidator. This is not the reaction the intimidator desires or expects. Following are a couple of examples of this sort of disarming humor reported by a Minnesota lawyer.

Example: *A deposition was being conducted in prison of a man who had killed another man by beating him with a pool cue. As the examining attorney began to grill the convict and tempers flared, the defending attorney stopped the deposition, took the examining attorney to the corner of the room and reminded him: they were in prison; there was no guard present; the* *door was locked; the person he was now making angry had already killed one person over this incident; and he was not going to keep this person from making it two. Civility quickly returned.*

* * *

Example: *In another deposition, the examining attorney was getting hotter and hotter under the collar. The other attorney leaned over the table and handed a pot of coffee to the examining lawyer while remarking: "Try the decaf."*

- Go to court. If you have to go to court to curtail the intimidator's conduct and you do not have a videotape of the deposition, you might consider getting an affidavit from the court reporter detailing the opposing lawyer's actions. If the attorney was loud and boisterous, you might try to get the court reporter's audiotape of the deposition to provide to the court.[119]

While dealing with an intimidator can truly try your patience, take solace in knowing that this type of abusive conduct can result in hefty monetary sanctions against the attorney, or even dismissal of the lawsuit in its entirety.[120] In one case, a federal court in Texas sanctioned an attorney for using vulgar language in a deposition. The court fined the attorney $7,000, calculated at the

---

[119] This audiotape also can come in handy if the opposing counsel or witness accuses you of raising your voice.

[120] *See, e.g.*, Crawford v. JPMorgan Chase Bank, N.A., 242 Cal. App. 4th 1265, 1267, 1271 (2015, as modified on denial of rehearing Jan. 4, 2016) (lawsuit terminated as sanction where attorney representing himself threatened defendants' counsel with pepper spray and a stun gun at a deposition).

rate of $500 to $1000 for each pejorative word or threat.[121] It's costly to be a jerk.[122]

5. The Professor

The professor is a close relative of the intimidator. This attorney likes to critique your deposition skills and to lecture you regarding your glaring inadequacies. The professor will contrast your meager deposition experience ("Is this your first deposition?") with his or her own vast experience ("I was taking depositions when you were just a glint in your father's eye.") and incomparable expertise ("I am about to be inducted in the Depositions Hall of Fame.").

You can react to this type of attorney in different ways. There is a natural tendency to get defensive and try to justify your experience and competence. This typically gets you nowhere and is just the kind of response the professor desires. Another equally problematic response is to let the professor dictate how you conduct the deposition. (Having said this, there are some situations where opposing counsel may make legitimate suggestions to you about how you might handle some matter such as dealing with various documents or asking about a particular fact. Just because the suggestion came from the opposing attorney does not mean it is necessarily flawed or mean-spirited.) The best initial response is to ignore the professor. If, however, the professor persists, try a mixture of humor and sarcasm, something like the following:

Example: *I think I'll just try to stumble through this this time. Perhaps you can give me a critique after the deposition.*

---

[121] Carroll v. Jaques, 926 F. Supp. 1282, 1293 (E.D. Tex. 1996).

[122] In one case, a judge imposed a creative sanction on an attorney who resorted to name-calling and cursing in a deposition ordering the attorney to sit down for a meal with his opponent. The judge said that she hoped that perhaps the adversaries in this case can be reinspired to achieve the Shakespearean vision and aspirational goals of the very rules of professional conduct by which counsel have pledged to abide. Order on Defendant's Motion for Protective Order and Sanctions at 1, Huggins v. Coatsville Area Sch. Dist., No. 07-4917, ECF No. 62, Order (E.D. Pa. Sept. 17, 2009).

This sort of response often will silence the professor and allow you to get on with your deposition without a running critique of your performance.

6. The Repeater (a/k/a Déjà Vu)

The repeater attorney, also known as Déjà Vu, generally asks legitimate questions in a deposition. The problem is the attorney asks the same questions over and over again in an attempt to elicit a "better" answer, to generate some inconsistencies in the witness's testimony, or simply because the attorney is disorganized.[123]

How do you handle this problem attorney? You might object to the repeated question on the ground it was "asked and answered" or, more properly, unreasonably repetitive and, thus, harassing the witness. The difficulty with this approach is that the rules do not authorize you to instruct a witness not to answer a question on the ground that it was already asked and answered,[124] and the attorney will simply carry on. This conduct generally does not rise to the level of ridicule or oppression that would warrant a protective order.

A better way to handle this situation is for the witness to reply that he or she already has been asked the same question several times and already has answered it several times. At that point, there is not much the déjà vu attorney can do. The attorney cannot force the witness to re-answer the question. While the attorney can go to court and ask the court to compel the witness to answer the question, it is unlikely the attorney will do this, especially if the attorney knows that you will point out to the court that the witness already answered the same question one or more times.

---

[123] Counsel generally are entitled to a certain amount of latitude in asking similar questions of a witness. In fact, this technique may be the only way to deal with certain evasive witnesses. The déjà vu attorney is one who essentially repeats the same questions over and over, hoping for a better response. As you might imagine, the line between appropriate probing and inappropriate repetition is not always clear, and where one thinks the line lies might vary depending on whether you are taking or defending the deposition.

[124] *See* FED. R. CIV. P. 30(c)(2).

7. The Timekeeper

The timekeeper is an attorney who constantly is trying to rush your examination by asking how much longer you will be, by noting how long you have taken so far, and by noting various other appointments the attorney and the witness have. This attorney has a solitary agenda – rush your examination and get out of the deposition as quickly as possible. With the seven hour deposition time limit contained in the Federal Rules limiting, the timekeeper will keep a meter running to track the time ("Counsel, we've now been here for five hours, 19 minutes and 38 seconds. Are you almost done?").

If the opposing counsel or witness states that he or she needs to be somewhere else, do not rush your questioning to accommodate their schedules. You can simply tell the attorney and witness that you will stop the deposition and resume it the following day to accommodate their other commitments. If you do not want to break up the deposition, insist on your right to complete the deposition.

C. Judicial Intervention

As discussed above, you may go to court for assistance in dealing with problem witnesses and problem attorneys. This usually should be a last resort. If you consider exercising this option, keep in mind the following.

- *Only go to court regarding important disputes.* Many things can happen in a deposition that do not go exactly your way. Typically, relatively few things, however, are important enough to bring to the attention of the court. If you ask the court to resolve unimportant disputes, you will look petty and lose credibility. You also will undermine your chances of getting the court's assistance when you really need it.

- *Only go to court if you are likely to win.* For the same reason you do not want to go to court over unimportant disputes, you also do not want to go to court if you are likely to lose. You are generally better off not going to court at all than going and losing.

- *Make a sufficient record before you go to court.* As discussed above, it is critical that you make an adequate record of whatever it is you plan to raise with the court. In the case of nonverbal conduct, this means you should describe the conduct on the record, get a videotape or audiotape depicting the conduct, and get affidavits of witnesses to the conduct (including the court reporter). In the case of oral conduct, get the verbatim transcript of the conduct to show to the judge. Do not rely on your characterization of what was said.

- *Try to resolve the problem yourself.* Make sure your efforts are on the record. Judges expect attorneys to try to work things out on their own before coming to court.

- *Know the judge's procedures for handling deposition disputes.* Even before you go into the deposition, you should know how your judge prefers to handle deposition disputes. For example, is your judge willing to receive phone calls during a deposition to provide an immediate ruling? If so, and if you anticipate that there may be problems in an upcoming deposition, you may want to call the judge's law clerk to find out if the judge will be available to receive such calls during your deposition. (Be careful to restrict the content of the call and to refrain from editorializing so as to avoid *ex parte* communication with the court.) Also, take the judge's phone number and the law clerk's name to the deposition.

There are, of course, other kinds of problem witnesses and problem attorneys in depositions not addressed here. For example, one of the authors knows an attorney who has been seen lowering the height of the deponent's chair before a deposition to obtain a height advantage. It is an unfortunate fact of life as a litigator that there always will be witnesses and lawyers who will find new and innovative ways to be difficult.[125] The above discussion is intended to help you

---

[125] There are various civility codes that contain guidelines for counsel's conduct in depositions. *See, e.g.*, ABA Litig. Sec. Civ. Disc. Standards 16-19 (1999); Minn. Professionalism Aspirations, Standard III.D (2001). While these are generally aspirational civility codes, you might consider citing to them if you get in a dispute before the court over opposing counsel's conduct at a deposition.

recognize some of the more common problem witnesses and attorneys and to give you some tools to deal with them.[126]

[126] One magistrate who was especially fed up with the deposition misconduct of counsel on both sides of a case resorted to public shaming:

> If I was an elementary school teacher instead of a judge I would require both counsel to write the following . . . on a blackboard 500 times:
>
>> I will not make speaking, coaching, suggestive objections . . . . I am an experienced lawyer and know that objections must be concise, nonargumentative and non-suggestive. I understand that the purpose of a deposition is to find out what the witness things, saw, heard or did. I know that lawyers are not supported to coach or change the witness's own words to form a legally convenient record. I know I am prohibited from frustrating or impeding the fair examination of a deponent during the deposition. I know that constant objects and unnecessary remarks are unwarranted and frustrate opposing counsel's right to fair examination. I know that speaking objections such as "if you remember," "if you know," "don't guess," "you've answered the question," and "do you understand the question" are designed to coach the witness and are improper. I also know that counsel's interjection that he or she does not understand the question is not a proper objection, and that if a witness needs clarification of a question, the witness may ask for the clarification.

Mazzeo v. Gibbons, No. 2:08-cv-01387, 2010 WL 3020021, at *2 (D. Nev. July 27, 2010).

CHAPTER 6

Expert Depositions

Experts have become commonplace in modern civil litigation. There are experts to testify about everything under the sun. Some expert referral services advertise that they have lists of experts on such topics as bleacher design, knots, mortuary science, odors, parachutes, and zippers. Expert testimony can be pivotal in a case. Jurors and, to a lesser extent, judges may put a lot of stock in what an expert says at trial. Accordingly, your expert, and your opponent's expert, may be the most important witnesses in your case. Their depositions, therefore, are critical.

This Chapter deals exclusively with the expert deposition. Included in this discussion is a review of basic expert deposition rules and requirements and general advice regarding preparing for and taking an expert deposition. At the end of the Chapter is a model outline of question topics for an expert deposition.[127]

[127] This Chapter does not address the circumstances under which you need or may desire expert testimony or how you locate an expert.

A. Expert Deposition Rules and Requirements

Following is an overview of the federal rules and requirements applicable to expert depositions. Individual state rules of procedure regarding expert depositions may vary somewhat.

1. Right to Depose Experts

Federal Rule of Civil Procedure 26 was amended in 1993 to provide that parties have a right to take the deposition of the experts expected to testify for the other side.[128] Prior to this amendment, Rule 26 permitted depositions of experts upon a motion and showing of good cause. In practice, however, parties frequently agreed to depositions of their respective experts, which ultimately led to the rule change in 1993.

Rules of civil procedure in some state courts still follow the pre-1993 version of Federal Rule 26.[129] If you are handling a case governed by these rules and are unable to convince your opponent to agree to depositions of your respective experts, you will need to bring a motion and establish good cause to take the expert's deposition. In bringing such a motion, you should consider arguing that the modern practice is to permit such depositions as a matter of right, as reflected in Federal Rule of Civil Procedure 26(b)(4)(A), and that because of the complexity of the issues in the case, you need to depose your opponent's expert to be able to prepare adequately to cross-examine the expert. You also can argue that your opponent's answer to your expert witness interrogatory is insufficient, and that you are willing to pay the expert a reasonable amount for the expert's time in his or her deposition to minimize any prejudice to your opponent.

While you have the right to depose experts expected to testify at trial in federal court, you do not have the right to depose experts retained by your opponent who are not expected to testify unless you can show exceptional circumstances that make it impractical for you to obtain facts and opinions on the

---

[128] FED. R. CIV. P. 26(b)(4)(A).

[129] *See, e.g.*, MINN . R. CIV. P. 26.02(d) (2001).

same subject by other means.[130] As one court has explained, there are several policy considerations that underlie this rule: (1) encouraging attorneys to obtain expert advice without fear of the adversary obtaining the information; (2) preventing unfairness from allowing an opposing party to reap the benefits from another party's expense and efforts; (3) preventing the chilling effect on experts serving as consultants if their testimony could be compelled; and (4) preventing unfairness that would result if an opposing party could compel the testimony of such experts who provided unfavorable opinions to the party who retained them.[131] The same rule applies to experts informally consulted by your opponent who are not expected to testify.[132]

2. Expert Reports

The 1993 amendments to Rule 26 also added a requirement that experts who are expected to testify prepare written reports regarding their opinions.[133] This requirement can be modified by stipulation, local rule, or court order.[134] Specifically, Rule 26(a)(2)(B) states that the expert's report must contain: (1) a complete statement of all opinions to be expressed; and the basis and reasons for

[130] FED. R. CIV. P. 26(b)(4)(B); *see also* Queen's Univ. at Kingston v. Kinedyne Corp., 161 F.R.D. 443, 448 (D. Kan. 1995) (denying defendant's motion to depose plaintiff's expert not expected to testify at trial). An expert who is "converted" from an expert expected to testify at trial to a non-testifying expert may be insulated from discovery. *See, e.g.,* Cooper v. Ciccarelli, No. 07-2434-GLR, 2009 W L 3053743, *3 (D. Kan. Sept. 18, 2009).

[131] Plymovent Corp. v. Air Tech. Solutions, Inc., 243 F.R.D. 139 (D.N.J. 2017).

[132] Ager v. Jane C. Stormont Hosp. & Training Sch. for Nurses, 622 F.2d 496, 501 (10th Cir. 1980); *but see* In Re Welding Fume Prods. Liab. Litig., 534 F. Supp. 2d 761, 767 (N.D. Ohio 2008) ("Although some cases characterize *Ager* as setting out the 'predominant view,' (citation omitted) it is clear that there is a split in authority. Many cases simply reject the ruling and reasoning set out in *Ager*, [at least as to the non-discoverability of even the identity of non-testifying consultants.]"

[133] As the Advisory Committee Notes indicate, the information disclosed under the former rule "was frequently so sketchy and vague that it rarely dispensed with the need to depose the expert and often was even of little help in preparing for a deposition of the witness."

[134] The requirement to provide a report also can be imposed on other witnesses offering testimony under FED. R. EVID. 702.

all such opinions; (2) the facts or data considered by the expert in forming the opinions; (3) any exhibits to be used as a summary of or support for the opinions; (4) the expert's qualifications including a list of all publications authored in the preceding ten years; (5) the expert's compensation; and (6) a list of other cases in which the expert has testified at trial or by deposition in the preceding four years.[135] If an expert's report does not disclose all of the expert's opinions, the court may exclude the undisclosed opinions at trial under Rule 37(c)(1). Testifying experts are required to supplement their reports if they are found to be incomplete or incorrect.[136] The 1993 Advisory Committee Notes indicate that the Rule does not preclude an attorney from assisting an expert in the preparation of the expert's report.[137] The expert must, however, sign the report.[138]

Federal courts typically set deadlines for the disclosure of expert reports in their Rule 16 pretrial scheduling orders. If the court does not do so, the reports are due at least 90 days before the trial date or the date the case is to be ready for trial.[139] As the 1993 Advisory Committee Notes indicate, in most cases, the party with the burden of proof on an issue should disclose its expert report on that issue before other parties are required to disclose their expert reports regarding the issue. You may want to consider negotiating such a staggered disclosure schedule or request that the court order such a schedule if your opponent has the burden of proof. In almost all instances, it is preferable to know what your opponent's experts' opinions are before your experts have to disclose their opinions.

---

[135] While certain expert witnesses (e.g., treating physicians, government accident investigators) are not required to provide a written report, Rule 26(a)(2)(C) requires a party to disclose the subject matter on which such an expert is expected to testify and a summary of the facts and opinions to which the expert is expected to testify.

[136] FED. R. CIV. P. 26(a)(2)(D), 26(e)(2).

[137] Some courts have, however, noted that expert reports authored in large part by attorneys are inherently suspect. *See, e.g.*, New York v. Anheuser-Busch, Inc., 811 F. Supp. 848, 869 (E.D.N.Y. 1993).

[138] For a good discussion of expert reports under Rule 26(a)(2), see Theodore C. Hirt, *Expert Reports*, 22 LITIG., Summer 1996, at 46.

[139] FED. R. CIV. P. 26(a)(2)(D)(i). Rule 26(a)(2)(D)(ii) allows an additional 30 days for disclosure of expert testimony that only rebuts another expert's expected testimony.

What do you do if your state court rules do not require the exchange of such expert reports? First, you should decide if that is a good thing in your case. Some attorneys prefer not to exchange expert reports. Second, if you would prefer to exchange such reports, you should convince your opponent to agree to do so. You might suggest that the parties follow Federal Rule of Civil Procedure 26(a)(2) in regard to the content and timing of these reports. If your opponent refuses to exchange reports, you might consider asking the court to require an exchange. Finally, if you are unable to persuade your opponent and the court to order the exchange of reports, you should consider trying to get an agreement or order allowing you to depose your opponent's experts. It is unusual for parties to provide sufficiently detailed interrogatory answers regarding expected expert testimony to allow for effective cross-examination of the expert at trial.[140]

3. Timing and Sequence of Expert Depositions

Federal Rule of Civil Procedure 26(b)(4)(A) provides that depositions of testifying experts must await the disclosure of the experts' reports. Many attorneys actually prefer to take expert depositions after the lay discovery in the case is completed in order to minimize the likely need for additional expert depositions to address newly acquired factual information. It is expected that an expert's report may eliminate the need for a deposition, or may at least shorten the length of the deposition.

The Rules do not provide any priority with respect to the taking of expert depositions. Courts sometimes order, and parties sometimes agree to, a staggered schedule for expert depositions similar to a staggered schedule for the disclosure of expert reports discussed above.

4. Location of Expert Depositions

Experts are treated like other non-party witnesses in regard to the location of their depositions. That is, they are usually deposed where they work or reside. A subpoena is needed to compel an expert to appear for a deposition. Parties often

[140] If, in the above circumstances, your opponent or the court agrees to one *or* the other of these options – an expert report or an expert deposition – but not both, you are probably better off to forego the report and to select the expert deposition.

agree to produce their respective experts at their depositions and thereby to dispense with the need for subpoenas.

You may decide that you would prefer that an out-of-state expert travel to where you are located for a deposition. While you have no right under the rules to compel this, you may be able to agree with your opponent that all experts will be deposed where counsel work. Typically, this may require you to pay the opposing expert's travel expenses or the parties may agree to pay for their own expert's travel expenses.

You may conversely decide that you would prefer to take the deposition of an expert at the expert's workplace. That way, you can get some impression of the expert's facilities. Moreover, if the expert references some documents or other items in the expert's files during the deposition that the expert did not bring to the deposition, you may be able to persuade the expert to go get the missing items at a break.

5. Costs of Expert Depositions

Federal Rule of Civil Procedure 26(b)(4)(C) provides that a party shall pay the expert a reasonable fee for time spent in responding to discovery. While disputes sometimes arise over whether an expert's fee is reasonable, it is usually not too difficult to determine this obligation in most expert depositions. One source of controversy is the issue of whether a party must compensate an expert for the expert's time spent preparing for the deposition. While the courts are not in agreement regarding this issue, a slim majority allow a party to recoup these costs.[141]

[141] The court in Borel v. Chevron, U.S.A., Inc., 265 F.R.D. 275 (E.D. La. 2010), addressed this issue and the split in authority on this issue. It also analyzed the factors that should be considered in determining the reasonableness of the fees. *Compare* S.A. Healy Co. v. Milwaukee Metro. Sewage Dist., 154 F.R.D. 212, 214 (E.D. Wis. 1994) (no compensation for expert's preparation time except in a "complex" matter "where there has been a considerable lapse of time between an expert's work on a case and the date of his actual deposition") *with* Hose v. Chicago & N.W. Transp. Co., 154 F.R.D. 222, 228 (S.D. Iowa 1994) (compensation for expert's preparation time allowed), *and* Boos v. Prison Health Servs., 212 F.R.D. 578, 580 (D. Kan. 2002) (compensation for expert's preparation time allowed, but at a reduced hourly rate).

Parties will sometimes agree to pay their own expert deposition expenses on the assumption that this expense will amount to a wash given the reciprocal obligation of the other side. You may, of course, not want to enter into such an agreement if the cost of deposing your experts will likely greatly exceed the cost of deposing your opponent's experts.

6. Recording Expert Depositions

There are no special rules regarding the recording of expert depositions. You do, however, need to decide whether you want to videotape an opposing expert's deposition. There are reasons you might want or not want to videotape the deposition. You might want to do this if the expert's analysis is demonstrative in nature. Conversely, if you suspect that the expert might not be available to testify at trial, you might not want to videotape the deposition so as not to preserve that format for the introduction of the expert's testimony at trial.

B. Preparing for the Expert Deposition

While many of the principles discussed in Chapters 2 and 4 are applicable to preparing to take and defend the deposition of an expert, there are some additional matters you need to consider. Because of the unique nature of expert testimony, your preparation to take an expert deposition generally will take on a different focus, as outlined below.[142]

1. Create a "Book" on the Expert

Preparing a "book" on the expert is probably the most important task in getting ready to take an expert's deposition. Typically, this involves finding out as much as you can about the expert and the expert's qualifications before you even

---

142 This part of the Chapter deals with preparing to take the deposition of your opponent's expert. You may also have occasion to depose your own expert. This typically arises if your expert is going to be unavailable to testify at trial. In fact, some courts allow plaintiffs to introduce the deposition testimony of treating physicians even if the physicians are not actually unavailable at trial within the meaning of the rules. The courts permit this to accommodate the busy schedules of the physicians. If you depose your own expert, you will want to treat the deposition as if it were a direct examination at trial.

get to the deposition. The following outline discusses the kinds of information you usually want to investigate regarding an expert before the deposition.[143]

a. Rule 26 Report

In federal court, you will almost always have your opponent's expert's Rule 26(a)(2)(B) report to review before the deposition as discussed above. If you do not have such a report, or are litigating in a state court that does not require the exchange of expert reports, you usually will have your opponent's answer to an interrogatory asking about the expected testimony of your opponent's expert. If you are fortunate to have a reasonably thorough expert report or expert interrogatory answer, these will greatly help you prepare your outline of questions.

b. Expert's Prior Testimony

Some of the most useful information you can get regarding an expert is the expert's prior testimony. This may be testimony from other trials, depositions, or other proceedings, such as legislative or agency hearings. Every once in a while you get lucky and find that the expert has testified inconsistently in another matter. How do you find this prior testimony? As noted above, the expert's Rule 26(a)(2)(B) report is required to list all cases within the preceding four years in which the expert has testified at trial or by deposition. While the expert may not be required to identify other and older testimony, you are not limited to this identified testimony. If you can get the expert's curriculum vitae, it often will contain a complete list of prior testimony. Moreover, if you can get one of the expert's recent deposition transcripts, you can often find out the other occasions in which the expert has testified. You may also be able to locate information regarding an expert's prior testimony from other attorneys in your firm or community or from various attorney associations. Some of these associations keep expert witness libraries or banks regarding recurring experts.

---

[143] Your law librarian can be a very valuable resource in tracking down non-legal information about experts you plan to depose. *See* Matthew Bird, *Researching an Expert's Background*, NAT'L L. J., July 16, 2001, at B20 (discussing how law librarians can help you find much information about experts).

Once you find and review this prior testimony, you need to decide what to do with it. You may find some prior testimony that looks like good impeachment material. At that point, you need to decide whether to disclose the testimony and impeach the expert during the deposition or whether to save the impeachment for trial. To avoid giving the expert time to reconcile the testimony, most attorneys would probably opt to save the impeachment material for trial.

c. Expert's Publications

Find out what publications the expert has authored. Again, the expert's Rule 26(a)(2)(B) report should disclose many of these publications. Otherwise, your law librarian can help you run searches to identify these publications, or you can do your own computer searches.

One problem you may encounter with respect to publications is the expert who cannot turn around without publishing something. This expert's curriculum vitae is roughly the length of a phone directory and contains a seemingly endless list of publications. You might ask your own expert to help you identify the most relevant publications to review. You can also ask the expert at his or her deposition to identify the most relevant publications.

d. Media Articles

Search for media articles in which the expert's name has appeared. You may come across interesting stories regarding the expert. You also may get useful information in op-ed pieces that the expert authored. Such articles often contain very opinionated remarks that you can use to show an expert's lack of objectivity on a subject.

e. Internet Information

There may be other information available regarding the expert on the Internet. For example, you may find a web site from the expert's firm that contains useful information about the expert's past work or other clients that may not appear in the expert's report or on the expert's curriculum vitae.

f. Licensure Boards/Professional Associations

Contact licensure boards or professional associations to which the expert belongs. Sometimes you can find out if the expert is in good standing or has a history of complaints against him or her. You also can verify certain basic information about the licenses that the expert has received, which you can check against what the expert tells you in the deposition.

g. Consultation with Other Attorneys and Associations

In preparing for an expert's deposition, it can be extremely helpful to confer with attorneys who already have examined (or retained) the same expert. These attorneys can provide you with a wealth of information not only about the expert's expertise and work but also about the expert's style, strengths, and weaknesses. You can often get similar information from some of the attorney associations that maintain expert files.

h. Check Expert's Credentials – Get Current Curriculum Vitae

You may want to do some preliminary checking into the expert's credentials before the expert's deposition. As noted above, you can check into licensure status. You might also be able to find out if an expert, in fact, graduated from a particular educational institution and whether the expert is a recipient of certain awards. Sometimes you get lucky and discover that an expert has lied about his or her credentials. If you discover that an expert has lied, you may want to save this information for your cross-examination at trial.

2. Use Your Expert and Client to Help You Prepare

Your own expert can be invaluable in helping you prepare to depose your opponent's expert. Your expert can suggest questions for you to ask regarding the other expert's qualifications and opinions and other materials for you to review on the subject matter. Also, do not overlook your own client as a valuable resource. For example, clients who are in a particular business may have substantial expertise about their products, markets, and competitors, and may be able to suggest very useful lines of questioning.

3. Get Expert's File Before the Deposition

Serve the expert you are to depose with a subpoena duces tecum requesting the production of various items. The only problem with this approach is that this subpoena gets you the requested materials at the deposition. Ideally, you would like to have these materials in advance so you can review them and prepare any necessary questions about them. Accordingly, you should consider negotiating an agreement with your opponent to produce these materials in advance of the deposition of the expert. Such advance production of these materials will invariably save time at the deposition. If your opponent will not agree to this, you might ask the court to order advance production of documents.

Typically, you will want to request the production of the following materials.

a. Reports/Drafts

While you already should have the expert's report, make sure you get the latest draft. While federal courts generally allowed parties to discover prior drafts of a testifying expert's report since the 1993 changes to Rule 26, a recent amendment to Rule 26(b)(4)(B) provides work product protection to such drafts of any report regardless of the form in which the draft is recorded.

b. Raw Data and Work Papers

Be sure to get the expert's underlying raw data and work papers. It is not at all uncommon to find that an expert has made simple arithmetic errors or other mistakes that can be fruitful material for cross-examination. You also may find limitations with or inaccuracies in the data the expert analyzed. You need the expert's data set if you want to replicate or verify the expert's calculations and analysis.

c. Communications with Counsel

You want to know what influence opposing counsel may have had on the expert's analysis. Rule 26 was amended in 1993 to provide that the expert must disclose all of the data or other information the expert "considered" in forming the expert's opinions. Previously, parties were only required to disclose what the expert "relied upon" in forming the expert's opinions.[144] Rule 26 was again amended in 2010 to provide work product protection to the communications between a party's attorney and a testifying expert. Rule 26(b)(4)(C) provides three exceptions to this work product protection. The new Rule does not extend work product protection to communications that (1) relate to compensation for the expert's study or testimony; (2) identify facts or data the party's attorney provided and the expert considered in forming the expert's opinion; and (3) identify assumptions the party's attorney provided that the expert relied upon in forming the opinions expressed in the expert's report. A party may be entitled to discover communications protected by this Rule, as well as prior drafts of reports otherwise not discoverable under the amended Rule, by making a showing of need and hardship sufficient to overcome this work product protection.[145]

Within the scope of amended Rule 26, make sure to request copies of all correspondence between the expert and opposing counsel and copies of all notes of any meetings or other oral conversations. Also be sure to ask specifically for copies of e-mail communications between the expert and opposing counsel. For many lawyers and experts, this has become the dominant communications medium.[146]

---

[144] See *Karn v. Ingersoll-Rand Co.*, 168 F.R.D. 633, 635 (N.D. Ind. 1996), for a good discussion of this issue and the competing policy considerations. *Compare* In re Pioneer Hi-Bred Int'l, Inc., 238 F.3d 1370, 1375 (Fed. Cir. 2001) (disclosure of privileged information, including core attorney work product, to expert expected to testify waives the protection and subjects the information to discovery) *with* Krisa v. Equitable Life Assurance Soc'y, 196 F.R.D. 254, 260 (M.D. Pa. 2000) (rejecting bright-line rule and concluding that core attorney work product communicated between attorney and expert remains protected).

[145] Keep in mind that the discoverability of communications between a party's attorney and a testifying expert, as well drafts of expert reports, may differ in state courts that do not recognize the same work product protection for these communications and drafts.

[146] You also may want to ask for the expert's document retention policy so that you can determine whether the expert may have improperly destroyed drafts and various forms of communication

d. Materials/Information Relied Upon

Always request the material and information the expert relied upon in forming his or her opinions. This may consist of computer data, photographs, videotapes, drawings, laboratory analyses, medical records, statements, deposition testimony, learned treatises, government reports, and other material. Because this material often is voluminous, you should try to get it in advance of the deposition. Without this underlying material, you may be unable to determine whether the expert made some errors in the expert's analysis or whether the expert's data was flawed.

e. Retainer and Invoices

The expert's retainer agreement should not only give you the expert's billing rate, but it also may describe the expert's assignments. The expert's invoices can reveal how much time the expert spent analyzing some matter, who did the work, and when the work was done. The invoices may additionally describe work the expert did that ultimately did not prove to be helpful to the other side's case.

4. Prepare Outline of Questions

Prepare an outline of your questions to the expert just as you would prepare such an outline for a lay witness deposition. While the content of such an outline will necessarily differ somewhat with each expert deposition you take, we have included at the end of this Chapter a model or generic outline that you can reference in preparing your own questions. This outline contains many of the topics that you are likely to want to address in your expert deposition.

C. Taking the Deposition

The following practice tips will help in taking the deposition of your opponent's expert.

---

with counsel. While there generally is no requirement that an expert retain earlier drafts or notes of communications with counsel, it is inappropriate for an attorney to request that the expert destroy these materials if that is inconsistent with the expert's usual practice. The nice, and also dangerous, thing about e-mail is that it rarely is truly destroyed.

1. Inquire About Production Requests

In most instances, you will have served a subpoena duces tecum on the expert, or you will have a written agreement from opposing counsel to produce materials in advance of the expert deposition. You should begin the deposition by marking the subpoena or agreement as an exhibit and then confirming that the expert has produced all material responsive to each of the requests.

2. Do Not Try to Destroy the Expert

As you take the deposition of your opponent's expert, resist the temptation to try to destroy the expert. First of all, your attempt to skewer the expert is highly likely to fail. Many of the experts you depose will have had their depositions taken many times and will be quite good at it. These experts are (usually) bright and very familiar with the kinds of traps attorneys like to set. They know how to avoid such traps, and can make you look unreasonable or even foolish. Second, even if you happen to be successful in slaying or mortally wounding your opponent's expert, your efforts are likely to be counterproductive. The other side will figure out how to rehabilitate the expert before trial or simply will get a new expert. While your destruction of the expert may be momentarily gratifying, it may do little or nothing to advance your overall case. The annihilation of your opponent's expert in a deposition is only likely to be productive as a show of strength for settlement purposes, and then only if you can convince your opponent that it will be difficult to get a new, more competent expert.[147]

3. Consider Having Your Expert Attend the Deposition

You may want to have your own expert attend the deposition of your opponent's expert. Your expert can help interpret the testimony of the deponent, especially if it is quite technical, and can suggest follow-up questions.

---

[147] The commentator described this "Colombo" approach to deposing experts: "Specifically, the questions should seem quite dumb, acting the part of a wide-eyed junior college student interested in learning all there is to know about the expert's expertise and about the opinions he has been paid to provide." Eliot G. Disner, *Taking Expert Depositions: The Role of "Dumb and Dumber,"* 51 FED. LAWYER 22, 23 (Feb. 2004).

4. Try Not to Educate the Expert About Your Analysis of the Case

One of the risks of deposing your opponent's expert is educating the expert regarding your theory of the case and the weaknesses in the expert's analysis. While you can try to minimize this risk, it is almost impossible to eliminate it if you do a thorough deposition. Your questioning will inevitably shed some light on your analysis of the case. You can try to disguise some of your analysis through various techniques. For example, if you question the expert regarding an alternative theory or explanation, you might ask the expert about multiple alternatives as opposed to only the one alternative you believe is most probable. Moreover, if you have discovered a flaw in the expert's analysis, you might stop short of revealing this in the deposition. You might also try to distribute and mix-up your questions in such a way as to avoid suggesting matters of particular interest to you.

5. Use Frequent Closure Questions

One of the most important techniques to employ in an expert deposition is the closure question – "Are those all of the opinions you plan to address in your testimony?", "Did you do any other tests?", and "Did you rely on anything else in formulating that opinion?" It is imperative to box the expert in to minimize the expert's ability to change or embellish the expert's testimony at trial. If you effectively contain the scope of the expert's testimony, you can better concentrate on attacking what you know is coming at trial. Some lawyers like to ask experts at the conclusion of their depositions if they had a sufficient opportunity to fully explain their opinions or whether the attorney failed to cover any significant aspect of the experts' analysis and expected trial testimony.

6. More Tips in Model Expert Deposition Outline

The model expert deposition outline found below contains some more specific tips regarding the taking of an expert's deposition.

7. Follow-up to Expert's Deposition

Following are several suggestions regarding the follow-up to the taking of an expert's deposition.

a. Get Supplemental Reports

If the expert testified at the deposition that the expert was preparing, or planned to prepare, a supplemental written report, make sure to get this report as soon as possible before trial. Also request that your opponent disclose prior to trial any material changes in the expert's deposition testimony.[148]

b. Take Another Deposition of the Expert

If the expert has not completed his or her analysis and, therefore, has not finalized the expert's opinions by the time of the expert's deposition, consider taking a subsequent deposition. While your opponent may object to a second deposition of the expert, the court likely will allow you to re-depose the expert in these circumstances.

c. Consider Getting a Different or Additional Expert

After you depose your opponent's expert, you may decide to get a different or additional expert of your own if, for example, it appears that your existing expert does not have the requisite expertise, if your opponent's expert plans to address a topic outside your expert's scope of expertise, or if you want to get another expert with greater expertise than your opponent's expert.

d. Give Transcript to Your Expert to Evaluate

If your expert did not attend the deposition of your opponent's expert, you should send the transcript or videotape of the deposition to your own expert to review.

---

148 With experts, unlike with other witnesses, the federal rules require a party to supplement deposition testimony if the testimony later turns out to be incorrect or incomplete in some material respect. FED. R. CIV. P. 26(e)(2).

D. Preparing an Expert to be Deposed

The preparation of an expert who is to be deposed is very similar to the preparation of other lay witnesses. Following are a few tips to keep in mind as you prepare your expert to be deposed. Note, however, as you review these tips that you really want your expert to tell you four things in preparation: First, what are the expert's opinions? Second, what assumptions underlie those opinions? Third, is there any information the expert has recently learned or would like to learn, that could impact on the opinions? Fourth, what are the likely attacks that the other side will mount against the opinions?

With those four key questions in mind, you may also want to consider the following possibilities.

1. Do Not Assume Expert Knows How to Testify

You may retain an expert who has never been deposed and is, therefore, just as unfamiliar about what to expect and how to testify as any lay witness. You also may encounter experts who have been deposed many times before but have never properly been prepared and, accordingly, testify rather poorly. Finally, you may prepare an expert who is very experienced and very skilled in a deposition. While the latter type expert should need less preparation, do not assume that all experts are of the latter type simply because they are experts.

A word of caution, however. Do not be condescending and do not waste time. The experts you hire presumably will be intelligent and they all will charge by the hour. If you are too patronizing in your general discussion about deposition basics you risk offending your expert and costing your client more than is necessary due to wasted time. If your expert has deposition experience, consider deferring discussion of general deposition instructions until after you have reviewed the four key substantive areas outlined above. These are discussions you need with any expert, and they never should be short changed because you have run out of time.

2. Review Theories of the Case

Even if your expert is very knowledgeable in his or her field and very skilled in testifying, it still is important that you brief the expert regarding your theories of the case and how the expert's testimony supports your position.

3. Discuss Testimony of Other Experts

In preparing your expert to be deposed, educate your expert as much as possible about what the other experts in the case have said or are likely to say. You would prefer to avoid having your expert say something inadvertently that helps your opponent's expert or undermines the testimony of another one of your experts.

4. Remember That Your Preparation May Be Discoverable

As discussed above, in federal court, some of your communications with your expert are discoverable under amended Rule 26(b)(4)(C) if they relate to the three exceptions to work product protection generally afforded to such communications. You should assume that your expert is like other non-party witnesses and that everything said in your deposition preparation session is discoverable. As also noted above, state court rules may differ as to the discoverability of these communications.

E. Model Expert Deposition Outline

Following is a model examination outline that you can tailor to use in nearly all expert depositions. Along with the outline of question areas are some specific comments and suggestions. You may decide to deviate from the order of question areas in this outline. For example, you might decide to delay your questions about the expert's credentials and assignment, and instead launch right into questions about the expert's opinions. This can be a bit disconcerting to the expert who was prepared to spend the first hour of the deposition reciting how utterly impressive his or her credentials are. Deferring background questions also helps minimize the risk of running out of time before you have completed critical substantive areas of inquiry.

▸ Expert's Qualifications

There are several topics you should cover in regard to the expert's qualifications. Hopefully, you can establish that your opponent's expert is less qualified than your expert or biased in favor of your opponent. Sometimes, if you get lucky, you may even discover that your opponent's expert falsified his or her credentials.[149]

- **Education**

  Ask about educational institutions attended, years attended, degrees received, majors/minors, and awards/recognition received.

- **Employment**

  Ask about employers, years of employment, positions held, job responsibilities, and reasons for leaving.

- **Publications**

  These are usually on the expert's curriculum vitae. Ask about any publications not listed on the expert's CV and about works in progress that the expert is currently authoring. If the expert's list of publications is voluminous, you might ask which of the publications are relevant, or most relevant, to the work the expert performed in your case.

- **Teaching Positions**

  Inquire about teaching positions the expert has held. You may find that an expert has articulated certain views in connection with his or her teaching that differ from the expert's views after retained as a litigation expert.

---

[149] For a good discussion of witnesses who falsify their credentials, and ways to use evidence of this kind of fraud, see Marcy Ressler Harris, *Getting Wise About Resume Lies*, 25 LITIG., Summer 1999, at 21.

- **Professional Affiliations**

Experts frequently include a long list of professional associations on their curriculum vitae. If you are not familiar with these associations, ask the expert about them. What are the qualifications for membership – is it an honorary association that you must be invited to join or can you just sign up? Also ask what the expert does in connection with the association – is he or she an officer or simply on a mailing list of members that receive periodic newsletters and other mailings? If you spend some time with this list, you will often find it is not nearly as impressive as it first appears and that you can show that many of these affiliations are not really relevant to the expert's opinions in your case.

- **Licensure/Certification**

Ask the expert about licensures and certifications. Some of these are very significant. For example, board certification is a very impressive accomplishment for a physician. Also ask whether the expert has ever been the subject of any attempted adverse licensure action such as censure, suspension, or revocation and the details concerning any such action.

In all of the above areas of inquiry regarding an expert's background, you need to use judgment regarding how much time to spend and how much depth and detail to go into. You likely have much data in the expert's curriculum vitae, which you should consider using to expedite your questioning. Get the expert to authenticate the curriculum vitae, and then ask only selected questions about important nuances, gaps, or additions. This approach allows you to short cut your background questions.

Example: *Q:* *You have in front of you Deposition Exhibit 1. This is a copy of your curriculum vitae, October 28, 2005 correct?*
A: *Yes.*
Q: *Is this the most recent version of your CV?*
A: *Yes.*

Q: *When did you prepare this version of your CV?*
A: *Last year.*
Q: *Does Exhibit 1 accurately reflect all of your post high school education, including degree work and non-degree work?*
A: *Yes.*
Q: *Does Exhibit 1 accurately reflect all seminars, conferences, and other non-degree educational opportunities you have participated in?*
A: *Yes.*
Q: *Does Exhibit 1 accurately reflect all articles, books and other pieces you have written or co-authored?*
A: *Yes.*
Q: *I would like to ask you a few questions about the second article listed, . . .*

▸ Experience with Procedure or Product at Issue

If your case involves a procedure or product about which the expert is going to testify, ask the expert about the expert's personal experience with the procedure or product. You may find, for example, that the expert physician who plans to testify that your client was negligent in delivering a baby has never delivered a baby, while your client has delivered a thousand babies. If an allegedly defective product is at issue, find out if the expert has ever owned or used the product. In one case, for example, an expert was planning to testify that a gas grill was dangerously defective because of a design flaw. In his deposition, the expert admitted that he used to own this same grill. When asked if he still owned the grill, the expert said that he gave it to his son and that, to his knowledge, his son still owned it. Needless to say, this little gem was tucked away for later use at trial ("The plaintiff's expert would have you believe that this grill is so dangerously designed it could explode at any time, yet he gave this same grill to his own son and has not caused his son to get rid of it.").[150]

▸ Experience as a Witness

The following topics relate to the expert's experience as an expert witness and the likelihood that the expert may be biased.

o Prior Deposition and Trial Testimony

As noted above, the expert is required to disclose in his or her report the cases in which the expert has testified by deposition or trial in the preceding four years. You are, of course, free to ask about deposition and trial testimony prior to this time period.

o Legislative/Agency Testimony

You should also ask if the expert has testified in other settings, such as proceedings before legislative or agency bodies. In testifying in these settings, the expert may come across as more of an advocate for some particular position which may give you grounds to question the expert's objectivity in your case.

o Percent of Time Spent and Income Received from Testifying

It is useful to know if the expert is a professional witness who spends almost all of his or her time, and earns all or most of his or her income from, testifying in cases.

[150] Similarly, the plaintiffs in an antitrust case retained a law professor to testify that the defendants' distribution system was anticompetitive. On cross-examination in the expert's deposition, the expert acknowledged that he had a side business venture. When asked what system he used to distribute his business's products, he admitted, after a very long pause, that he used the same system as the defendants.

- **Testimony for Plaintiffs v. Defendants**

When asked how often experts testify for plaintiffs versus defendants, most experts invariably say about half and half. Do not believe them. If you get such a response and you suspect it is not true, ask the expert to identify the last 10 or 20 cases in which the expert testified and for which side the expert testified in each of these cases. You will very often find that the expert's work is not broken down nearly as evenly as the expert claims.

- **Fees**

The expert must disclose his or her fee in the expert's report. There may be little else that you want to ask about this in the expert's deposition. Often this issue is a wash because your expert is charging a similar fee. You may want to inquire more into the matter of fees if your opponent's expert is charging much more than your expert. Some attorneys also like to estimate how much the expert has charged in other cases for the same attorney or party to try to establish the expert's bias.

- **Relationship to Opposing Party and Attorney**

Ask about the expert's relationship to the party on whose behalf the expert is testifying and to the attorney who hired the expert. Has the expert had some past dealings with the party (e.g., a consulting relationship) that might suggest that the expert is biased? Is the expert joined at the hip to opposing counsel and likely to say anything counsel desires so as not to upset the expert's gravy train? You might also find out if the expert had a prior relationship with your client that could disqualify the expert, although typically you would know this before the deposition.

- **Assignment**

Ask in detail about the assignment the expert was given. The following topics relate to the expert's assignment.

- **When Contacted**

Find out when the expert was first contacted. The timing of the expert's retention can be revealing insofar as it follows some particular development in the litigation. It may also be worth knowing if the expert was brought into the case at the eleventh hour.

- **What Told/Given About the Case**

As noted above, experts must disclose in their reports what they considered in formulating their opinions. Find out what the expert was initially told about and given regarding the case. Does it appear that the information provided to the expert was incomplete or misleading, which would likely have tainted the expert's opinion of the case? For example, was the expert given only selected photographs or excerpts of certain witnesses' deposition testimony that supported the other side's case? Also inquire about what the expert requested from counsel. This can be revealing. And find out whether the expert asked not to be given or told about any type of information.

- **What Asked to Do**

Find out what the expert was asked to do in the case. The nature and scope of the expert's initial assignment and later assignments can reveal how your opponent is analyzing the case. The expert's assignment also may have tainted the expert's analysis.

▸ Work Performed

Once you have asked what the expert was told to do, you need to find out what the expert actually did.

- **What Did Expert Do/Review and When**

Review exactly what work the expert performed. In organizing this line of questioning, you may choose to proceed chronologically or topically regarding the work done relative to each opinion.

- **How Much Time Was Spent**

Determine how much time the expert spent on the various tasks performed. This may reveal whether the expert's work was thorough or cursory and thereby subject to attack.

- **Who Did Work/Tests/Calculations/Analysis**

Ask the expert who performed the various tasks. It should not surprise you that much of the underlying work forming the basis of an expert's opinion was actually done by some graduate student or other underling.

- **Qualitifications of Those Doing the Work**

If the expert employed others to do some of the underlying work, find out the qualifications of these individuals. You may argue that the reliability of the expert's opinions is only as good as the credentials of the least qualified individuals who did parts of the work. In some cases, this may have been college students.

- **Types of Equipment Used/Calibrations Required**

In some cases, the type of equipment the expert used may be important. Certain equipment may be more accurate than other kinds. Your expert may have more sophisticated equipment, which may account for a discrepancy in the experts' analyses. In some cases, you may want to inquire about when and how the expert calibrated his or her equipment. If the expert examined a product or other samples of physical evidence, you should inquire about the chain of custody of the product or other evidence.

▸ **Areas/Issues Not Investigated**

It can be useful to identify the areas or issues the expert decided not to investigate, especially if these are areas your expert did investigate and found significant.

▸ **Any Work Left to Do – Why and When**

Ask whether the expert plans to do any more work before trial and when such work will be done. You may need to re-depose the expert if the expert's analysis still is incomplete. Try to find out why the expert needs to do this additional work and how important the work is. You may be able to use this later at trial if the expert never completes work the expert said was necessary to finish.

▸ **Reports/Drafts/Calculations**

Find out what reports were prepared including the drafts of each such report. If not already reflected in the expert's report, find out what calculations were performed and the results of the calculations.

▸ **Opinions**

Ultimately, you will want to ask the expert about the opinions the expert formed and the basis of those opinions. Rule 26(a)(2)(B) requires the expert to set forth his or her opinions and the basis for the opinions in the expert's report. You should use the report as a roadmap for questioning the expert as to these topics.

o **Opinions Formed**

Have the expert identify the opinions he or she formed. Try to get the expert to articulate his or her opinions as precisely as possible and make sure to elicit all of the opinions to which the expert plans to testify at trial.

o Bases of Opinions

Ask the expert for the basis of each of the expert's opinions. The basis of an opinion may be the combination of several things. The expert may rely upon certain facts observed by the witnesses (e.g., it was raining at the time of the accident, there was a great deal of blood at the site of the incision) as well as certain principles the expert may apply to the situation (e.g., gravity, chemical reactions, economic forces). One expert, when asked for the basis of the expert's opinion, took the attorneys and court reporter down the hall to the expert's library and made a simple dramatic sweeping gesture with his arm to indicate that all of the books in his library helped form the basis of his opinion.

Make the expert explain the basis of the expert's opinions in detail. If the expert employs technical jargon that you cannot understand, make the expert explain his or her testimony in simple English. Do not gloss over this part of the deposition because you are concerned that you will look ignorant by asking for clarification. In fact, you might even employ the "Columbo" technique to ask these kinds of follow-up questions even if you are quite sure you understand the expert's testimony.

If the expert's opinions are based upon somewhat dubious science, you should inquire as to whether the expert's analysis, reasoning, or methodology is scientifically valid and can be applied to the facts in the case. An expert's testimony must rest on a reliable foundation and be relevant.[151] Find out if the expert's theory or technique has been tested, whether it has been subjected to peer review and publication, whether it is based upon any standards controlling its operation, and whether it has been accepted in the relevant scientific community. You may decide to bring a motion to exclude the expert's trial testimony based largely on the expert's answers to such deposition questions. You also may try to exclude

---

[151] For federal standards regarding the admissibility of an expert's testimony, see FED. R. EVID. 702.

the testimony of a professional expert who has no specialized expertise in the subject matter at issue.[152]

- **Assumptions**

One of the most fertile areas for attacking an expert is the expert's assumptions. Experts often make certain assumptions for the purpose of forming their opinions. If you can establish what these assumptions are and can then prove at trial that the assumptions were erroneous, you will undermine the expert's testimony, especially if the expert also admits in the deposition that the assumptions the expert made are important and that the expert's opinion may differ if these assumptions turn out to be false.

- **Degree of Certainty**

Inquire about the expert's level of certainty in regard to each opinion expressed. Sometimes experts will state an opinion but be reluctant to express much confidence in it. You can capitalize on this uncertainty at trial, especially if your expert comes across as quite confident of his or her contrary opinions. For certain types of expert testimony (e.g., medical malpractice cases), it may be necessary for the expert to state his or her opinion to a reasonable degree of certainty for the opinion to be admissible.

- **Other Reasonable/Plausible Explanations**

Try to get the expert to admit that there may be legitimate differences of opinion on the subject to which the expert is testifying. This can be a very useful concession if your expert happens to have such a difference of opinion.

---

[152] *See* Edward J. Imwinkelried, *Expert Witness - An Unheralded Change*, NAT'L L.J., Feb. 5, 2001, at A10 (discussing growing reluctance of courts to accept testimony of such generalized professional expert witnesses). Accordingly, you may want to encourage your opponent's expert to identify at length the many areas of his or her purported expertise.

- **Discussions with Others**

Identify other individuals with whom the expert has talked about the case and the expert's opinions. This might include colleagues, witnesses, and other experts. You may want to talk to some of these individuals about conversations they had with the expert and what influence they may have exerted over the expert's opinions. These individuals may have heard the expert express some useful reservations or concerns about the expert's analysis.

▸ **Other Authoritative Sources**

You often can identify useful cross-examination material by getting the expert to identify sources that the expert believes are authoritative. Following are some question areas directed to eliciting this information.

- **Authoritative Treatises/Periodical Subscriptions**

Ask the expert to identify authoritative treatises in the field and the professional periodicals the expert subscribes to and considers reliable.

- **Other Respected Views on the Issue**

As noted above, try to get the expert to acknowledge that there are other respected views on the issue in the expert's field. Ask the expert to identify individuals who hold contrary views. You may want to go hire one of them.

- **Other Experts in the Field**

Ask the expert to identify other prominent experts in the field even if some of these individuals may share the same views as the expert.

- **Other Experts with Greater Expertise**

It can be helpful, and even fun, to ask the expert if there are other experts or types of experts with more expertise regarding the subject at issue (e.g., "Doctor, would you agree that a pediatric neurologist has more expertise than you to identify the cause of this infant's brain injuries?"). This can be a difficult question for the expert to answer. If the expert claims to have more expertise than anyone else, the expert can come across as quite pompous. On the other hand, if the expert identifies others with greater expertise, the expert must realize you may go out and hire one of these other experts.

CHAPTER 7

Uses of Depositions

There are a variety of ways to use a deposition. You should plan in advance your intended use, as that may affect your approach during the course of the deposition. You also should consult the rules of evidence and civil procedure, as those rules govern the uses to which deposition testimony may be put.

A. Use With Motions

One extremely effective use of depositions is as evidence in support of motions, particularly summary judgment motions.[153] Depositions are sworn testimony and contain the words of the deponent rather than the attorney. This makes them particularly persuasive.

---

[153] Rule 56 of the Federal Rules of Civil Procedure specifically contemplates the use of deposition testimony in connection with summary judgment motions. Admissibility of the testimony contained in the deposition is subject to the rules of evidence in the same way that the rules govern admissibility of allegations contained in an affidavit. *Cf.* Starr v. Pearle Vision, Inc., 54 F.3d 1548, 1555 (10th Cir. 1995) (hearsay testimony contained in deposition inadmissible to support or oppose summary judgment).

You may use deposition excerpts both in support of and in opposition to summary judgment motions. In support of such a motion, deposition testimony may provide evidence to prove the elements of a claim or defense. In defense against a motion, you may use deposition testimony to refute a factual allegation or to prove the existence of a factual dispute.[154] Mechanically, you simply attach the excerpt to an affidavit that identifies and authenticates the deposition.[155]

---

[154] If you have pinned down a witness in a deposition and the witness subsequently submits an affidavit containing contrary testimony in connection with a summary judgment motion, the deposition testimony prevails and the affidavit testimony is disregarded. *See* Martin v. Merrell Dow Pharm., Inc., 851 F.2d 703 (3d Cir. 1988); Wilson v. Westinghouse Elec. Corp., 838 F.2d 286, 289 (8th Cir. 1988); Marathon Ashland Petroleum v. Int'l Bhd. of Teamsters Local No. 120, 300 F.3d 945, 951 (8th Cir. 2002). Some courts and commentators have described this as the "sham affidavit" doctrine. *See, e.g.*, Malave-Torres v. Cusido, 919 F. Supp. 2d 198 (M.D. Ga. 1987); David F. Johnson & Joseph P. Regan, *The Competency of the Sham Affidavit as Summary Judgment Proof in Texas*, 40 ST. MARY'S L.J. 2005 (2008).

Some cases have cited *Videon Chevrolet, Inc. v. Gen. Motors Corp.*, 992 F.2d 482, 488 (3d Cir. 1993), to distinguish the facts of their case from those of *Martin*. For example, *Wise Invs., Inc. v. Bracy Contracting, Inc.*, 232 F. Supp. 2d 390 (E.D. Pa. 2002), distinguished *Martin* as involving a factual question (date medication was ingested), and cited *Videon* for the proposition that "judicial estoppel should not apply where a party most likely was confused or did not intend to address an ultimate legal issue such as the characterization of a surcharge." *Id.* at 401. Similarly, *Armour v. County of Beaver*, 271 F.3d 417 (3d Cir. 2001), cited *Videon* as standing for the proposition that *Martin* only applies in the "extreme circumstances" where the affidavit is "flatly contradictory" and contains "no explanation for her change in position." *Armour*, 271 F.3d at 431, n.5. The *Armour* court then identified an explanation for the discrepancy in testimony that could have been accepted by the fact-finder. *Id.*

In re Safeguard Scientifics, 2004 WL 2644393, at *2 (E.D. Pa. 2004), contains a succinct explanation of the two different types of affidavits involved in these cases, and *Pittman v. Atlantic Realty Co.*, 754 A.2d 1030 (Md. 2000), contains a list of the factors to be considered "[i]n distinguishing between a sham affidavit . . . and a correcting or clarifying affidavit." *Id.* at 1042; *see also* Cothran v. Brow, 592 S.E.2d 629, 633 (S.C. 2004) (listing the factors as: "(1) whether an explanation is offered for the statements that contradict prior sworn statements; (2) the importance to the litigation of the fact about which there is a contradiction; (3) whether the nonmovant had access to this fact prior to the previous sworn testimony; (4) the frequency and degree of variation between statements in the previous sworn testimony and statements made in the later affidavit concerning this fact; (5) whether the previous sworn testimony indicates the witness was confused at the time; (6) when, in relation to summary judgment, the second affidavit is submitted"). The holding in *Pittman* has been superseded by state rule in Maryland. *See* Marcantonio v. Moen, 959 A.2d 764, 772 (Md. Ct. App. 2008). *Pittman's* discussion of sham affidavits, however, is still useful.

If you anticipate before taking a deposition that you may use it in conjunction with a motion, you should try to organize and phrase your questions in a way that will provide you with a crisp and orderly excerpt. Some questions you may want to script in advance.

Additionally, do not overlook the opportunity cross-examination may provide. If the witness is your own, the witness probably will be available to provide an affidavit if necessary. However, because depositions are in the witness's own words, while affidavits typically are drafted by attorneys, the testimony may appear more compelling when in a deposition. On the other hand, such cross-examination may tip your hand and invite additional questioning from opposing counsel. In the end, you must make a judgment call about whether cross-examination will quickly and cleanly provide evidence for use in connection with motions or will open the door to additional questioning that may not be advantageous to your case or that may muddy the record in a way that may defeat a summary judgment motion. Generally speaking, this weighing of the pros and cons may persuade you to forego using cross-examination in an attempt to support a summary judgment motion, but cross-examination may be an effective tool to defeat a summary judgment motion.

B. Use at Trial

In addition to being an extremely useful trial preparation tool, a deposition may be used a number of ways at the trial itself. Following are some of the situations in which you may use a deposition in a trial setting, along with procedural suggestions.

1. Deposition Testimony as Substantive Evidence

Deposition testimony may be used as substantive evidence at trial if the witness is unavailable and the deposition qualifies as former testimony under Fed. R. Evid. 804(b)(1), or if the deposition contains the admissions of a party opponent under Fed. R. Evid. 801(d)(2), or if the witness testifies at trial and the

---

[155] *See* FED. R. CIV. P. 56(e); *see also* Stuart v. Gen. Motors Corp., 217 F.3d 621, 635 n.20 (8th Cir. 2000).

deposition testimony qualifies as a prior inconsistent statement of the witness under Fed. R. Evid. 801(d)(1)(A).

a. Witness Unavailable

If a witness is unavailable to testify live at trial, you may use the witness's deposition testimony as if the witness were present and testifying so long as the testimony offered is otherwise admissible under the rules of evidence and so long as certain procedural requirements are met.[156] Under Rule 32(a)(4) of the Federal Rules of Civil Procedure, a witness is unavailable for purposes of substituting deposition testimony if the witness is dead, the witness is more than 100 miles away, the witness is unable to testify live because of age, illness, infirmity or imprisonment, or the party has been unable to procure the witness's attendance by subpoena.[157] Even if the witness's deposition was noticed by another party, you may offer the deposition at trial as if you noticed it yourself.[158] Depositions taken in connection with other actions also may be offered if the witness is unavailable and if the party against whom the deposition is offered was present at the

[156] *See* FED. R. CIV. P. 32. Parties may even be able to take their own depositions to preserve testimony for trial. This typically arises when parties realize in advance that they will not be available for trial. *See, e.g.*, Richmond v. Brooks, 227 F.2d 490 (2d Cir. 1955) (plaintiff allowed to offer her own deposition at trial against former husband); Chandler v. Scott, 427 S.W.2d 759 (Mo. Ct. App. 1968) (U.S. Marine on active duty in Vietnam had right to take his own deposition to be used as evidence in divorce suit filed by Marine against his wife). Such a deposition may be taken via a Rule 31 written deposition, as described in Chapter 8.

[157] *See also* FED. R. EVID. 804(a)(4), 804(a)(5); FED. R. CIV. P. 32(a)(4). Rule 32(a)(4) also contains a good cause exception, under which a party can apply to the court to allow deposition testimony to be used when "exceptional circumstances make it desirable-in the interest of justice and with due regard to the importance of live testimony in open court-to permit the deposition to be used." Live testimony is strongly favored, however, *see* Loinaz v. EG&G, Inc., 910 F.2d 1, 8 (1st Cir. 1990), and courts read this exception restrictively, *see, e.g.*, Griman v. Makousky, 76 F.3d 151, 153 (7th Cir. 1996). Note, of course, that even though "admission of deposition testimony as evidence under Fed. R. Civ.P. 32(a) is dependent upon meeting the requirements of the rules of evidence . . . the reverse is [not] true." Long Island Sav. Bank, F.S.B. v. United States, 63 Fed. Cl. 157, 163-64 (2004).

[158] *See* Savoie v. Lafourche Boat Rentals, Inc., 627 F.2d 722, 724 (5th Cir. 1980); Nichols v. Am. Risk Mgmt., Inc, 2000 WL 97282 (S.D.N.Y. Jan. 28, 2000) (party may use expert deposition of settling party against remaining opposing party); Weiss v. Wayes, 132 F.R.D. 152, 154 (M.D. Pa. 1990).

deposition and had a similar motive at that time to examine or cross-examine the witness.[159] Note, however, that you cannot use the deposition of a deponent who is unavailable at trial because you procured that witness's absence, although you may be estopped from objecting to the other side's use of the deposition.

If you think you may use a deposition in place of live testimony at trial, you need to be vigilant about meticulously following all procedural requirements when you notice and take a deposition. Otherwise, you risk losing the ability to use the deposition at trial even if the deposition goes forward in the face of an objection.[160] Similarly, if potentially valid objections are raised to the form of your questions, it is prudent to re-phrase; if the judge sustains the objection at trial, the opportunity to re-phrase no longer exists.

You also must meticulously follow certain pretrial procedures if you intend to use a deposition at trial. First, as part of your pretrial disclosures, you must designate all testimony you intend to present in the form of deposition rather than live witness testimony.[161] Your disclosure must identify not only the witnesses you intend to present through deposition testimony, but the specific

---

[159] FED. R. EVID. 804(b)(1); *see, e.g.*, In re Beiswenger Enters. Corp. v. Carletta, 46 F. Supp. 2d 1297, 1299 (M.D. Fla. 1999); Leger v. Tex, EMS Corp., 18 F. Supp. 2d 690, 694 (S.D. Tex. 1998).

[160] *See, e.g.*, FED. R. CIV. P. 32(a)(5):

> **(A)** *Deposition Taken on Short Notice.* A deposition must not be used against a party who, having received less than 14 days' notice of the deposition, promptly moved for a protective order under Rule 26(c)(1)(B) requesting that it not be taken or be taken at a different time or place--and this motion was still pending when the deposition was taken.
> **(B)** *Unavailable Deponent; Party Could Not Obtain an Attorney.* A deposition taken without leave of court under the unavailability provision of Rule 30(a)(2)(A)(iii)must not be used against a party who shows that, when served with the notice, it could not, despite diligent efforts, obtain an attorney to represent it at the deposition.

See also Lauson v. Stop-N-Go Foods, Inc., 133 F.R.D. 92, 94-95 (W.D.N.Y. 1990).

[161] FED. R. CIV. P. 26(a)(3)(A)(ii).

passages you intend to introduce.[162] If the deposition was recorded other than stenographically, you must provide a transcript of your selected excerpts.[163]

Generally, a pretrial order will specify the sequence and timing of deposition disclosures. If not, however, keep in mind that the pretrial disclosure requirements are not triggered by request or demand but are required automatically under the federal rules,[164] and must be in writing, signed, served on all parties and filed with the court unless local rules or a court order directs otherwise.[165] If you do not properly disclose the deposition testimony you intend to use, you may be precluded from introducing it at trial.[166]

As a practical matter, you should seek rulings in advance on all objections to the testimony you intend to offer through deposition. That way, you can introduce it at trial without the distraction of objection interruptions.

At the trial itself, the deposition testimony is accepted as if the witness were present, subject to the same evidentiary objections that would apply were the testimony live.[167] When you present the testimony, it generally is most effective to have another person "act" as the witness, unless you are using a video deposition.[168] The person reading the part of the witness will take the witness stand, although the person will not be sworn. If possible, have a stand-in who is

---

[162] As you select your deposition passages, you should be mindful of the right of the opposing party to require you also to offer portions of the deposition that, in fairness, should be offered with the portion you intend to introduce. *See* FED. R. CIV. P. 32(a)(6).

[163] FED. R. CIV. P. 26(a)(3)(A)(ii).

[164] *See* FED. R. CIV. P. 26(a)(3).

[165] FED. R. CIV. P. 26(a)(3)(A), 26(a)(4).

[166] *See* Advisory Committee Note to 1993 Amendment, FED. R. CIV. P. 26.

[167] FED. R. CIV. P. 32(b). As discussed in Chapter 4, however, certain objections will be deemed waived if not presented initially at the deposition itself. FED. R. CIV. P. 32(b), (d)(3).

[168] The Federal Rules allow a party to offer deposition testimony in stenographic or nonstenographic form, but if the trial is before a jury, any party may require that the testimony be presented in nonstenographic form, unless it is offered for impeachment or the court orders otherwise for good cause. FED. R. CIV. P. 32(c). Any party offering testimony in nonstenographic form must provide the court with a transcript of the portions offered. *Id.*

the same gender and approximate age as the deponent and who presents an image or demeanor that corresponds to the image you want the jury to have of the real deponent. Then read the questions you have marked, word-for-word, and have the witness read the answers, word-for-word. The person standing in as the witness may use normal inflections, which is one of the advantages of proceeding in this way, but the stand-in witness should not be overly dramatic (except in those unusual instances in which the real deponent was dramatic), or you will draw an objection and perhaps lose your opportunity to have someone read the witness's responses.[169]

If you anticipate at the time you notice a deposition that you may want or need to use it at trial as substantive evidence, you should consider the pros and cons of having it videotaped. While your initial inclination may be to have it videotaped, we do not necessarily recommend it. Deposition videos are not the kind of high quality video jurors are used to seeing, and they do not show a complete picture of the deposition room. In fact, the videos frequently are scratchy, they do not show you as the questioner, and the sound picks up the rustling of papers. The view of the witness will show him or her taking exhibits from someone's hands but without a full view, and there will be pauses as the witness reviews documents. All of this can add up to a distracting and not very persuasive presentation for the jury. Therefore, if the deponent is a good witness for you, it may be more effective to recreate the testimony with a stand-in witness than to present it through videotape. On the other hand, there may be situations in which the deponent is not a very appealing witness, and it is advantageous for the jury to see the real person in the real deposition. If you do use a video deposition at trial, you should produce an edited copy containing only the portions that you have been allowed to offer. Fast forwarding to relevant parts – even if done with pinpoint accuracy – tries everyone's patience and risks compromising the persuasive impact of the testimony.

If you are the party against whom deposition testimony is being presented, you also must be mindful of certain procedural requirements or you will waive your right to present otherwise valid objections.

---

[169] Some lawyers hire a real actor to play the part of the witness. This is perfectly acceptable so long as the actor understands that this is not an opportunity to secure an Oscar nomination.

- Be careful to preserve your rights at the time of the deposition itself. Generally speaking, objections to questions or to procedural irregularities that if timely made would allow the other party to cure the defect, are deemed waived at trial if not made on the record at the deposition itself.[170] For example, objections to the form of the question, such as an objection to leading the witness, are waived if not made or otherwise preserved at the deposition itself.[171]

- Within 14 days of a party's pretrial disclosure of intent to use deposition testimony, you must serve and file your objections to such use.[172] You should include in this filing your designation of any additional portions of the deposition that you believe in fairness should be considered together with the part the offering party proposes to introduce.[173] In this way, if the offering party proposes to take passages out of context, you need not wait until cross examination to introduce testimony that provides a more accurate depiction of the witness's intent.[174]

- Unless the court rules in advance on objections to specific deposition questions, you must renew the objections at trial or they will be deemed waived.[175]

---

170 *SEE* FED. R. CIV. P. 32(d).

171 *See* FED. R. CIV. P. 32(d)(3)(B)(i); *see also* Boyd v. Univ. of Md. Med. Sys., 173 F.R.D. 143, 147 n.8 (D. Md. 1997) (listing ten most common objections to form of question).

172 FED. R. CIV. P. 26(a)(3)(B).

173 *See* FED. R. CIV. P. 32(a)(6).

174 *See* FED. R. EVID . 106; Trepel v. Roadway Express, Inc., 194 F.3d 708, 718-19 (6th Cir. 1999).

175 *See* Advisory Committee Note to 1993 Amendment to Rule 26 of the Federal Rules of Civil Procedure.

b. Admissions of Party Opponent

You may use as substantive evidence depositions that contain admissions of a party opponent even though the deponent in such cases generally is in attendance at trial.[176] This applies to officers, directors and managing agents of a party organization, as well as to persons designated to testify on behalf of the organization.[177] The rule also applies to co-defendants with adverse interests. When using a deposition in this way, you typically will use a very brief passage, which you should reproduce for use as an exhibit.

c. Prior Inconsistent Statement

If a witness's trial testimony is inconsistent with the witness's deposition testimony, you may offer that portion of the deposition as substantive evidence at trial.[178] In such a situation, you need not have disclosed in advance of trial your intent to use the deposition.[179]

2. Deposition for Impeachment

Any party may use deposition testimony to impeach a witness when the witness's trial testimony contradicts the witness's deposition testimony.[180] Pretrial disclosure of your intent to use a deposition is not required when its use is solely

---

[176] FED. R. CIV. P. 32(a)(3) ("An adverse party . . . may use for any purpose the deposition of a party . . ."); *see also* FED. R. EVID. 801(d)(2). Be mindful that you also may use a deposition from a previous case. One attorney did this, for example, to show a plaintiff's ever-changing account of why he was fired.

[177] FED. R. CIV. P. 32(a)(3).

[178] FED. R. EVID. 801(d)(1).

[179] *See* FED. R. CIV. P. 26(a)(3) (pretrial disclosures need not include evidence used solely for impeachment).

[180] *See* FED. R. CIV. P. 32(a)(2); *see also* FED. R. EVID. 613. "The credibility of a witness may be attacked by any party, including the party calling the witness." FED. R. EVID. 607.

for impeachment.[181] Follow the rules relating to impeachment and use the transcript as you would any other writing.

Example:

Q: *Ms. Smith, you said you fired Mr. Jones because you discovered he falsified information on his resume?*
A: *Yes, that's correct.*
Q: *There's no question in your mind that this was the reason you fired Mr. Jones?*
A: *Correct.*
Q: *You gave a deposition in this case, didn't you, Ms. Smith?*
A: *Yes.*
Q: *You attended the deposition with your lawyer, correct?*
A: *Yes.*
Q: *And you took an oath to tell the truth at the deposition, just as you took an oath to tell the truth today?*
A: *Yes.*
Q: *You did tell the truth at the deposition, didn't you?*
A: *Yes, I did.*
Q: *After the deposition, you had an opportunity to read your testimony to make sure it was accurate, didn't you?*
A: *Yes.*
Q: *And you, in fact, signed a statement verifying that the testimony as transcribed by the court reporter was accurate?*
A: *Yes.*
Q: *It is now a year-and-a-half since Mr. Jones was fired, isn't it?*
A: *Yes, approximately.*

---

[181] FED. R. CIV. P. 26(a)(3). You may need to be a bit cautious, however, as courts apply different interpretations of the "solely for impeachment" requirement. *See generally* Hayes v. Cha, 338 F. Supp. 2d 470, 503-05 (D.N.J. 2004); Halbasch v. Med-Data, Inc., 192 F.R.D. 641, 648-50 (D. Or. 2000).

Q: *Your deposition was taken just six months after Mr. Jones was fired, wasn't it?*
A: *I suppose it was about six months.*
Q: *Your Honor, may I approach the witness? [Permission granted.] I am going to read from your deposition beginning on page 35, line 6. Please follow along while I read:*
Q: *Why did you fire Mr. Jones?*
A: *Because the quality of his work failed to meet my standards.*
Q: *Is there any other reason why you fired Mr. Jones?*
A: *No.*
Q: *Did I read the deposition transcript correctly?*
A: *Yes.*

3. Deposition to Refresh Recollection and as Past Recollection Recorded

A deposition transcript, when properly annotated for quick reference, is useful at trial as a tool for refreshing the recollection of a witness.[182] You can use a deposition transcript for this purpose in the same way you would use any other writing to refresh recollection. Similarly, a transcript may be used as a past recollection recorded if the witness was also the deponent and viewing the excerpted portion of relevant deposition testimony fails to refresh the witness's recollection.[183] Used in this way, you may read the relevant excerpt into the record, but may not offer the transcript as an exhibit.[184]

---

[182] *See* FED. R. EVID. 612.

[183] *See* FED. R. EVID. 803(5).

[184] *Id.*

C. Use in Settlement Negotiations

A less formal but extremely effective use of deposition testimony is in settlement negotiations. Do not be shy about citing and quoting particularly useful passages. Most cases settle, and they will settle more favorably if the opposing party is aware of the strength of your case and the weakness of their own. Do not make the mistake of assuming you need not cite your devastating deposition testimony because opposing counsel was present at the time. Sometimes the golden nuggets are buried in the middle of not terribly illuminating testimony and will have gone unrecognized or overlooked by opposing counsel; sometimes lead counsel for the opposing party will be unaware of the golden nuggets because less senior co-counsel will have been present and not have fully briefed lead counsel for the case; and sometimes it assists settlement negotiations if the opposing *party* understands that you have obtained helpful deposition testimony and that you know how to use it.

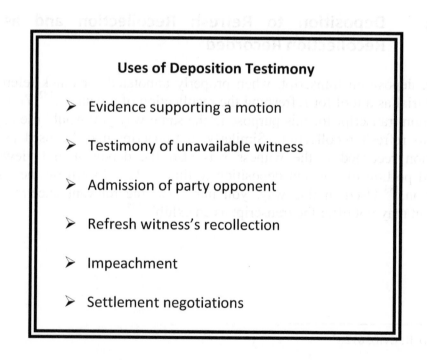

Uses of Deposition Testimony

- Evidence supporting a motion
- Testimony of unavailable witness
- Admission of party opponent
- Refresh witness's recollection
- Impeachment
- Settlement negotiations

In addition to the usefulness of citing favorable deposition testimony in written settlement offers, it is extremely useful to use such testimony in moderated settlement discussions. If a judge or mediator is overseeing pretrial settlement discussions, be prepared to use especially effective passages to educate the settlement intermediary of the strength of your case.

CHAPTER 8

Miscellaneous Deposition Issues

Following is a brief discussion of a variety of miscellaneous deposition issues, including compensation of fact witnesses and issues relating to taking depositions by non-standard means.

A. Compensation of Fact Witnesses

Can you pay a fact witness to prepare for and attend a deposition? The answer is it depends on the controlling law in the applicable jurisdiction, the identity of the fact witness, the purpose of the payment, the time for which you paying the witness, and the amount of the payment.[185]

[185] For a thorough discussion of this issue, see Douglas R. Richmond, *Compensating Fact Witnesses: The Price is Sometimes Right*, 906 HOFSTRA L. REV. [Vol. 42-905] (2014).

ABA Model Rule of Professional Conduct 3.3(b) and ABA Ethics Opinion 96-402 (1996) address this issue and provide that fact witnesses may be compensated for time spent preparing to testify and testifying in depositions, including time spent in deposition preparation sessions with attorneys, if the payment is not for the substance or efficacy of the witness's testimony or an inducement to tell the truth. If not prohibited by local law, witnesses also may be compensated for time spent in researching and reviewing records that are germane to their anticipated deposition testimony. The amount of the compensation must be "reasonable" and should equate to the witness's direct loss of income related to the witness's time spent in connection with the deposition. If there is no such direct loss, the lawyer must demonstrate the reasonable value of the witness's time based on relevant circumstances.[186]

You should be aware that, notwithstanding the ABA's position on this issue, some states prohibit the compensation of fact witnesses. For example, in its Advisory Opinion 1984-01, the New Mexico State Bar Ethics Advisory Committee interpreted its rules to prohibit any compensation to fact witnesses for their wages lost from preparing to testify or testifying. A New Mexico statute[187] also prohibits "fees for services," not just "fees for testifying," which arguably prohibits payments of fees to fact witnesses for preparing to testify in or testifying in a deposition. Accordingly, you should make sure to research the applicable local law to determine if payment to a fact witness is permitted.[188]

The federal bribery statute[189] also is germane to this issue. This statute makes it a crime to "corruptly" give, offer, or promise anything of value to any person with intent to influence that person's testimony under oath. It excepts, however, from this prohibition the payment of "the reasonable cost of travel and

---

[186] *See, e.g.*, Cal. State Bar Comm. Prof'l Responsibility, Formal Op. 1997-149 (1997) (describing various factors to consider in deciding whether a payment is reasonable including, for example, what other persons earn for comparable activity).

[187] N.M. Stat. Ann. § 38-6-4(A).

[188] Model Rule 8.5(b)(1) provides that the forum court governs ethical issues. In complex litigation involving numerous lawsuits, it may be necessary to consult the ethics rules of more than one state.

[189] 18 U.S.C. § 201.

subsistence incurred and the reasonable value of time lost in attendance at any such trial, hearing or proceeding." A payment to a fact witness violates the statute if the payment was "for" or "because of" the witness's testimony.[190] Courts have generally held that reasonable payments for time that the witness spends not just testifying, but also reviewing documents and meeting with attorneys does not constitute a payment "for" or "because of" testimony in violation of the statute.

Assuming that you can ethically compensate a fact witness, should you do so? Any payment can later arguably be characterized as, and perceived to be, an attempted bribe to obtain the witness's favorable testimony. Accordingly, you should avoid paying fact witnesses if you can. On the other hand, some witnesses (e.g., police officers) routinely insist that you compensate them for their time. In that case, you may have little choice but to pay the witness. You may feel less concerned about compensating fact witnesses if you know the other side is doing the same thing.

If you compensate a fact witness, here are some practical tips:

- Do *not* pay the fact witness for favorable testimony or condition payment on a favorable outcome in the litigation.
- Research the law of the applicable jurisdiction regarding your ability to compensate the fact witness.
- Pay only a reasonable amount to the fact witness, which is best determined by the value of the direct loss of income from the witness's time.
- Avoid paying a fact witness who was formerly employed by the other party or hostile to your client.[191]

---

190 Consol. Rail Corp. v. Grand Trunk W. R.R., No. 09-cv-10179, 2012 WL 511572, at *8 (E.D. Mich. Feb. 16, 2012).

191 Courts look critically at payments made to a fact witness who was affiliated with an opposing party. *See* Fla. Bar v. Wohl, 842 So.2d 811, 814-15 (Fla. 2003).

- Document in a letter that: (1) you are paying the witness "as the witness requested;" (2) the payment is "for the witness's time" in meeting with you to prepare for the witness's deposition; and (3) the payment is based on the witness's direct loss of income based on the witness's actual rate of pay."[192]
- Be aware that you will have to divulge this payment if sought during discovery.

B. Depositions on Written Questions

Although rarely used, Federal Rule of Civil Procedure 31 authorizes depositions upon written questions, and sets forth the procedures by which a party can notice and take such a deposition.[193] The Rule allows a party to take such a deposition of a governmental entity or corporation in accordance with the procedure for designated deponents under Rule 30(b)(6). The procedure also allows for the service of cross, redirect and re-cross questions.

When would you consider using this deposition method? You might use it if the deponent is far away, or in ill health, or if you merely wish to elicit non-controversial objective testimony, such as authentication of documents. Depositions on written questions may be a useful alternative to interrogatories in some situations, even if written depositions generally are less useful than live depositions. For example, written deposition questions, as opposed to interrogatory requests, may be directed to a particular individual within an organization.[194]

---

[192] Some attorneys also like to state in such a letter that this payment is not in any way a payment for the substance of the witness's testimony or an inducement to tell the truth. Other lawyers do not believe this is necessary and prefer not to even mention this point at all lest it appear that they or the witness would ever even entertain the thought of such a bribe.

[193] The 2015 Amendment to Rule 31 incorporates the "proportionality" provision discussed *supra* at Chapter 9.A.

[194] *Compare* FED. R. CIV. P. 31 *with* FED. R. CIV. P. 33.

The disadvantages of written depositions over live depositions are numerous and generally significant. For example, you cannot observe the deponent's demeanor while the deponent answers your questions. You cannot ask spontaneous follow-up questions.[195] And, perhaps most significant of all, you are not likely to get the testimony of the deponent. Rather, the written response to your questions will, like interrogatories, be crafted with the assistance of an attorney.

Example: *Q:* *What was the color of the traffic light for the northbound traffic as your brother's car entered the intersection?*

A: *When my brother drove his car, with his hands on the steering wheel at the 10:00 and 2:00 positions, on his way to donate toys to the children's orphanage using the same care that a reasonable person would use under like circumstances, I noticed with my 20/20 vision that the traffic light facing us was the deepest shade of emerald green I had ever seen in my life, the span of which, of course, has been tragically shortened as a direct and proximate result of the unspeakable injuries I suffered when the Defendant's car illegally and recklessly rocketed right through the bright crimson red light into the side of my brother's car, which had the clear legal right of way.*

Given these disadvantages, depositions on written questions generally are of limited value unless they deal with relatively non-controversial requests for objective information.

---

[195] Some commentators note that a party can serve successive sets of written questions under Rule 31. It is unclear, however, whether this is permitted in light of the limitation on the number of times a person can be deposed in Rule 30. In fact, Rule 31(a)(2)(A) provides that written questions can be sent to a person already deposed only by court order or written consent of the parties. If a person who receives and answers an initial set of written deposition questions under Rule 31 is considered "already deposed," then a party would have no right to serve successive sets of written deposition questions on a witness.

C. Telephone and Videoconference Depositions

Rule 30(b)(4) expressly authorizes the recording of a deposition by telephonic or remote electronic (e.g., satellite television) means.[196] To record a deposition by these means, the party must obtain the consent of counsel or a court order. While these procedures are used relatively infrequently, they can be quite useful, especially when the witness is far away or unable to travel, when the deposition is expected to be short and the testimony relatively non-controversial (e.g., authentication of documents), or when you have a limited litigation budget. You might also use this procedure if your opponent notices a deposition far away and you would prefer not to travel to it.[197]

The mechanics of setting up a telephone deposition are not terribly complicated. You need to figure out where everyone will be during the deposition and connect them to a conference call. The deponent will be wherever the deponent is. Opposing counsel can be: (1) in the same room with you; (2) in the same room with the witness; or (3) at some other location such as his or her office. The court reporter is usually in the room with you or in the room with the witness.

There are several advantages to this deposition recording method. The major advantage is the cost-saving. It may be prohibitively expensive to travel to take the deposition of a particular witness or to pay the witness's expenses to travel to you. This procedure provides a low-cost alternative to get the sworn testimony of such a witness.

There also are several disadvantages to this type of deposition. The principal disadvantage is the inability of counsel taking the deposition to observe the witness's demeanor while testifying. Generally, this should not be very important if the witness is not especially critical. On the other hand, if it is important that you see with your own eyes the blood drain out of the deponent's

[196] A Rule 30(b)(4) deposition is considered taken at the place where the deponent answers the questions rather than where the questions are propounded.

[197] There is nothing that prohibits one party's counsel from participating in a deposition by telephone while the other party's counsel attends in-person.

face when you ask those go-for-the-jugular questions, you may not want to use this recording method. Another disadvantage is that it can be somewhat difficult to question the witness about documents in such a deposition. There are, however, ways to deal with this difficulty, such as sending the documents to the witness in advance. You also can "hand" the documents to the witness via a fax machine.

Attorneys also may be reluctant to take a telephone deposition if they know that opposing counsel, or the witness's own counsel, will be with the witness while the witness is testifying. They fear that they will not be able to see the other counsel signal the witness on how to answer the questions (e.g., counsel holding up a big sign stating: "The answer to this question is 'No'").[198] While this is a risk that counsel takes in using this deposition procedure, the risk may be mitigated if the court reporter or another neutral person is present in the same room with the witness and opposing counsel and can observe any such impermissible coaching.

Counsel can avoid some of the disadvantages of a telephone deposition by taking the deposition via a videoconference system. These systems are becoming increasingly popular and some law firms have these systems in-house. If your firm does not have such a system, you usually can rent one. You can also have a videoconference connection via readily available programs like "Skype". The attorneys and court reporter can be situated in the same way as in a telephone deposition. The split or multiple-screen capability of many videoconference systems allows for the participants to be in multiple locations and to still see each other.

The principal advantage of a videoconference deposition over a telephone deposition is that it allows the participants to see each other throughout the deposition. As such, the attorneys can observe the witness's demeanor almost as well as if they were in the same room. The video link also allows attorneys to watch for improper signaling of the witness by counsel. It also is relatively easy to work with documents using such a system. The systems often have a separate camera that displays documents to the witness and counsel in a split screen format or on a separate monitor. The principal disadvantage of this recording method is the cost. All of the participants need to have access to compatible systems. While the rental and transmission charges of such a deposition will invariably exceed

198 The court can prevent other persons from interfering in such a deposition this way by ordering that no one else be present while the witness is testifying.

that of a telephone deposition, they may still be significantly less than the cost of traveling to the witness for an in-person deposition.

D. Videotaped Depositions

Videotaped depositions have become very popular in the last 25 years. This means of recording presents some obvious advantages over purely oral and even stenographic recording. The videotape not only records what was said, but how it was said, including the fidgeting, hesitation, and aversion of the eyes that tell much about the witness's credibility.

1. Rules/Requirements

Rule 30 does not say much about this type of recording, except that the camera or sound recording cannot distort the appearance or demeanor of the deponents and attorneys (e.g., no *60 Minutes*-style close-ups on the deponent's shaking hands or sweaty brow).[199] The Uniform Audio-Visual Deposition Act addresses certain procedures to be followed in videotaping a deposition, including: the preliminary statements to be made at the start of the deposition, the use of a time counter index to prevent unauthorized editing, and the marking, handling, and filing of the videotapes.[200]

It is advisable to hire a professional videographer and to film with high quality video equipment. The use of a professional usually will result in a much higher quality tape. Some courts have held that the fact that a lawyer or an employee of the lawyer's firm operated the videocamera is not sufficient to invalidate the recording absent any apparent irregularities. While not required, it often is helpful to have a stenographic recording made of a deposition that is videotaped.

If you videotape a deposition, you need to be mindful of various logistical issues such as the background, the camera view, and the lighting. Some attorneys prefer a softer, more natural and interesting background, such as the interior of an office. Others prefer a stark, completely blank background, especially if the

---

199 FED. R. CIV. P. 30(b)(5)(B).

200 12 UNIF. AUDIO-VISUAL ACT §§ 1-9, 12 U.L.A. 11.

witness is an opposing party. The camera is typically aimed only at the witness, and you may insist (and a court may order) that the cameraperson not use a zoom feature (e.g., to zoom in on the beads of sweat on your client's forehead). Finally, while many videographers like using extra lights to eliminate shadows and get a better quality tape, these lights can make the room very hot and very uncomfortable.

Given the risk of later manipulation of deposition videotapes, care must be taken in the editing of any deposition videotapes. A deposition videotape may need to be edited before it is played back at trial to eliminate inadmissible questions and testimony and extraneous footage. If the deposition is edited for use at trial, the original unedited tape should be retained. Courts will sometimes issue editing orders to spell out what can and cannot be done with such a videotape.

2. Advantages and Disadvantages

There are several advantages and disadvantages associated with videotaped depositions. A video deposition has the potential to be powerful and more interesting to the trier of fact than a written transcript. The videotape allows the trier of fact to observe the witness's demeanor in a way that a plain written transcript does not.[201] As such, this form of recording may be well suited for depositions taken to preserve a witness's testimony for trial.[202]

A videotaped deposition also is well suited for demonstrative testimony in which the witness describes an action, such as a physical assault. A written transcript can never replicate a videotaped reenactment. Likewise, videotaped depositions can be very effective when a physician uses anatomical models to explain the location and type of an injury, or when an accident reconstruction

---

[201] While a videotape can be more interesting than a written transcript, it can also be every bit as boring. Just because the deposition is videotaped does not mean it will be riveting to the jury. If you do a long, dull examination of the witness, the videotape will not magically make it interesting. In fact, the videotape may even highlight how dull the deposition was. Most jurors are accustomed to much slicker video presentations and much better production quality than one generally finds in a video deposition.

[202] Some courts permit parties to take a prior "discovery deposition" of a deponent whose deposition is going to be taken by videotape and used at trial in lieu of the deponent's live testimony.

expert uses a diagram of a scene and vehicle models to show the location of impact and the movement of a vehicle during a rollover accident.

An especially useful and sometimes overlooked advantage of a videotaped deposition is as a device to curtail abusive tactics by a witness or opposing counsel. Even the most abusive witnesses and attorneys tend to clean up their act when they are on videotape. The videotape also may be able to detect impermissible nonverbal coaching or signaling of a witness by an attorney.[203]

Some attorneys videotape depositions in order to have the videotapes to use in connection with video settlement brochures. The attorneys splice selected excerpts of the video depositions into their overall video brochure. When combined with other videotape, such as videotaped witness statements, day-in-the-life videos, and news media videotape, the resulting product can be very persuasive.

There also are some disadvantages to videotaped depositions. One downside is the cost. The cost of these recordings is, however, likely to decline in the future as video recording equipment gets less and less expensive. Another downside of video depositions is the effect of the camera on certain witnesses. Some witnesses "freeze up" or get extremely nervous when the camera is rolling and they become much less effective. Moreover, just as any deposition can perpetuate unfavorable testimony, videotaped depositions can perpetuate the same testimony even more powerfully. Finally, videotaped depositions can present logistical difficulties when used at trial. For one thing, the court may order on-the-spot additional editing due to newly-sustained objections. Furthermore, you may not be able to play back the deposition at trial while you are waiting for a live witness to show up because of the set-up time required. You may have more flexibility by reading a deposition transcript into the record in these circumstances.

---

[203] *See* Riley v. Murdock, 156 F.R.D. 130 (E.D.N.C. 1994).

E. International Depositions

To take a deposition in a foreign country, begin by consulting Federal Rule of Civil Procedure 28(b). Depending on the rules of the country in which the witness is located, you may take a foreign deposition:

- *"[U]nder an applicable treaty or convention."*[204] If you need to take a deposition in a foreign country, always consult the Hague Convention, including all treaty supplements.[205] Some countries have treaties with the United States that will assist you; others do not. If there is a treaty that applies, you need to follow it.
- *"[U]nder a letter of request, whether or not captioned a 'letter rogatory'."*[206] A letter of request also may be called a letter rogatory. You may seek a letter of request or letter rogatory from a federal court. All federal courts are authorized to issue letters rogatory. Evidence obtained from a letter of request need not be excluded even though rules applicable to other depositions are not followed. For example, testimony obtained pursuant to a letter of request may not be under oath or may not be provided in the form of a verbatim transcript. If you use a letter of request, you may want to channel it through the State Department, which may transmit the letter for you and receive and return the response.[207]
- *"[O]n notice, before a person authorized to administer oaths either by federal law or by the law in the place of examination."*[208] The person may be so authorized either by the laws of the foreign country or by the laws of the United States.

---

[204] FED. R. CIV. P. 28(b)(1)(A).

[205] You can find the Hague Convention on the Taking of Evidence Abroad in Civil or Commercial Matters reproduced in a note to 28 U.S.C.A. § 1781 and on Westlaw.

[206] FED. R. CIV. P. 28(b)(1)(B).

[207] 28 U.S.C. § 1781(a)(2). Note that this section only references letters rogatory.

[208] FED. R. CIV. P. 28(b)(1)(C).

- *"[B]efore a person commissioned by the court."*[209] To obtain a commission, you apply to a federal court, which shall issue the commission on terms that are just and appropriate. The commission may designate the person before whom the deposition is to be taken either by name or by descriptive title. A court may issue both a letter of request and a commission in appropriate cases.

F. Internet Depositions

The technology now exists to take depositions over the Internet, and some lawyers have begun to take advantage of this new medium.[210] The advantages and disadvantages of using the Internet to take a remote deposition mirror the advantages and disadvantages of telephone and videoconference depositions. The advantage of Internet depositions over telephone depositions is the ability to see the witness; the advantage of Internet depositions over videoconference depositions is that Internet streaming technology allows the video, audio, and text to display simultaneously and as a continuous stream. With new on-line deposition services, you can see and hear the witness in real time, receive a real time transcript as the court reporter types it, and send private encrypted messages to selected participants at other locations.

An additional advantage of Internet depositions over videoconference depositions relates to cost and convenience. To do a videoconference deposition the participants need to own or rent costly equipment and may need to travel to another location to access the equipment. Internet depositions can be done with relatively in expensive equipment that most law offices already may have. So long as you have a high speed Internet connection, an online deposition service provider will take care of everything else.

---

[209] FED. R. CIV. P. 28(b)(1)(D).

[210] For a good discussion of Internet depositions, including logistics, advantages and disadvantages, see Rebecca Porter, *The next step: taking depositions online*, TRIAL, Aug. 1, 2001, at 12. For a discussion of some of the unique ethical concerns posed by online depositions, see Lynn Epstein, *The Technology Challenge: Lawyers Have Finally Entered the Race but Will Ethical Hurdles Slow the Pace?*, 28 NOVA L. REV. 721, 730-32 (2004).

Internet Depositions

- See and hear witness in real time
- Receive real time transcript
- Send and receive private messages to and from remote participants
- Multiple participants in multiple locations
- Remote monitoring of on-site associate
- Save travel time and expense
- Limited ability to assess witness
- Limited ability to monitor coaching of witness
- Limited ability to monitor participation of others (e.g., experts)

This new technology provides exciting possibilities for particular situations, but it is not a panacea because of logistical issues and the importance in many situations of seeing the deponent and potential trial witness live. Internet depositions are especially useful for peripheral witnesses being deposed by co-counsel in multiparty cases and in situations where you otherwise may use a telephone deposition. This new technology also is useful if multiple attorneys or an expert want to attend a particular deposition without incurring the additional time and expense of traveling to a distant location. Similarly, Internet depositions could provide useful backup and monitoring of less experienced attorneys.

Logistically, the court reporter should be with the witness. In most cases, we would not recommend Internet depositions in situations where opposing counsel is with the witness, while you as the deposing attorney are the only remote participant.

G. Depositions of Electronic Data Custodians

We live in an increasingly electronic world. This means you are almost certain to become involved in litigation in which you will need to discover electronic data ("e-data") from your client's opponent. Following is a brief discussion of the types of questions you should consider asking the opposing entity's e-data designated custodian to get a "lay of the land" for your opponent's e-data.[211] This discussion does not include various other important issues regarding e-discovery, including, for example, the permissible scope of e-discovery, e-data production options and requirements, the costs of e-discovery, e-data spoliation, and privilege waivers.[212]

1. Get Help from Your Own E-Data Expert

Particularly in complex or high stake cases, consider consulting with your own e-data expert before taking the deposition of your opponent's e-data custodian. In such cases it is advisable to have your expert attend this deposition with you. E-data tends to be quite complex and you may find yourself in over your head if you are not highly trained regarding this kind of data. Your expert can help you navigate the murky waters in which you opponent's e-data are likely to be found.[213]

---

[211] You can depose such a custodian using FED. R. CIV. P. 30(b)(6).

[212] Some of the uncertainties regarding e-discovery have been and hopefully will continue to be resolved through amendments to the Federal Rules of Civil Procedure. For an expanded discussion of e-discovery issues, review such resources as Michele C.S. Lange and Kristin M. Nimsger, ELECTRONIC EVIDENCE AND DISCOVERY: WHAT EVERY LAWYER SHOULD KNOW (ABA 2004).

[213] Some commentators contend that e-discovery is so complex that it is best left to outside e-data experts. *See, e.g.,* Jason Krause, *Don't Try This at Home*, A.B.A. J., March 2005, at 59.

2. E-Data Custodian's Background and E-Data Policies

Ask questions to determine the expertise of the e-data custodian. Is this a highly educated and experienced person who is managing the entity's e-data or is this someone who is assigned job duties they are not especially qualified to handle? Where does the custodian fit in the entity's organization chart? What is the size of the custodian's budget to manage the entity's e-data? Also ask about the custodian's staff, if any, including their respective areas of responsibility and expertise.[214]

Be certain to inquire about the entity's e-data policies. These policies can help explain the e-data operations, including, for example, e-data retention protocols. Find out if there has been any deviation from the entity's formal e-data policies and, if so, explore any such deviations in detail.

3. Locations of E-Data

While you might principally think of e-data as the large volume of bits and bytes on the entity's central main server, this type of data actually can be found in many other places within an entity, including, for example:

- E-mail systems
- Workstation computer hard drives
- Laptop and home computers
- CDs, DVDs
- Cell phones (including instant messages)
- Personal data assistants
- Thumb drives
- Voice mail
- Pagers
- Video camera data

---

[214] Companies may find themselves paying much more attention to the management of their e-data operations in the wake of a Florida trial judge's decision to impose a partial default judgment against Morgan Stanley as punishment for its failure to locate and produce a large amount of e-data. A jury then awarded a $1.45 billion fraud verdict against Morgan Stanley. *See* Paul D. Boynton, *A $1.45B 'wake up call' on E-Discovery*, MINN. LAWYER, Sept. 26, 2005, at 1. There have been many situations in which companies have been sanctioned for spoliation of evidence for not retaining, or intentionally destroying e-data.

- Copier/fax machine/printer buffers
- Access control systems
- Archive/back-up storage media

Ask the e-data custodian about the different types of e-data media your opponent uses, e-data found on fixed media, such as a server or hard drive, and e-data contained on removable media, such as CDs and DVDs.

Another type of corporate communication is instant messaging. Instant messaging is increasingly replacing oral communications. Instant messaging works like e-mail but is faster and allows for the exchange in real time of written communications among several participants. The retention of instant messages is more complicated than e-mail because many instant messages are deleted as soon as the computer is turned off. There are, however, some instant message software programs that allow for the archiving of instant messages. Suffice it to say, instant messaging may turn out to be an important source of e-data in your litigation. Ask about it.

4. E-Data Hardware and Software, Access Types, Formats, Storage Media, and File-Naming

Find out what type of electronic hardware and software the entity uses and the location and number of hardware components. This hardware and software may not be uniform throughout the entity. Inquire as to the entity's operating systems and end user applications.

You should inquire about the forms of access to your opponent's e-data. E-data may exist in various forms, such as:

- *Active data.* This is data that is currently readily accessible to end users and should be easily available to discover without special restorative processes.

- *Archive or legacy data.* This includes data found on back-up tapes or other media that is not immediately accessible.

- *Deleted/residual data.* This includes data that has been deleted but is nonetheless still recoverable via special forensic techniques.

E-data files also may be found to exist in different formats including *text files* and *image files*. The latter e-data, which are akin to photographs of documents, may be in formats such as PDF or TIF. Your opponent also may use other, and even out-dated proprietary, data formats that may make your discovery of your opponent's e-data considerably more difficult. If the entity maintains one or more large electronic databases, ask for a general description of what is contained in the database as well as the format, and ask for a field or coding manual, which should describe the specific content of each database.

You should also inquire as to whether the entity keeps its e-data in its *native* format in the usual course of its business. Unlike data in image formats such as PDF, data in this format can be manipulated. Obtaining data in its native format may enable you to access *embedded* or *metadata*. This is data about data, including, for example, data that reflects changes made in a document. Such historical metadata may prove extremely useful; it may, for example, help prove that your client had notice of some fact or considered and actually rejected incorporating some term in an important document. Reading data in its native format generally requires using the same software application used to create the data. Ask about the software applications used and about the entity's file-naming conventions and standards. This information should help you understand the data you eventually receive.

5. E-Data Preservation/Retention

E-data preservation is an important area of inquiry. How, and how often, is the entity's e-data backed up? Is there a formal e-data retention policy that provides a schedule for the destruction of certain e-data after certain prescribed periods? If the entity has such a retention policy, find out if it is actually followed. If not, information that "should" have been destroyed may, in fact, still be available.

If the custodian testifies that certain types of e-data, such as e-mails, are "deleted," inquire as to whether the data is nonetheless recoverable. That is, find out when "delete" does not really mean "irretrievable." Many people assume that e-mails are forever erased once the end user hits the "delete" key. In fact, many deleted e-mails are recoverable.

Also inquire about what steps the custodian and entity have taken to preserve e-data that may be relevant to the litigation which might otherwise be destroyed. Include questions regarding the notice, if any, that was given to your opponent's employees to preserve e-data. Inquire as to the destruction of any relevant e-data that has already occurred, and, if you have not already done so, make a formal record of your demand that all potentially relevant e-data be preserved. As recent cases have shown, the spoliation of relevant e-data can lead to serious consequences.[215]

6. Access to E-Data

Determine who has access to the entity's e-data. This could help you determine who may have destroyed certain data. This information also may be relevant to your opponent's claim of a privilege with respect to certain e-data. A privilege claim may be unsuccessful if the entity has not taken reasonable steps to secure the e-data.

7. How E-Data is Used

Be sure to ask about how certain of the e-data is used. If the entity maintains some large electronic databases, inquire as to the original source of the information entered into the databases and what types of reports are generated from the databases or how end users access the databases interactively. You may request the production of samples of some such reports or end user screens. You also may want to inquire about whether particular information you desire is readily accessible from your opponent's files or whether the production of the data you need would require the creation of a new programming application. In

---

[215] *See, e.g.*, Zubulake v. UBS Warburg LLC, 229 F.R.D. 422, 439-40 (S.D.N.Y. 2004) (sanctions imposed and adverse inference instruction given as discovery sanction); Metro. Opera Assoc., Inc. v. Local 100, 212 F.R.D. 178, 190-91, 231 (S.D.N.Y. 2003) (plaintiff's motion for judgment as to liability and other discovery sanctions granted). *See also* Leon v. IDX Sys. Corp., 464 F.3d 951, 959-61 (9th Cir. 2006) (employee's destruction of electronic data sufficient to support dismissal of employee's claim under federal False Claims Act).

the latter circumstance, you might still be able to obtain the data, but you may be required to pay the cost of creating the new application.[216]

[216] *See generally* Corinne L. Giacobbe, Note, *Allocating Discovery Costs in the Computer Age: Deciding Who Should Bear the Cost of Discovery of Electronically Stored Data*, 57 WASH. & LEE L. REV. 257 (Winter 2000).

CHAPTER 9

Deposition Rules and Procedures

The Federal Rules of Civil Procedure govern such deposition mechanics as scope, number, location, timing, order, and recording. Many battles are waged over these logistical matters. In fact, the actual deposition may be quite anti-climactic after the parties spar over where the deposition will be held, who can attend, and whether it can be videotaped. This Chapter discusses various logistical issues regarding deposition rules and procedures, including some of the threshold issues that tend to spur satellite litigation skirmishes.

A. Scope of Depositions

Generally speaking, the permissible scope of a deposition is governed by Federal Rule of Civil Procedure 26(b)(1), which provides in general that a party may take discovery regarding:

> any non-privileged matter, that is relevant to any party's claim or defense and proportional to the needs of the case, considering the importance of the issues at stake in the action, the amount in controversy, the parties' relative access to relevant information, the parties' resources, the importance of the discovery in resolving the issues, and whether the burden or expense of the proposed discovery outweighs its likely benefit. Information within this scope of discovery need not be admissible in evidence to be discoverable.[217]

Rule 26(b)(2) also notes the authority of federal courts to limit discovery, including depositions, considered to be cumulative or excessive.[218] The court can regulate the scope of depositions through protective orders.[219] The court can prohibit the taking of certain depositions, or even any depositions at all, and can restrict the scope of questioning, the length of the deposition, and other matters.

The Federal Rules encourage parties to negotiate the scope of discovery to be taken, including the scope of, and procedures for taking, depositions. For example, Rule 26(f) requires parties to conduct a discovery conference early in the litigation to discuss and prepare a discovery plan. The Rule directs the parties to consider the subjects on which discovery is needed and any necessary changes in the limitations on discovery imposed under the Rules. Rule 29 also allows parties to provide via a written stipulation that depositions be taken before any person, at any time or place, upon any notice, and in any manner.[220]

---

[217] FED. R. CIV. P. 26(b)(1). The proportionality language of the 2015 amendment is likely to lead to new arguments regarding appropriate deposition limits and scope.

[218] Specifically, the court can limit discovery that is unreasonably cumulative or duplicative, that is obtainable from another more convenient and less burdensome and expensive source, where the party had ample opportunity to obtain the information sought, and where the burden of the discovery outweighs its benefits considering the needs of the case, the amount in controversy, the parties' resources, the importance of the issues, and the importance of the discovery in resolving the issues. FED. R. CIV. P. 26(b)(2)(C).

[219] The court can, for example, preclude attempted discovery of privileged information.

[220] Some state rules of civil procedure allow oral stipulations under their counterparts to the Federal Rules. *Compare* FED. R. CIV. P. 29 *with* MINN. R. CIV. P. 29. Because such stipulations are

B. Number of Depositions

Federal Rule of Civil Procedure 30(a)(2)(A) limits the number of depositions that can be taken in a case to ten per side.[221] Because this is a limitation on the number of depositions per side, and not per party, multiple parties on the same side are expected to confer and agree as to which depositions are most needed.[222] As the Advisory Committee noted when this limitation was imposed in 1993, the purpose of the limitation is to ensure judicial review under Rule 26(b)(2) standards before any side is allowed to take more than ten depositions and to emphasize to counsel their professional obligation to develop a cost-effective discovery plan.

Notwithstanding this limitation, the parties can stipulate in writing to a larger limit pursuant to Rule 30(a)(2). In fact, parties frequently agree to a larger number of depositions, especially in large and complex cases, since both sides often want to take more than ten depositions. It is expected that the parties will consider this deposition limitation at the Rule 26(f) discovery conference and at the time of the Rule 16(b) scheduling conference.

Rule 30(a)(2) also authorizes the court to enlarge the number of depositions otherwise permitted. A party seeking such an enlargement will emphasize such factors as the number and complexity of the claims and defenses, the number of individuals having knowledge of important facts in the case, and the number of co-parties.

The Advisory Committee Notes to the 1993 Amendments to Rule 30 also recognize a situation in which more than ten persons can be deposed per side

---

usually as enforceable as court orders, you should be cautious about any informal oral agreements you make with opposing counsel.

221 Some state court rules do not limit the number of depositions. *See, e.g.,* MINN. R. CIV. P. 30. Minnesota used to limit the number of depositions that could be taken prior to a discovery conference to three. This limitation was eliminated in 1993 because it was almost universally ignored.

222 This task may be considerably more difficult if the co-parties have cross-claims against each other. If co-parties cannot resolve this issue, they can refer the dispute to the court.

without a stipulation or court order. This can occur because Rule 30(b)(6) designated depositions are regarded as a single deposition for purposes of the ten-deposition limit, even if more than one person is designated to testify.[223]

Parties also can request, and the court can order, that fewer than ten depositions per side be permitted in a given case. A party seeking a reduced limit should bring a motion for a protective order under Rule 26(c).

Rule 30(a)(2)(A) also provides that a person can only be deposed once in a case. Once again, the parties can stipulate otherwise and the court can order that a deponent be redeposed. This one-deposition limitation does not apply if the deposition was temporarily continued for the convenience of counsel or of the deponent or to gather additional materials before continuing.[224] There are some circumstances in which a court will permit a party to be deposed more than once. For example, if a case is nearing trial and several years have transpired since the plaintiff in a personal injury case was last deposed, the court might allow the defendant to redepose the plaintiff to evaluate the extent and permanence of the plaintiff's injuries. Courts will also sometimes permit a second deposition of a witness if there is newly acquired evidence in the case or if the witness or a party previously failed to disclose certain information and/or documents. Misbehavior by deponents or their counsel also may justify a second deposition of a witness.

Courts also permit second depositions of deponents where new claims have been added to the complaint or new parties have joined the suit since the deponent's initial deposition. If a court permits a second deposition of a witness,

---

[223] While parties could arguably try to circumvent the ten-deposition limitation by serving very broad Rule 30(b)(6) deposition notices, deposing numerous corporate representatives, and arguing that all such depositions constitute only a single deposition, the court can always prevent such attempts to end-run the rule. In one decision, a federal district court refused to permit a party to take a second Rule 30(b)(6) deposition which it claimed was necessary because of an amended complaint. The court reasoned that Rule 30(a)(2) does not allow a party to depose a person who has already been deposed in a case and that since there had already been a deposition of the corporate person, the new deposition within the same case was invalid. *In re* Sulphuric Acid Antitrust Litig., 2005 U.S. Dist. Lexis 17420, at *8 (N.D. Ill. Aug. 19, 2005).

[224] The Advisory Committee Notes suggest that in the latter situation the parties should consider completing the deposition by telephone.

the court may limit the second deposition to questions pertaining to the new evidence, claims, or parties, and preclude a full-blown second deposition.[225]

C. Notice Requirement

Federal Rule of Civil Procedure 30(b)(1) requires you to serve reasonable written notice of the taking of a deposition on the other parties in the case. The notice shall state the time and place for the deposition, the name and address of the deponent and, if the deponent's name is not known, a general description sufficient to identify the person or particular class or group to which the person belongs.[226] The notice also shall include a description of any materials requested in a subpoena duces tecum as well as the method by which the testimony shall be recorded. The notice to a party deponent may be accompanied by a request for production of documents. A sample deposition notice is included at Appendix A.

Disputes regarding deposition notices most often concern the issue of whether "reasonable" notice was provided as required by Rule 30(b)(1). What is reasonable notice for a deposition?[227] As frequently is the case in the law, it depends on the circumstances; there is no fixed time requirement. Courts have addressed challenges to deposition notices of varying lengths of time.[228] As a rough litmus test, you can probably figure that notice of less than one week is

---

225 In a rather unusual example of multiple depositions of an individual, a colleague of one of the authors was permitted to take multiple depositions of a plaintiff who had multiple personalities. Each of the personalities had an independent recollection of the events giving rise to the lawsuit. The plaintiff's psychiatrist elicited each personality at the deposition. Each personality was then separately sworn in and multiple depositions were taken of the separate personalities.

226 You can draft a single deposition notice for multiple depositions occurring on different dates and at different times.

227 There are rules regarding the timing of depositions that will also affect the service and content of your deposition notices. For example, if you seek to take a deposition before the time allowed under Rule 26(d), Rule 30(a)(2)(A)(iii) requires that your deposition notice certify that the deponent is expected to leave the United States and be unavailable for examination in this country unless deposed before that time.

228 If you decide to challenge the timing of a deposition, you should bring a motion for a protective order under Rule 26(c)(1).

likely to elicit an objection.[229] Rule 32(a)(5)(A) implies that fourteen days notice is presumptively sufficient. If you give notice of a week or more, chances are the notice will be upheld if challenged.[230] Several courts have noted that scheduling conflicts of this sort are easily avoided if counsel exhibit some minimal professional courtesy and contact each other before scheduling depositions.[231]

Parties sometimes battle over whether a deposition can be scheduled on a weekend or in the evening. While one court ruled that Sunday depositions are not permitted,[232] there is no provision in the Rules barring depositions on certain days or at certain times. Once again, the reasonableness of a weekend, holiday, or evening deposition is likely to depend upon the exigency under the circumstances.

Can you give oral notice of a deposition? Courts have generally held that you can dispense with written notice only in the most unusual circumstances.[233] Parties can, however, waive the formal deposition notice requirement. It is common, for example, in large cases involving many depositions on both sides for counsel to schedule depositions of the parties by phone, confirming the schedule by letter rather than by formal deposition notices of the type described above.

---

[229] *Compare* Lloyd v. Cessna Aircraft Co., 430 F. Supp. 25, 26 (E.D. Tenn. 1976) (two days-notice unreasonable where no need shown for such haste) *with* Natural Organics, Inc. v. Proteins Plus, Inc., 724 F. Supp. 50, 52 n.3 (E.D.N.Y. 1989) (one day notice reasonable given expedited discovery schedule and sudden, unexpected need for deposition).

[230] *See, e.g.*, Pearl v. Keystone Consol. Indus., Inc., 884 F.2d 1047, 1052 (7th Cir. 1989) (giving six days-notice complied with Rule 30 absent showing why such notice was unreasonable); United States v. Woods, 2008 WL 2115130, at *2 (E.D.N.C. May 16, 2008) (notice received one week prior to deposition was reasonable); James v. Ann Arbor Pub. Sch., 2000 WL 33418959, at *2 (Mich. Ct. App. May 30, 2000) (one week constitutes reasonable notice for taking of depositions, especially where deponents are not unknown witnesses).

[231] *See, e.g.*, Judicial Watch, Inc. v. U.S. Dep't of Commerce, 34 F. Supp. 2d 47, 50 (D.D.C. 1998) (dispute over two-day deposition notice could have been avoided if lawyers would have demonstrated minimal level of professional courtesy toward one another); Seabrook Med. Sys., Inc. v. Baxter Healthcare Corp., 164 F.R.D. 232, 233 (S.D. Ohio 1995) (counsel should, as a matter of professional courtesy, jointly schedule third-party depositions to avoid conflicts).

[232] Shenker v. United States, 25 F.R.D. 96, 98 (E.D.N.Y. 1960).

[233] *See, e.g.*, C & F Packing Co. v. Doskocil Cos., 126 F.R.D. 662 (N.D. Ill. 1989).

Must the opposing party receive your deposition notice? Some courts have held that nonreceipt does not affect the validity of a properly served deposition notice.[234]

D. Timing and Order of Depositions

Federal Rule of Civil Procedure 26(d) provides that parties cannot take any depositions in a case until after the Rule 26(f) conference.[235] There is an exception to this rule under Rule 30(a)(2)(A)(iii). Under the latter rule, a party need not wait until the Rule 26(f) conference if the deposition notice contains a certification, with supporting facts, that the person to be deposed is expected to leave the country and be unavailable for examination unless deposed before the Rule 26(f) conference. There are several issues that can arise regarding the timing and order of the depositions in a case.

1. Priority/Sequence

It is not uncommon for parties to battle over the order of the depositions taken in a case. The 1970 Amendments to Rule 26(d) eliminated any deposition priority based on which party noticed a deposition first. The Advisory Committee noted several reasons why such a priority rule is unsatisfactory. Rule 26(d) provides that the fact that a party is conducting discovery does not operate to delay any other party's discovery. The court also has the authority to set a sequence for the taking of depositions in a case upon motion.

---

[234] *See, e.g.*, Lock 26 Contractors v. John Massman Contracting Co., 127 F.R.D. 542 (D. Kan. 1989); *see also* Fattah v. Killeen, 2005 WL 2234644, at *3 (M.D. Pa. Sept. 14, 2005) (non-receipt of mailed notice does not affect validity of notice); 4A C. WRIGHT & A. MILLER, FEDERAL PRACTICE AND PROCEDURE § 1148 (2d ed. 1987).

[235] State court rules of civil procedure often contain different timing limitations. For example, MINN. R. CIV. P. 30.01 provides that a plaintiff cannot take a deposition, without leave of court, until 30 days after the service of the summons and complaint unless the defendant has served a deposition notice or otherwise conducted discovery. The Rule permits a defendant to take a deposition any time after commencement of the action.

2. Multiple Tracking

Especially in cases involving many depositions or an impending discovery deadline, the parties will engage in multiple tracking of depositions – the simultaneous taking of depositions of multiple deponents.[236] One advantage of multiple tracking is that it may prevent collusion between witnesses deposed on opposing tracks since they are not able to observe or read each other's testimony. Parties sometimes schedule depositions for the same time with the hope that they can prevent such collusion or that they can prevent certain opposing attorneys from defending particular deponents. If you cannot schedule the depositions of hostile witnesses for the same time, you may alternatively want to schedule them back-to-back to try to minimize the likelihood of any effective collusion.

3. Rule 27 Pre-Action Depositions

Federal Rule of Civil Procedure 27 permits the taking of depositions before the commencement of a lawsuit. This procedure is most often invoked when a deponent is about to leave the country or subpoena power of the court or is otherwise unlikely to be available to be deposed at a later date (e.g., the deponent is dying).[237] This procedure cannot be used by a party to determine if there is a basis for bringing a lawsuit. It is also not available to a party if the party is able to commence the lawsuit and conduct discovery in the usual fashion. Consequently, this procedure is most likely to be invoked by a prospective defendant who wishes to preserve a witness's testimony before the plaintiff commences the action. This procedure also may be available to a plaintiff if there

---

[236] While counsel usually agree to multiple tracking of depositions, it is not entirely clear whether a party can unilaterally schedule more than one deposition for the same time. While the Advisory Committee to the 1970 Amendments noted (in commenting on Rule 26(d)) that Rule 30 does permit parties to set concurrent depositions, it did not address whether the same party could schedule multiple depositions at the same time over another party's objection.

[237] But as the Eleventh Circuit Court of Appeals decided in *Lombard's, Inc. v. Prince Mfg., Inc.*, 753 F.2d 974 (11th Cir. 1985), the fact that witnesses are "not immune from the uncertainties of life (and death)" is not enough to justify the taking of a Rule 27 deposition. So, if you seek permission to take such a deposition, you ought to allege more than that it is merely possible the deponent could be struck by lightning, eaten by a shark, or spontaneously implode.

is something that prevents the plaintiff from commencing the action (e.g., a statutory waiting period).[238]

4. Tactical Considerations

There are some basic strategic considerations regarding the timing and order of depositions. Some attorneys prefer to depose an opposing party or critical witness as early as possible in the case to "pin down" the deponent's story.[239] This can effectively limit the ability of such witnesses to mold their testimony to conform to the testimony of other witnesses.[240] The downside of taking early depositions is that the attorney may still not know critical facts and issues in the case and may still be trying to understand and to develop the client's theme of the case. Because the attorney is not likely to be able to re-depose the witness, the attorney may lose the chance to question the witness regarding this later acquired information. Because they typically get only one shot at a witness, some attorneys prefer to take depositions of opposing parties and other critical witnesses later in the course of the litigation. The disadvantage of this approach, of course, is that the deponents will have seen how the other witnesses testified and may conform their testimony accordingly.

Because there is no clear right or wrong approach to this dilemma, make sure that you consider the ramifications of your approach in your specific case. Do not simply take a deposition right away because other lawyers you know do. If, for example, you are pretty confident that you can use other discovery devices (such as interrogatories and requests for admissions) to obtain the necessary

---

[238] Some courts also recognize an equitable cause of action to take discovery, including depositions, independent of a lawsuit where exceptional circumstances exist. *See, e.g.*, Lubrin v. Hess Oil Virgin Islands Corp., 109 F.R.D. 403 (D.V.I. 1986); Temple v. Chevron U.S.A. Inc., 840 P.2d 561, 563-66 (Mont. 1992). Some states refuse to recognize such equitable discovery actions. *See, e.g.*, Austin v. Johnston Coca-Cola Bottling Group, Inc., 891 P.2d 1143 (Kan. App. 1995).

[239] The witnesses' memories also are likely to be fresher the earlier they are deposed. Such early depositions may help to preserve other evidence in the case before it is lost or destroyed.

[240] Similarly, some attorneys schedule early depositions in a case to try to force the other side to question the deponent before the other side has completed its preliminary investigation. It is not entirely clear whether an attorney can reserve the right to question a deponent at a later date because the other side has scheduled the deposition before the attorney is ready to depose the witness.

information from a deponent regarding later acquired information in the case, you may decide that it is worth the risk to depose the witness early. Conversely, if you already have the witness pinned down through other means (such as a signed statement), you may opt to forego pinning the witness down in an early deposition, and wait until you have more facts and a better understanding of the case.

There also are strategic considerations regarding the order or sequence of the depositions. For example, you may want to take the deposition of an opposing party or critical witness before your clients are deposed so that your clients can hear what other witnesses have said before they are deposed. You may want to depose a higher-level employee of an opposing corporate party before deposing that employee's subordinates if you think the higher-level employee's testimony is likely to be helpful, or not all that harmful, and you think the subordinates will be subtly pressured to testify the same way when they are deposed. Of course, just the opposite may be true in some cases.

There are also strategic considerations regarding the deposition of certain types of witnesses. Some attorneys prefer to begin with an early round of Rule 30(b)(6) designated depositions to identify witnesses, documents, and other forms of proof, and to get a general "lay of the land" for the case. There also are tactical considerations regarding the timing of expert depositions. Such depositions usually are done later in the case, after the experts have submitted their Rule 26(a)(2)(B) reports. Defense counsel often will seek a staggered expert deposition schedule under which the plaintiff's expert is deposed first and the defendant's expert is deposed second. Courts frequently issue such scheduling orders for expert discovery. Parties also may leave some time for additional lay witness discovery after the expert depositions so that they can obtain certain important factual information discussed by the experts.

E. Location of Depositions

There are several general statements that can be made about the location of depositions. First, the location of a deposition lies ultimately within the sound discretion of the court. Second, a party has the unilateral right to specify the location of the deposition.[241] Third, a deposition should ordinarily occur in the community where the deponent works or resides.

1. Location of Particular Types of Depositions

Notwithstanding the general rules noted above, the courts have developed several additional principles regarding the location of the depositions of certain kinds of deponents. Following is a summary of these rules:

a. Plaintiffs

Plaintiffs are usually deposed where they work or reside or where the action was brought. Courts have generally held that the defendant can examine a non-resident plaintiff in the forum state where the action was brought.[242] This is basically an exception to the general rule that one ought to be deposed where one is. Defendants can compel non-resident plaintiffs to be deposed in the state where they brought the lawsuit. Courts can alter this rule if it would impose an undue hardship on the plaintiff that outweighs any prejudice to the defendant were the deposition taken elsewhere.

b. Defendants

Defendants are normally deposed where they work or reside.[243] Consequently, if the defendant is a non-resident, the plaintiff has to go to where the defendant works or resides to take the defendant's deposition. This is subject to modification by the court. A non-resident defendant also can be deposed while otherwise in the forum state.

---

[241] *See* FED. R. CIV. P. 30(b)(1).

[242] *See* Clem v. Allied Van Lines Int'l Corp., 102 F.R.D. 938 (S.D.N.Y. 1984). *But see* Connell v. City of New York, 230 F. Supp. 2d 432, 437 (S.D.N.Y. 2002) (permitting video conferencing deposition of indigent plaintiff in Boston); Normande v. Grippo, 2002 WL 59427 (S.D.N.Y. Jan. 16, 2002) (permitting telephone deposition of plaintiff in Brazil).

[243] *See* Bank of N.Y. v. Meridien Biao Bank Tanz. Ltd., 171 F.R.D. 135 (S.D.N.Y. 1997); *cf.* Fausto v. Credigy Servs. Corp., 251 F.R.D. 427, 429 (N.D. Cal. 2008).

c. Corporations

The general rule regarding corporations is that officers, directors, and managing agents must be deposed at the corporation's principal place of business or where these individuals reside.[244] This is not an inflexible rule. In ruling on requests to alter this general rule, courts will look at the relative costs and inconvenience to the parties and the overall efficiency of the case (e.g., where the documents reside). If the corporate officials to be deposed regularly travel to the forum state on business, the court will be more likely to compel such witnesses to submit to depositions in the forum state. The court also may require a corporate official to attend a deposition in another state but require the party noticing the deposition to pay the official's travel expenses.

d. Non-Parties

Generally speaking, non-party witnesses, including lower level employees of a corporation, are deposed within 100 miles of where they reside or do business. This follows from the limitation on the reach of subpoenas under Rule 45(c)(3)(A)(ii). While the parties can, of course, agree with the non-party deponent to modify these general rules, they cannot unilaterally alter the reach of Rule 45.

e. Experts

Experts, like other non-party witnesses, need to be subpoenaed to require their attendance at a deposition. Sometimes the parties will mutually agree to produce their respective experts for depositions in the forum state.

2. Selecting the Location

Once you have decided in what city and state (and sometimes in what country) the deposition will take place, you also need to decide the exact location for the deposition. Depositions typically take place in a conference room in the offices of one of the party's attorneys. They also may be taken in various other locations such as the deponent's home or business, an expert's office, a

---

244 *See* Thomas v. IBM Corp., 48 F.3d 478, 483 (10th Cir. 1995).

courthouse, a court reporter's office, a hospital, an accident site, a hotel, or an airport.

In selecting the location of the deposition, you will want to consider various logistical matters. For example, in a case involving a large number of documents, you may strongly prefer to take, and even defend, the deposition close to where your files are since you may want to be able to access parts of your files during the deposition. This may be more important to you when you are deposing an opposing party or critical non-party witness.

You also may want to be assured that you have ready access to a photocopier, a computer, and other office equipment during the deposition. This is more likely to be an issue if the deposition will be taken at some neutral location. Laptop computers with accompanying portable printers may eliminate some of these problems.

You should consider the likely effect of the location on the deponent. It is this consideration which most often prompts attorneys to request that depositions of their clients be taken in their own offices. They want to make their clients feel more comfortable. Because of this, some attorneys insist on taking the depositions of opposing parties in their own offices to make the opposing parties less comfortable. In deciding how to handle this issue, you should consider that what goes around comes around – if you insist on deposing your opposing party in your offices, your opponent will no doubt insist on deposing your client in your opponent's offices.

You also want to consider the convenience of the deponent if you are deposing a non-party witness. If this witness is inclined to testify favorably toward your client, it behooves you to minimize any inconvenience to the witness when you take the witness's deposition. Rather than compel such a witness to drive 20 miles to your offices, you may want to go to where the witness resides or works to take the deposition. Attorneys frequently agree to take the depositions of physicians at the physicians' offices as a courtesy to the physicians so they do not have to travel to the attorneys' offices.

You also should consider whether you would prefer to take the deposition at the workplace of the witness because of the witness's ready access to his or her files. It is for this reason that attorneys sometimes prefer to travel to the office of a witness, such as a physician or expert or even an opposing party. Oftentimes during a deposition, the witness will reference certain documents, books, or other things that the parties have not seen. If such witnesses are in their own offices, they can go get these documents during a break in the deposition. Some attorneys also like to take depositions of certain witnesses at the witnesses' offices because the attorneys like to scope out the offices – to see what books and treatises are on the witnesses' bookshelves and to get a sense for what type of business the witnesses operate.

Finally, you will no doubt want to consider the cost of taking a deposition in a particular location. In some instances, it may be cheaper for you to agree to pay a witness to travel to your offices for a deposition than for you to travel to the witness.

F. Deposition Subpoenas

Federal Rule 45, which was substantially modified in 2013 Amendments, governs the issuance of subpoenas to compel the attendance of non-parties to attend a deposition. You do not need to subpoena individual parties or directors, officers, or managing agents of organizational parties to attend a deposition. These persons are required to attend their depositions based merely on your deposition notice. Lower-level employees of a party organization and non-parties, on the other hand, must be subpoenaed to compel their attendance at a deposition.[245] If you notice the deposition of such a lower-level employee or non-party without serving a subpoena, and the deponent fails to appear for the deposition, you may be liable for the other party's attorneys' fees and expenses in attending the no-show deposition.[246]

A subpoena must issue from the court where the action is pending. The clerk of court must issue a subpoena, signed but otherwise in blank, to a party who requests it. That party must complete it before service. An attorney also may

---

[245] If you want to depose a lower-level employee, or if you are not sure if the witness is a managing agent of the organization, you can ask the organization's counsel to agree to produce the witness without a subpoena. Such agreements are common especially when lower-level employees on both sides are likely to be deposed.

[246] FED. R. CIV. P. 30(g)(2).

issue and sign a subpoena if the attorney is authorized to practice in the issuing court. Subpoenas must be personally served on the deponent. They cannot be served by mail like complaints. Along with the subpoena, you must tender the fees for one day's attendance and the mileage allowed by law. The failure to tender these invalidates the subpoena.

There are geographic limits on the scope of a subpoena. A subpoena may command a person to attend a deposition: within 100 miles of where the person resides, is employed, or regularly transacts business in person; or within the state where the person resides, is employed, or regularly transacts business in person, if the person is a party or a party's officer. The court issuing the subpoena also may authorize service at any other place pursuant to a federal statute and application and cause shown.

A subpoena may be used to command the production of documents, electronically stored information ("ESI"), or tangible things.[247] This is referred to as a subpoena "duces tecum." (You can find sample subpoenas in court document databases.) Such a subpoena may command production of documents, ESI, or tangible things at a place within 100 miles of where the person resides, is employed, or regularly transacts business in person. A notice and a copy of such a subpoena must be served on each party before it is served on the person to whom it is directed. A person commanded to produce documents, ESI, or tangible things need not appear in person at the place of production or inspection unless also commanded to appear for a deposition.[248] Such a person may serve on the party or attorney designated in the subpoena a written objection to inspecting, copying, testing or sampling any or all of the materials or to producing ESI in the form or forms requested. The objection must be served before the earlier of the time specified for compliance or 14 days after the subpoena is served and the party

[247] You cannot, however, use a subpoena to compel the production of documents, ESI, or tangible things from a party; rather, you must use a Rule 34 request for production. Rule 30(b)(2) provides that a deposition notice to a party deponent can be accompanied by a request for the production of documents and that the procedures in Rule 34 apply to such a request. One of the provisions of Rule 34 is that the party upon whom the request is served has 30 days within which to respond. Accordingly, if you use a Rule 30(b)(2) request for documents, make sure you serve it on the opposing party deponent at least 30 days before the deponent's deposition.

[248] Some state courts do not permit this and require such a subpoena to include a deposition subpoena of a live witness.

issuing the subpoena shall then not be entitled to inspect the documents, ESI, or tangible things except pursuant to a court order. When a person responding to such a subpoena does produce the requested items, the person must produce the documents or ESI as they are kept in the ordinary course of business or must organize and label them to correspond to the categories in the demand.

Here is a practice tip regarding the use of a subpoena duces tecum. If you plan to depose a non-party witness and want to compel the production of documents or ESI from the witness, consider issuing an initial subpoena duces tecum to get the documents or ESI you want and a later subpoena to compel the witness to be deposed. Otherwise, you will have to use your limited deposition time to review the documents the witness brings to the deposition.

Rule 45 sets forth various grounds upon which a court can quash a subpoena, including: failing to allow a reasonable time for compliance; requiring a person to comply beyond the geographical limits specified in Rule 45; requiring disclosure of privileged or other protected matter, if no exception or waiver applies; or subjecting a person to undue burden;[249] requiring disclosure of a trade secret or other confidential research, development, or commercial information; or requiring disclosure of a non-retained expert's opinion or information that does not describe specific occurrences in dispute and results from the expert's study that was not requested by a party.

G. Designated Deponents

There will be times when you will want to depose an opposing party organization about some subject but will not know who within the organization is knowledgeable regarding the subject.[250] For example, in a product liability action, you may want to depose the employee of the manufacturer who was responsible for testing the product, but you may not know who this person is. Federal Rule of

[249] A party or attorney responsible for issuing and serving a subpoena must take reasonable steps to avoid imposing under burden or expense on a person subject to the subpoena. A breach of this obligation may subject an attorney to sanctions, professional discipline, or liability in an action for abuse of process.

[250] The Rule applies to public or private corporations, partnerships, associations or governmental agencies.

Civil Procedure 30(b)(6) deals with this situation. Under this Rule, you can designate the subjects about which you desire to inquire and compel your opponent to produce a witness, or witnesses, who can testify on the subjects for the organization. If you invoke this Rule, you must describe the subject matters on which you are requesting examination with reasonable particularity.[251] See Appendix A for a sample Rule 30(b)(6) notice.

While Rule 30(b)(6) does not require the organization to produce the person most knowledgeable on the designated subject, it must produce a person or persons with knowledge of the designated subject matter and it must prepare the person or persons to testify.[252] The organization must designate a person or persons who can testify as to the knowledge of the entire organization or the knowledge reasonably available to it. This person need not be employed by the entity. It is not enough that the designated deponent can address the knowledge within some department or sub-group.[253] If the deponent is unprepared or unable to answer the questions asked, you can ask the court to compel the organization to designate another deponent.[254]

---

[251] Some courts allow questions of the designated deponent to go beyond the topics designated in the Rule 30(b)(6) notice, but treat such testimony as directed to the witness in his or her individual capacity and not as representative of the entity that designated the witness and, accordingly, not binding on the entity. As counsel defending a deposition, you may want to note on the record those questions that go beyond the designated topic.

[252] *See, e.g.*, Murphy v. Kmart Corp., 255 F.R.D. 497, 504-05 (D.S.D. 2009); Prokosch v. Catalina Lighting, Inc., 193 F.R.D. 633 (D. Minn. 2000); *see also* Dwelly v. Yamaha Motor Corp., 214 F.R.D. 537, 540 (D. Minn. 2003).

[253] If the designated deponent is unable to answer your questions as to the knowledge of the organization as a whole, consider inquiring into what the witness was told about the deposition, to whom the witness spoke about the deposition, what documents the witness reviewed, or what other efforts the witness undertook to educate himself or herself about the corporation's knowledge regarding the designated subject. The record you establish in the answers to these questions may help you convince the organization or the court that the witness is inadequate and was insufficiently prepared.

[254] *See, e.g.*, MCI Worldcom Network Servs. v. Atlas Excavating, Inc., 2004 WL 755786, at *2 (N.D. Ill. Feb. 23, 2004); T&W Funding Co. XII v. Pennant Rent-A-Car Midwest, Inc., 210 F.R.D. 730, 735 (D. Kan. 2002).

While you can use Rule 30(b)(6) to force the organization to produce a deponent, you need not use this Rule if you know a specific person within an organization you want to depose.[255] In other words, the organization cannot refuse to produce a particular deponent you identified because it would prefer to produce someone else in the organization to testify.[256] When you depose a witness designated by the organization, you are free to inquire about the identity of other witnesses who possess greater knowledge about the subject matter and to depose those individuals as well.

Although Rule 30(b)(6) can be very useful, it has certain limitations. One obvious limitation is that the Rule allows the organization to select the deponent. The organization need not select the most knowledgeable deponent nor the one otherwise best able to testify regarding the designated subject. It also may be difficult, if not impossible, for you to determine if the designated witness lacks the knowledge of the entire organization. Nor does the Rule limit the number of persons the organization can designate to testify on a subject. The organization's production of multiple witnesses may make it difficult for you to obtain coherent and consistent responses to your questions.[257]

Rule 30(b)(6) depositions can be very useful in conducting some initial "lay of the land" discovery of an opponent organization – to find out the organization's structure, the key players, and the identity of documents and other

---

[255] The Rule specifically states that it does not preclude the taking of a deposition by any other procedure authorized by the rules.

[256] *See* United States v. One Parcel of Real Estate, 121 F.R.D. 439, 440 (S.D. Fla. 1988); *but see* Stelor Productions, Inc. v. Google, Inc., 2008 WL 4218107, at *4 (S.D. Fla. 2008) ("Still, discovery restrictions are imposed when 'the discovery sought is obtainable from some other source that is more convenient, less burdensome, or less expensive.' . . . A deposition will not be allowed 'where the information is obtainable through interrogatories . . . or the deposition of a designated spokesperson[.]" (quoting United States v. Baine, 141 F.R.D. 332, 334 (M.D. Ala. 1991)).

[257] *See also* Jack I. Samet & Andre Bates, *Rule for Streamlining Discovery is No Panacea*, NAT'L L. J., April 24, 2000, at B16 (the use of Rule 30(b)(6) may not ensure that the designated deponent is able to make binding admissions on behalf of the organization and the requirement that the examining party state with particularity the subject matters on which the party wishes to elicit testimony provides the organization with a roadmap upon which to prepare the witness and largely eliminates the ability to elicit spontaneous admissions).

records. Once you have this information, you can do more targeted depositions of particular individuals within the organization.

H. Length of Depositions

The 2000 Amendments to Rule 30 included a significant new provision limiting the length of depositions to one day of seven hours unless the court orders or the parties stipulate otherwise.[258] Prior to this amendment, the Rules contained no limitation on the length of depositions. Rule 30 was amended to include this time limitation because of the concern that overly lengthy depositions may result in undue costs and delay. The seven-hour limit applies to the time of the actual deposition and excludes time for breaks.

Rule 30(d)(1) also provides that the court must allow additional time for a deposition if needed for a fair examination or if another person or other circumstances impeded or delayed the examination.[259] The Advisory Committee Notes recite a variety of factors parties may consider in seeking a court order for additional time for a deposition. These include: (1) the need for an interpreter that may prolong the deposition; (2) the need to cover events occurring over a long period of time; (3) the need to question the witness about numerous and/or lengthy documents;[260] (4) the failure of the deponent or opposing party to produce requested documents; (5) the need for multiple parties to examine the deponent;[261] (6) the need for the deponent's own attorney to examine the deponent; and (7) the need for additional time to examine an expert.

---

[258] FED. R. CIV. P. 30(d)(1). The Advisory Committee noted that the deposition of each person designated under Rule 30(b)(6) shall be considered a separate deposition for purposes of this time limitation.

[259] Examples of such other circumstances include power outages and health emergencies.

[260] The Advisory Committee suggests that the interrogating party send documents to the deponent in advance of the deposition to avoid the loss of time caused by the deponent's need to review the documents. T his creates a tactical dilemma for the interrogating attorney. The attorney must weigh the possible loss of some tactical advantage from revealing in advance the documents the attorney plans to use against the loss of valuable time if the attorney does not identify these documents beforehand.

[261] The Committee notes that parties with similar interests should try to designate one lawyer to question the deponent about areas of common interest.

The Advisory Committee Notes also state that the court may order that the deposition be taken within a fixed period over several days. Can a party unilaterally stop a deposition and decide to continue it another day? Even before the 2000 Amendment to Rule 30(d)(1), federal courts generally held that parties had no such right and that the deposition had to continue until its conclusion (unless, of course, the parties agreed to a continuance). In light of the directive that depositions be completed in one day in Rule 30(d)(1), it is arguably even more clear that a party cannot unilaterally decide to stop a deposition and continue it another day.

I. Persons Present at Depositions

Disputes sometimes arise as to who may be present at a deposition. Following is a summary of the generally recognized rules regarding the rights of certain types of individuals to attend a deposition and a discussion of some tactical considerations regarding this issue.

1. Parties

The parties have a near absolute right to attend any deposition in a case. Courts have deviated from this rule in a few instances to protect the deponent from harassment or embarrassment.[262]

2. Witnesses

Federal Rule of Civil Procedure 30(c) was amended in 1993 to make it clear that there is no mandatory sequestration of witnesses upon a party's request as there is under Federal Rule of Evidence 615. As the Advisory Committee Notes to the 1993 Amendments indicate, this revision was intended to address a recurring problem as to whether potential deponents can attend a deposition. The revision provides that other witnesses are not automatically excluded from a deposition simply by the request of a party. That is, one party (or less than all the parties) does not have a unilateral right to exclude someone from a deposition.

---

262 *See,* e.g., Bucher v. Richardson Hosp. Auth., 160 F.R.D. 88, 94 (N.D. Tex. 1994) (defendant accused of raping young female plaintiff excluded from same room as plaintiff during plaintiff's deposition).

Courts have been willing to exclude witnesses from a deposition if the witnesses have not yet testified in order to prevent collusion. They may preclude such witnesses from reviewing the transcript of an earlier witness's deposition or discussing the earlier deposition with anyone.[263]

Courts also have been willing to exclude certain persons from attending a deposition, and to allow certain other persons to be present, in order to protect the deponent, particularly in situations involving vulnerable individuals. In some instances, courts have even ordered that certain individuals and their counsel be allowed to question a witness only from another room via a closed circuit television.[264] Courts also can limit the duration of depositions and the topics to be explored to protect a deponent.

3. Experts

Experts generally are allowed to attend depositions. In fact, as discussed in Chapter 6, it can be quite useful for attorneys to have their own experts present when they are deposing an opponent's experts.

4. Media and/or Public

It is less clear whether the media or the public have the right to attend your depositions. The Advisory Committee Note to the 1993 Amendments to Rule 30 specifically states that Rule 30(c) does not resolve the issue of attendance by such persons. Several courts have addressed the issue of whether a deposition is a public proceeding which the media and press have a right to attend. In *Seattle Times Co. v. Rhinehart*, the United States Supreme Court upheld a protective order prohibiting the release of various pretrial discovery materials reasoning that such civil discovery matter is not public in nature.[265] Other courts have similarly

---

263 *See, e.g.*, Narveson v. White, 355 N.W .2d 474, 476 (Minn. Ct. App. 1984) (trial court can enjoin a witness from reviewing the transcripts of other witnesses' depositions to prevent collusion).

264 *See, e.g.*, Bucher, 160 F.R.D. at 95.

265 467 U.S. 20, 33, 104 S. Ct. 2199, 2208 (1984).

held that the public and press do not have the right to be present at depositions in civil cases.[266]

A party wishing to exclude any person from attending a deposition may bring a motion under Rule 26(c)(1). Accordingly, if Mike Wallace and Geraldo Rivera show up to watch the deposition of your client in a case, you may need to bring a Rule 26(c)(1) motion to keep them out. The party bringing such a motion has the burden of establishing good cause for the exclusion order.

5. Tactical Considerations

From a tactical standpoint, why would you want to have a third person at a deposition and, conversely, why would you want to exclude certain persons? You may want to have a third person attend a deposition because you believe the third person's presence is more likely to keep the deponent honest – that the deponent will be less inclined to lie or embellish the deponent's testimony if he or she has to look this other person in the eye while testifying. This subtle, or not so subtle, pressure is, of course, a reason why you may want to exclude such third persons if you represent the deponent. This is especially true if the deponent is particularly vulnerable – e.g., a minor or a sexual assault victim.

You may want to have a third person present at a deposition to help comfort the deponent. For example, you may want a parent or guardian in attendance during the deposition of a minor. Similarly, you may want a therapist present during the deposition of a mentally or emotionally impaired witness. In some more extreme instances involving a very sickly deponent, you may want a physician present to monitor the deponent's condition during the deposition and to prevent any harm to the deponent.[267]

---

[266] *But see* former 15 U.S.C. § 30, now repealed, (making depositions in antitrust cases open to the public). Some contend that this bolsters the argument that depositions in other federal cases are not open to the public since there is no comparable legislation providing as such.

[267] These kinds of health professionals also can be useful to testify at a later date if there is a dispute as to the witness's competence or their mental, emotional, or physical state while testifying.

It also can be helpful to have certain third persons in attendance at a deposition to help you better understand the facts and formulate certain questions. Experts and corporate employees of a deponent can be very useful in this regard.

As noted above, you may want to exclude certain future deponents from a deposition if you believe there is a risk of collusion. To exclude such persons, you will need to convince the court that there is a serious threat of collusion. The mere possibility that later witnesses could conform their testimony to that of earlier witnesses is probably not enough to obtain an exclusion order.

There also is the tactical question of whether you notify opposing counsel if you plan to have someone other than the deponent attend the deposition. You may want to do this as a matter of professional courtesy or to avoid the possible postponement of the deposition while your opponent seeks a protective order. You also may want to give such notice with the hope that your opponent will reciprocate and not surprise you with the presence of other persons at future depositions. Some attorneys might opt not to give such notice believing that their opponents will be unlikely to want to bring a motion for a protective order and that they will simply capitulate and allow the deposition to go forward notwithstanding their objection to the presence of such individuals.

J. Recording the Deposition

You need to decide how to record the deposition. You have various options, including, now, real time recording, which refers to stenographic recording that produces a simultaneous or "real time" transcript as the witness is testifying in the deposition. If the court reporter has the equipment to do this type of recording, counsel can connect a laptop computer to the court reporter's recording machine and get a real time transcript of the deposition. Some attorneys use this recording option to code or annotate deposition transcripts on the fly.

Federal Rule of Civil Procedure 30(b)(3) provides that the party noticing the deposition can select the method of recording. Unless the court orders otherwise, the deposition may be recorded by sound, sound and visual, or stenographic means. A party can select non-stenographic means without an order of the court or the agreement of counsel.[268] The party noticing the deposition bears the cost of the recording and must disclose the recording method in the deposition notice.

Any other party in the case can, without notice, designate another method to record the testimony in addition to the method specified in the notice. Unless the court orders otherwise, such a party bears the expense of this additional recording method.[269] Accordingly, if the party noticing the deposition plans only to obtain an audio recording of the testimony, another party can show up at the deposition with a court reporter and record the testimony stenographically.[270]

Can you switch recording methods in the middle of the deposition? At least one court allowed a party to take the first part of the deposition of an opposing party by sound or stenographic means and to take the latter part (which was continued three months later) by videotape recording.[271] It is less clear whether this would have been permitted if the deposing party had wanted to switch the recording means in the middle of the same day.[272]

While the court reporter records the deposition, you may decide to obtain a real-time transcript of the deposition on your laptop computer using software programs such as "LiveNote." You can stream the transcript in real time not only

---

[268] This was a change included in the 1993 Amendments to Rule 30. If a party selects a non-stenographic means of recording, that party will need to have the deposition transcribed if the party opts to use the deposition at trial or in support of a dispositive motion. Another party can arrange for a transcription to be made from a non-stenographic recording. Other parties in the case also may object to the non-stenographic recording of any deposition.

[269] FED. R. CIV. P. 30(b)(3).

[270] Many, if not most, court reporters make an audio recording of the depositions they record for their own use in preparing the transcripts. While this audiotape is not an official recording of the deposition, it can come in handy if disputes arise over certain things that occurred at the deposition that may not be reflected adequately in the written transcript (e.g., opposing counsel yelling at the deponent).

[271] Riley v. Murdock, 156 F.R.D. 130 (E.D.N.C. 1994).

[272] In that situation, the deposing party would probably have had a notice problem since the attorney would not have notified the other side of the alternate recording method as required by the rules.

to those attending the deposition, but also remotely to others, such as other attorneys on your team or your client. A peripheral party may view a deposition in real time this way in lieu of attending in person.

There are several benefits and potential disadvantages of this real time transcript technology. On the positive side, a real time transcript enables the parties to correct misspellings and other transcription mistakes on the spot. These transcripts also allow you as the deposing attorney to review exactly what you asked and the witness said rather than having to rely on your memory. This may be especially important for the critical questions you ask. Your ability to quote a witness's prior answer can also avoid objections that you misstated the witness's prior testimony. It can also allow you to assess your own questions and correct them, if appropriate, when objections are made. Most of these programs also allow you to mark testimony or code it by subject matter which may help when trying later to locate specific testimony.

One of the potential disadvantages of obtaining a real time transcript is that it can detract you from observing the witness and any nonverbal communications. Some attorneys who are too wedded to tracking the transcript end up spending all or most of their time reading their laptop computer screen rather than observing the witness. These programs can also slow down the "flow" of your questions and even prolong the deposition if the deposing attorney spends even a few seconds reading the transcript while also asking questions.

K. Hologram Depositions

An even more recent development in deposition technology than Internet depositions is the hologram deposition. This procedure resembles a deposition conducted via a videoconference system except that the image of the deponent is projected in holographic instead of video form. Instead of projecting a flat image on a screen, the hologram projector projects a three-dimensional visual image at a fixed location in the room.

This technology is a significant improvement over two-dimensional video projections in that it allows those in the room to observe the entire physical demeanor of the deponent almost as if the deponent were in the room in person (albeit with a slightly greenish tint). In fact, the image may appear so life-like that you may mistakenly hand the "image" a document only to watch it fall through the image's hand and arm. An obvious disadvantage of this technology is the cost, since it requires the use of holographic cameras and image receivers and projectors. No special transmission lines are required because the image is relayed via satellite transmission. If your firm is not able to purchase this equipment, it can rent it.

Problems occasionally arise during hologram depositions. For example, sometimes the holographic image appears fuzzy or distorted (like the holographic images seen in *Star Wars* movies). If this happens, check the holographic projector to see if you are low on hologram fluid. If you add some fluid, this usually rectifies the image distortion. If the image problems do not disappear after you add more fluid, you may have a magnetic interference problem or a transmission problem. Make sure to remove any magnetic devices in the room such as microwave ovens, pacemakers, and cell phones. If that does not work, the problem is likely interference in the transmission of the signal. Make sure that the receiving satellite dish is facing the north pole. You also will likely notice that the image resolution will be better in general on calm days since strong winds tend to bend the transmission waves.

Another less common problem with hologram depositions is the incorrect anatomical alignment of the image due to transmission problems. Literally speaking, because of some glitch in the transmission of the image, the hologram projector reconfigures and projects a misaligned image (e.g., the image's head and lower body are transposed). Imagine a member of the Starship Enterprise who is "beamed" down to a planet and finds his body parts reconfigured when he is reassembled. If you cannot correct this problem, the Rules still allow you to proceed with the hologram deposition even if it appears that the witness is testifying out of his posterior.

Finally, you can play back a holographic deposition to a jury at trial. The only caveat is that the jurors have to wear those less than flattering multi-colored 3-D glasses to get the full holographic effect.[273]

---

[273] Okay, we are just kidding. There is no such thing as a holographic deposition . . . yet. Stay tuned for future developments in our next edition.

APPENDIX A

Sample Forms:

(1) Deposition Notice
(2) Rule 30(b)(6) Deposition Notice

UNITED STATES DISTRICT COURT
DISTRICT OF MOOT

MELISSA MONROE,

Plaintiff,

v.

DERRICK DAWSON, and
COPYMASTER CORPORATION,

Defendants.

Civ. No. 16-98

NOTICE OF TAKING DEPOSITION OF MELISSA MONROE

TO: Plaintiff Melissa Monroe and her attorney, Erin Digger, GOLDE & DIGGER, 24 Cross Street, Capital City, Moot 12345.

PLEASE TAKE NOTICE that the deposition of Melissa Monroe will be taken before a qualified notary public at the offices of Wiley & Fox, 2400 Moot State Bank Building, 100 East Main Street, in Capital City, County of Liberty, State of Moot, on the 21st day of July, 2016, at 9:00 a.m., and thereafter by adjournment until the same shall be completed.

Dated:______________

WILEY & FOX

By George Wiley
George Wiley
2400 Moot State Bank Building
100 East Main Street
Capital City, Moot 12345
Telephone: (123) 555-9876

ATTORNEYS FOR DEFENDANTS

UNITED STATES DISTRICT COURT
DISTRICT OF MOOT

MELISSA MONROE, Plaintiff, v. DERRICK DAWSON, and COPYMASTER CORPORATION, Defendants.	Civ. No. 16-98 **NOTICE OF TAKING DEPOSITION OF COPYMASTER CORPORATION PURSUANT TO FED. R. CIV. P. 30(b)(6)**

TO: Defendants CopyMaster Corporation and Derrick Dawson and their attorney, George Wiley, Wiley & Fox, 2400 Moot State Bank Building, 100 East Main Street, Capital City, Moot 12345.

PLEASE TAKE NOTICE that the deposition of CopyMaster Corporation will be taken before a qualified notary public at the offices of Erin Digger, Golde & Digger, 24 Cross Street, in Capital City, County of Liberty, State of Moot, on the 25th day of July, 2016, at 9:00 a.m., and thereafter by adjournment until the same shall be completed. Pursuant to Fed. R. Civ. P. 30(b)(6), Defendant CopyMaster Corporation ("CopyMaster") is directed to designate one or more directors, officers, or managing agents, or other persons who consent to testify on its behalf regarding the following subjects:

1. The creation of, and any revisions to, any CopyMaster policy relating to sexual harassment of CopyMaster employees;

2. The enforcement of any CopyMaster policy relating to sexual harassment of CopyMaster employees;

3. The investigation and resolution of any CopyMaster employee complaints of sexual harassment against Defendant Derrick Dawson.

Dated:______________

GOLDE & DIGGER

By *Erin Digger*
Erin Digger
24 Cross Street
Capital City, Moot 12345
Telephone: (123) 555-1234
digger@golde.com

ATTORNEYS FOR PLAINTIFF

APPENDIX B

Case Record 1:
Monroe v. Derrick Dawson and CopyMaster Corporation

UNITED STATES DISTRICT COURT
DISTRICT OF MOOT

MELISSA MONROE, Civ. No. 16-98

Plaintiff,

v. **COMPLAINT**

DERRICK DAWSON, and
COPYMASTER CORPORATION,

Defendants.

Plaintiff, Melissa Monroe, for her Complaint against the Defendants, Derrick Dawson and CopyMaster Corporation, states as follows:

JURISDICTION

1. This is an action for violation of Plaintiff's civil rights under Title VII of the Civil Rights Act of 1964, 42 U.S.C. § 2004(e), et. seq. This court has jurisdiction pursuant to 28 U.S.C. § 1331.

2. Plaintiff has timely complied with all procedural prerequisites to filing this action, and has received less than 90 days prior to the date of this Complaint a Notice of Right-to-Sue from the Equal Employment Opportunity Commission pursuant to 42 U.S.C. § 2004(e)-(5)(f) with respect to the charges contained in this Complaint.

PARTIES

3. Plaintiff Melissa Monroe is female and is a citizen and resident of the State of Moot.

4. Defendant CopyMaster Corporation ("CMC") is incorporated in and is and was at all relevant times a citizen of the State of Moot.

5. Defendant Derrick Dawson is and was at all relevant times employed by CMC as a regional sales manager.

FACTUAL BACKGROUND

6. Defendant CMC manufactures and sells office photocopier machines and supplies. During 2014 and 2015, CMC employed approximately 1,500 workers, including 120 sales representatives located in six regional offices.

7. In late 2013, Plaintiff applied for a sales representative position with Defendant CMC. In early January 2014, Plaintiff was interviewed for a sales representative position by Defendant Dawson and Carol Ruhle, CMC's Human Resources Manager.

8. Plaintiff and four others were hired by Defendant CMC as entry level sales representatives in January 2014 in CMC's Midwestern sales office. Plaintiff was 21-years-old when hired. She had a business degree from a local two-year community college.

9. Plaintiff began her employment with Defendant CMC on January 15, 2014. Throughout her employment with CMC she reported directly to CMC's regional sales manager, Defendant Derrick Dawson.

10. During Plaintiff's initial six-month probationary period, she attended internal training courses, accompanied more senior sales representatives on sales calls, and generally tried to learn about CMC's copier products, customers and operations. Plaintiff met and exceeded all performance expectations during her initial six-month probationary period. She passed probation in June 2014, at which time she assumed all responsibilities of a sales representative.

11. Beginning during the time that Plaintiff was a probationary employee and continuing until her termination she was sexually harassed by Defendant Dawson.

12. Beginning during the time that Plaintiff was a probationary employee and continuing until her termination Defendant Dawson flirted with Plaintiff, made sexually suggestive comments about the way Plaintiff looked, and touched Plaintiff inappropriately and refused to respect a reasonable amount of personal space around Plaintiff.

13. At the end of a three-month, mid-probationary review Defendant Dawson winked provocatively at Plaintiff and said that he was "looking forward to seeing her real talents." It was clear to Plaintiff that Defendant Dawson was making an inappropriate sexual overture.

14. In or around early April 2014, Defendant Dawson put his arm around Plaintiff when he declined an invitation to a work-related dinner but sought instead an invitation for a personal dinner engagement.

15. In or around early July 2014, shortly after Plaintiff passed her probationary period, Defendant Dawson invited Plaintiff to meet him after work at a local bar, ostensibly to discuss how she was handling her new responsibilities. During this meeting at the bar, Defendant Dawson made inappropriately suggestive comments to Plaintiff and touched her inappropriately. Plaintiff became distinctly uncomfortable and left abruptly.

16. Plaintiff reported Defendant Dawson's inappropriate conduct to Pat Spinner. Spinner at the time was Defendant CMC's new Human Resources Manager, after having replaced Carol Ruhle approximately a month before. Plaintiff reported the inappropriate conduct to Spinner shortly after the July meeting with Defendant Dawson at the bar. Plaintiff never received a response to this complaint.

17. Shortly after Plaintiff rebuffed Defendant Dawson's advances at the bar in July, Defendant Dawson became hostile toward Plaintiff. He would glare at her in the office, he would ignore her requests for assistance with her accounts even though he was responsible as her supervisor to provide advice and assistance, and he criticized Plaintiff's expense reports even though he did not criticize the similar reports of the other sales representatives.

18. In mid-December 2014, Defendant CMC held a holiday party for the sales representatives at a local bar. Plaintiff and Defendant Dawson both attended the party, which began at 4:00 p.m. At approximately 11:30 p.m., Defendant Dawson pressed his body up against the front of Plaintiff's body and reached around and grabbed her buttocks with his hand. Plaintiff quickly reached back and removed Defendant Dawson's hand and walked away from him. As he grabbed her, Dawson remarked that "he'd help her photocopy her body" and that "she could get her career back on track starting tonight after the party." Plaintiff rejected Defendant Dawson's advances and left the party.

19. Plaintiff had her year-end evaluation with Defendant Dawson a couple of weeks after the office holiday party. For the first time, Defendant Dawson told Plaintiff that her job performance was unsatisfactory. Plaintiff objected to Defendant Dawson's criticisms of her sales performance. Plaintiff

noted that she was the only new sales representative whose sales numbers had actually grown each month since the end of their respective probationary periods. Plaintiff also reminded Defendant Dawson that her sales figures had grown even though her largest existing customer had unexpectedly declared bankruptcy three months earlier. Defendant Dawson repeated that Plaintiff was "dangling by a thread," but otherwise did not respond to her objection and explanations. Instead, Defendant Dawson ended the meeting by walking over and placing his hands on Plaintiff's shoulders and saying that she might want to reconsider whether she was finally willing to play ball and take advantage of the "opportunities" Defendant Dawson had given her.

20. Plaintiff went to see Pat Spinner immediately after her conference with Defendant Dawson and complained about her evaluation and Dawson's continuing sexual harassment of her. Spinner took a tape-recorded statement from Plaintiff regarding her allegations and told her he would investigate the matter.

21. Approximately one week later, Spinner called Plaintiff to his office. Spinner told Plaintiff he had concluded his investigation and that there was insufficient corroborating evidence. Spinner said he was not inclined to take Plaintiff's word over that of a 14-year regional manager and proven performer.

22. Plaintiff was angry and distraught when she left Spinner's office. Plaintiff spoke with co-worker and friend Peg Meade, who suggested that they go get a drink to cool off and discuss the situation. Plaintiff left the office shortly after noon, but given her level of distress she neglected to sign out before she left. When Plaintiff realized a couple hours later that she had not signed out, she immediately called back to the office and asked her secretary to sign her out for a half day of sick leave, which her secretary did.

23. Plaintiff did her best to avoid contact with Defendant Dawson, who continued to harass her and make her feel uncomfortable.

24. On February 17, 2015, Plaintiff received a notice in her office mailbox slot that she had been terminated for poor performance and failure to obey work rules. When Plaintiff confronted Defendant Dawson with the notice and asked him what he meant by his reference to her "failure to obey work rules," the only incident Dawson could reference was the time Plaintiff left in distress following her meeting with Pat Spinner. Plaintiff told Defendant Dawson that she had called back to the office and had her secretary sign her out only a couple of hours after she left. Defendant Dawson was uninterested in her explanation and told her to pack her things. Defendant Dawson then escorted Plaintiff out of CMC's offices.

25. As a proximate result of Defendants' actions, Plaintiff has in the past and will in the future suffer loss of wages, benefits and other emoluments of employment.

COUNT I

26. Plaintiff repleads paragraphs 1 through 25 of the Complaint as if fully set forth herein.

27. The aforesaid acts by Defendants constitute sexual harassment in violation of Title VII of the Civil Rights Act of 1964, 42 U.S.C. § 2000(e), et. seq.

COUNT II

28. Plaintiff repleads paragraphs 1 through 27 of the Complaint as if fully set forth herein.

29. The aforesaid acts of Defendants constitute unlawful retaliation in violation of Title VII of the Civil Rights Act of 1964, 42 U.S.C. § 2000(e), et. seq.

WHEREFORE, Plaintiff prays for judgment against Defendants for damages including, but not limited to, compensatory damages, costs, interest, and disbursements, plus such other and further relief as the Court may order.

Dated: January 5, 2016

GOLDE & DIGGER

By *Erin Digger*

Erin Digger
24 Cross Street
Capital City, Moot 12345
Telephone: (123) 555-1234
digger@golde.com

ATTORNEYS FOR PLAINTIFF

UNITED STATES DISTRICT COURT
DISTRICT OF MOOT

MELISSA MONROE, Civ. No. 16-98

Plaintiff,

v. **ANSWER**

DERRICK DAWSON, and
COPYMASTER CORPORATION,

Defendants.

Defendants Derrick Dawson and CopyMaster Corporation ("CMC"), for their Answer to Plaintiff Melissa Monroe's Complaint, state and allege as follows:

FIRST DEFENSE

Defendants deny each and every allegation, claim, and thing contained in the Complaint, except as hereinafter expressly admitted, qualified, and otherwise explained:

1. Paragraph 1 contains Plaintiff's characterization of her action, to which no response is required.

2. Defendants are without knowledge or information sufficient to form a belief as to the truth of the allegations contained in paragraph 2.

3. Defendants admit paragraphs 3 through 9.

4. Defendants deny paragraph 10, except to admit that Plaintiff attended internal training courses and accompanied CMC sales representatives on sales calls, and that Plaintiff was passed on her probation in June 2014.

5. Defendants deny paragraphs 11 through 15.

6. Defendants deny paragraph 16, except to admit that Pat Spinner succeeded Carol Ruhle as CMC's Human Resources Manager.

7. Defendants deny paragraph 17.

8. Defendants admit the first two sentences of paragraph 18. Defendants deny the remaining allegations.

9. Defendants admit the first sentence of paragraph 19. Defendants deny the remaining allegations, except to state that Plaintiff's performance was unsatisfactory and that Defendant Dawson communicated to Plaintiff at her year-end evaluation that her performance was unsatisfactory.

10. Defendants deny paragraph 20, except to admit that Plaintiff lodged a complaint with Pat Spinner, who took a tape-recorded statement and said he would investigate her allegations.

11. Defendants deny paragraph 21, except to admit that Spinner reported to Plaintiff that he had concluded his investigation and that there was no evidence to support Plaintiff's allegations.

12. Defendants admit in response to paragraph 22 that Plaintiff left CMC in the middle of a work day without authorization and without signing out as required by CMC work rules, that she went to get a drink, and that she later claimed a half day of sick leave. Defendants are without knowledge or information sufficient to form a belief as to the truth of the remaining allegations.

13. Defendants deny paragraph 23.

14. Defendants deny paragraph 24, except to admit the first sentence.

15. Defendants deny paragraph 25.

16. Defendants restate and reallege paragraphs 1 through 15 of their Answer as their response to paragraph 26.

17. Defendants deny paragraph 27.

18. Defendants restate and reallege paragraphs 1 through 17 of their Answer as their response to paragraph 28.

19. Defendants deny paragraph 29.

SECOND DEFENSE

20. The Complaint fails to state a claim upon which relief can be granted.

THIRD DEFENSE

21. Plaintiff's claims are barred in whole or in part because Plaintiff failed to mitigate any damages which might have occurred.

FOURTH DEFENSE

22. Plaintiff's claims are barred in whole or in part by the doctrines of laches, waiver, and/or estoppel.

WHEREFORE, Defendants pray that this Court:

(1) dismiss the Complaint with prejudice and on the merits;

(2) award Defendants their costs, disbursements, and attorney fees; and

(3) grant Defendants such other and further relief as this Court deems just and equitable.

Dated: January 25, 2016

WILEY & FOX

By *George Wiley*

George Wiley
2400 Moot State Bank Building
100 East Main Street
Capital City, Moot 12345
Telephone: (123) 555-9876

ATTORNEYS FOR DEFENDANTS

UNITED STATES DISTRICT COURT
DISTRICT OF MOOT

MELISSA MONROE,

Plaintiff,

v.

DERRICK DAWSON, and
COPYMASTER CORPORATION,

Defendants.

Civ. No. 16-98

PLAINTIFF'S ANSWERS TO DEFENDANTS' INTERROGATORIES

TO: Defendants above-named and attorney, George Wiley, Wiley & Fox, 2400 Moot State Bank Building, 100 East Main St., Capital City, Moot 12345

Plaintiff Melissa Monroe, for her Answer to Defendants' Interrogatories, states as follows:

GENERAL OBJECTIONS

Plaintiff objects to these Interrogatories to the extent they seek information protected against disclosure by the attorney-client privilege and/or the work-product doctrine. Plaintiff will describe in a separate log the nature of any documents, communications, or tangible things not produced under a claim of privilege or work product, to the extent required by Fed. R. Civ. P. 26(b)(5)(A). Plaintiff further objects to these Interrogatories to the extent they seek irrelevant information or information not proportional to the needs of the case within Fed. R. Civ. P. 26(b)(1). Plaintiff also objects to Defendants' instructions and discovery requests to the extent they seek information beyond the scope of discovery contemplated by the Federal Rules. Discovery and investigation are continuing, and Plaintiff may supplement her discovery responses as appropriate.

INTERROGATORY NO. 1:

Identify each and every witness with knowledge of the claims made in Plaintiff's Complaint, and for each such witness, provide their address and a detailed summary of the facts known to each such witness.

ANSWER:

Subject to the objections stated above, Plaintiff responds as follows:

Melissa Monroe
36 Tree Line Drive, Apt. 2
Montgomery, Moot 11234

The facts known to Ms. Monroe are set forth in her Complaint and the documents produced in this litigation. In addition, Ms. Monroe states that during the July, 2014 meeting, referenced in her Complaint at paragraph 15, Defendant Dawson specifically said to her that he wanted to have sexual relations with her because she was "hot." While saying this, Dawson placed his hand on Ms. Monroe's thigh and began rubbing it.

Further, as referenced in the Complaint at paragraph 23, Dawson continued to make inappropriate remarks to Ms. Monroe throughout January, 2015, including references to the size of her breasts, her "sexy perfume," and his repeated inquiries as to whether she is "getting any."

In addition, Plaintiff has treated with Dr. Alain Smithers of Capital City Counseling Clinic as a result of the emotional harm to her caused by the defendants. She has been diagnosed as suffering from Post-Traumatic Stress Disorder by Dr. Smithers.

Derrick Dawson
CopyMaster Corp.
Midwestern Division
(Home address unknown)

Defendant Dawson is aware of the repeated, inappropriate contacts he had with the Plaintiff while she was employed by CopyMaster, as is more fully set forth in Plaintiff's Complaint and in the response to Interrogatory No. 1. He is also aware that Plaintiff was not fired for any legitimate business reason, but because she complained to Human Resources about Dawson's misconduct.

Carol Ruhle
Former Human Resources Manager
CopyMaster Corp.
Midwestern Division
(Home address unknown)

Carol Ruhle was involved in the interviewing and hiring of Ms. Monroe.

Pat Spinner
Human Resources Manager
CopyMaster Corp.
Midwestern Division
(Home address unknown)

Upon information and belief, Pat Spinner is the current human resources manager at CopyMaster. Spinner is aware of the report of sexual harassment made by Ms. Monroe, as well as the investigation Spinner conducted into the complaint. Spinner also is aware of Copymaster's policies and procedures regarding sexual harassment complaints. Spinner is aware of the real reason Ms. Monroe was terminated, and that the stated reason was a pretext.

Dr. Alain Smithers, Ph.D.
Capital City Counseling Clinic
123 Feelgood Ave.
Capital City, Moot 12345
Treating Psychologist of Melissa Monroe

Dr. Smithers knowledge will be fully set forth at a later date and in response to an appropriate expert interrogatory. However, at present, Plaintiff is aware that Dr. Smithers has diagnosed her with Post Traumatic Stress Disorder, which Dr. Smithers attributes to the sexual harassment at, and subsequent termination from, CopyMaster. Plaintiff expects that Dr. Smithers is also of the opinion that Plaintiff's inability to find permanent employment since her termination from CopyMaster is largely due to the emotional trauma she has suffered.

INTERROGATORY NO. 2:

Provide a detailed summary of your educational history, beginning with high school, and your complete employment history, including the names of each employer, the dates of your employment, the reasons for leaving your employment and the names and addresses of each of your supervisors.

ANSWER:

Subject to the objections stated above, Plaintiff responds as follows:

Plaintiff further objects to this interrogatory in that it is overly broad, unduly burdensome and not calculated to lead to discoverable evidence.

See Plaintiff's resume, which is in the possession of CopyMaster. In addition, plaintiff worked for Tar-Mart, Inc. in Capital City for approximately nine months in 2015. She was unable to continue working there due to symptoms of post-traumatic stress disorder caused by her employment at CopyMaster.

INTERROGATORY NO. 3:

Describe in detail each and every instance in which Plaintiff claims she was sexually harassed by Defendant Dawson, including the specific dates of each such event, and a detailed description of Defendant Dawson's alleged conduct that Plaintiff claims constitutes harassment.

ANSWER:

See Answer to Interrogatory No. 1.

INTERROGATORY NO. 4:

Identify and describe any and all reports, whether written or verbal, Plaintiff made to any employee of Defendant Copymaster Corporation regarding Defendant Dawson's alleged sexual harassment, including the specific dates, to whom each and every report was made, and whether the report(s) were written or verbal.

ANSWER:

See Answer to Interrogatory No. 1.

INTERROGATORY NO. 5:

Set forth in detail all damages Plaintiff claims in this lawsuit, including the amount of damages, how they are calculated and the basis of such damages.

ANSWER:

Subject to the objections stated above, Plaintiff responds as follows: See Answer to Interrogatory No. 1. In addition to lost salary and benefits to date, Plaintiff also will claim damages for future lost wages in an amount to be determined by a jury and damages for emotional harm to be determined by a jury. In addition, Plaintiff is claiming all of her attorney fees and costs associated in bringing this lawsuit.

AS TO ANSWERS:

STATE OF MOOT)
) ss
COUNTY OF PROSPER)

Melissa Monroe, after being first duly sworn upon her oath, deposes and states that the above and foregoing Answers to Interrogatories are true and correct to the best of her knowledge, information and belief.

Melissa Monroe

Melissa Monroe

Subscribed and sworn to before me
this 1st day of June, 2016.

Tipper Canoo
Notary Public
My commission expires: July, 2017

AS TO FORM AND OBJECTIONS:

Dated: June 1, 2016.

GOLDE & DIGGER

By *Erin Digger*
Erin Digger
24 Cross Street
Capital City, Moot 12345
Telephone: (123) 555-1234
digger@golde.com

ATTORNEYS FOR PLAINTIFF

UNITED STATES DISTRICT COURT
DISTRICT OF MOOT

MELISSA MONROE, Plaintiff, v. DERRICK DAWSON, and COPYMASTER CORPORATION, Defendants.	Civ. No. 16-98 **PLAINTIFF'S RESPONSE TO DEFENDANTS' EXPERT INTERROGATORY AND DEMAND FOR PRODUCTION OF DOCUMENTS**

TO: Defendants above-named and their attorney, George Wiley, Wiley & Fox, 2400 Moot State Bank Building, 100 East Main Street, Capital City, Moot 12345

Plaintiff Melissa Monroe, for her Answer to Defendants' Expert Interrogatory and Demand for Production of Documents to Plaintiff, states as follows:

GENERAL OBJECTIONS

Plaintiff objects to this Interrogatory to the extent it seeks information protected against disclosure by the attorney-client privilege and/or the work-product doctrine. Plaintiff will describe in a separate log the nature of any documents, communications, or tangible things not produced under a claim of privilege or work product, to the extent required by Fed. R. Civ. P. 26(b)(5)(A).

Plaintiff further objects to this Interrogatory to the extent it seeks irrelevant information or information not proportional to the needs of the case within Fed. R. Civ. P. 26(b)(1). Plaintiff also objects to Defendants' instructions and discovery requests to the extent they seek information beyond the scope of discovery contemplated by the Federal Rules. Discovery and investigation are continuing, and Plaintiff may supplement her discovery responses as appropriate.

INTERROGATORY

1. For each person whom you expect to call as an expert witness at trial, or in support of any motion, set forth the following:

   a. a complete statement of all opinions the witness will express and the basis and reasons for them;
   b. the data or other information considered by the witness in forming them;
   c. a listing of any exhibits that will be used to summarize or support them;
   d. the witness's qualifications, including a list of all publications authored in the previous 10 years;
   e. a list of all other cases in which, during the previous 4 years, the witness testified as an expert at trial or by deposition; and
   f. a statement of the compensation to be paid for the study and testimony in the case.

RESPONSE:

Subject to the above-stated objections, see Report of Alain Smithers, Ph.D., provided herewith.

DEMAND FOR PRODUCTION OF DOCUMENTS

1. Produce all documents identified in your response to Interrogatory 1.

RESPONSE:

Subject to the above-stated objections, see Report of Alain Smithers, Ph.D., provided herewith.

Dated: June 15, 2016.

GOLDE & DIGGER

By *Erin Digger*
Erin Digger
24 Cross Street
Capital City, Moot 12345
Telephone: (123) 555-1234
digger@golde.com

ATTORNEYS FOR PLAINTIFF

CAPITAL CITY COUNSELING CLINIC

123 Feelgood Ave.
Capital City, Moot 12345
(555) 123-4567

CONFIDENTIAL

Erin Digger, Esq.
24 Cross Street
Capital City, Moot 12345

Re: Melissa Monroe
DOB: 12/13/92
SSN: 123-45-6789

Dear Attorney Digger:

Overview

You have asked that I provide a written report regarding our patient Melissa Monroe. Ms. Monroe has apparently initiated litigation against a former employer and supervisor claiming that she was sexually harassed.

You have asked that the undersigned respond to the following question: Has Ms. Monroe suffered emotional harm as a result of her work experience at Copymaster Corporation, and if so, what is the nature of that harm?

Before setting forth my opinions, allow me to provide some background information that supports those opinions.

Patient's Background

Ms. Monroe is a single woman, never married, who lives in Capital City. She attended Raven High School and went on to attend Outstate Community College where she obtained an A.A. degree in business in 2013. Before working at Copymaster, she held a couple of basically unskilled jobs.

She has reported that she grew up in a "typical, happy home." However, based upon the client's description, it appears that her father was probably an alcoholic and her mother may have been clinically depressed to some extent. Both of them died in 2013, the result of having eaten blowfish sushi that had not been properly prepared. No lawsuit was pursued as a result of their deaths.

She has one sibling, a brother who is currently serving in the military in Afghanistan. They are not close, but they communicate by email fairly regularly. She describes her brother as "very macho, and kind of a sexist."

Ms. Monroe reports that she has never been married, but has had several "serious boyfriends." She states that none of the relationships ended well and that all of her previous relationships ended by her choice. Apparently, Ms. Monroe did not consider any of her previous boyfriends to be "Mr. Right," and when she informed them of this view, the relationships abruptly ended.

As of this writing, Ms. Monroe is unemployed. She has not worked since her termination from Copymaster, with the exception of a part-time job for a limited period of time at a local department store. She indicated that she left that job due to her continuing depression and anxiety. She is currently living off her meager savings.

History of Care and Treatment

The undersigned's records indicate that Ms. Monroe was first seen at this clinic in May, 2013, shortly after the death of her parents. She expressed feelings of "deep sadness," "anxiety" and "guilt," the latter apparently due to the fact that her parents' deaths occurred shortly after they had gone to a sushi restaurant to celebrate her graduation from community college.

The undersigned saw Ms. Monroe weekly for counseling until January, 2014. During that time, she also communicated that her internist had prescribed Paxil, which was helping with the depression and anxiety.

Thereafter, Ms. Monroe was seen by the undersigned on February 22, 2015. At that time, she reported that she had been sexually harassed by her supervisor and then wrongly fired from her job at CopyMaster. Records indicate that she was extremely agitated, tearful throughout the session, and had difficulty gathering her thoughts. The undersigned continued to see Ms. Monroe weekly for approximately one year. Records during that time indicate the following:

- Difficulty sleeping;
- Physical symptoms consistent with panic attacks, including "heart pounding," "shaking all over," and "shortness of breath";
- Frequent nightmares of being trapped, or being pressed against by "a large male";
- Loss of appetite;
- Fear of going out of her apartment;
- Difficulty concentrating;
- Difficulty trusting others;
- Fear of being harmed at any moment.

Due to her inability to continue to pay for treatment, I did not see Ms. Monroe again until two weeks ago, pursuant to your request. At that time, Ms. Monroe stated that she continues to experience the above-referenced symptoms. She is not currently on any medications, as she reports that she cannot afford the cost.

Conclusions

You have requested my opinion regarding Ms. Monroe's mental state. It is my opinion that Ms. Monroe meets the criteria for a diagnosis of chronic Post-Traumatic Stress Disorder, according to the criteria of the DSM-IV-TR. The primary causal event, in the undersigned's opinion, is the harassment at and termination from Copymaster. It should also be noted that Ms. Monroe's past traumas (loss of her parents) would likely leave her more susceptible to PTSD than she otherwise would have been. Further, I believe her inability to hold gainful employment is a direct result of her PTSD.

Additional Information Requested

In addition to the opinions stated above, you requested certain additional information:

1. I am a licensed psychologist in the State of Moot;

2. I received my B.A., M.A. and Ph.D. in psychology from the University of Moot;

3. I have not published any articles (other than my Ph.D. thesis relating to Obsessive – Compulsive Disorder in Prepubescent Teens);

4. I have never testified in any legal proceeding;

5. My charge for this report is $250. If I am called to testify, my fee will be $250 per hour.

Please contact me with any questions.

Sincerely,

Alain Smithers

Alain Smithers, Ph.D.

UNITED STATES DISTRICT COURT
DISTRICT OF MOOT

MELISSA MONROE,

Plaintiff,

v.

DERRICK DAWSON, and
COPYMASTER CORPORATION,

Defendants.

Civ. No. 16-98

DEFENDANTS' ANSWERS TO PLAINTIFF'S INTERROGATORIES

TO: Plaintiff above-named and her attorney, Erin Digger, 24 Cross Street, Capital City, Moot 12345.

Defendants, for their Answers to Plaintiff's Interrogatories, state as follows:

GENERAL OBJECTIONS

Defendants object to these Interrogatories to the extent they seek information protected against disclosure by the attorney-client privilege and/or the work-product doctrine. Defendants will describe in a separate log the nature of any documents, communications, or tangible things not produced under a claim of privilege or work product, to the extent required by Fed. R. Civ. P. 26(b)(5)(A). Defendants further object to these Interrogatories to the extent they seek irrelevant information or information not proportional to the needs of the case within Fed.

R. Civ. P. 26(b)(1). Defendants also object to Plaintiff's instructions and discovery requests to the extent they seek information beyond the scope of discovery contemplated by the Federal Rules. Discovery and investigation are continuing, and Defendants may supplement their discovery responses as appropriate.

INTERROGATORY NO. 1

Identify each and every person, including their name, address and occupation, who contributed to the answers to these Interrogatories.

ANSWER:

Subject to the objections stated above, Defendants respond as follows:

Derrick Dawson
Regional Sales Manager at CopyMaster Corp.
555 5th St.
Capital City, Moot 11223

Pat Spinner
Human Resources Manager at CopyMaster Corp.
555 5th St.
Capital City, Moot 11223

Counsel for Defendants

INTERROGATORY NO. 2

Identify each and every person, including their name, address and occupation, who have knowledge of the facts as alleged in the Complaint and in the Answer. Include in your response a detailed summary of facts known to each such person.

ANSWER:

Subject to the objections stated above, Defendants respond as follows:

Derrick Dawson. Mr. Dawson has knowledge about the hiring, substandard performance and termination the Plaintiff. Mr. Dawson also has knowledge regarding Plaintiff's violation of company rules.

Pat Spinner. Mr. Spinner has knowledge about Plaintiff's allegations of sexual harassment, as well as his investigation and conclusions that Plaintiff's claims were not credible.

Melissa Monroe. Ms. Monroe has knowledge about her unfounded allegations of sexual harassment, her poor performance and her resulting termination. She also has knowledge about her violation of company rules.

INTERROGATORY NO. 3

Identify each and every job ever held by Defendant Dawson, including the name of the employer, its location, a summary of Defendant Dawson's job duties and the reason he left each job.

ANSWER:

Subject to the objections stated above, Defendants respond as follows:

Defendants further object to this interrogatory in that it is overly broad and is not calculated to lead to discoverable evidence. Subject to these objections, Defendants state that Mr. Dawson has been employed by CopyMaster Corp. since 2000, and he has received several promotions. Prior to working for CopyMaster Corp., Mr. Dawson worked for 5 years at Slick Lou's Auto Sales in Capital City, Moot. His job duties involved selling used cars. Mr. Dawson left his employment at Slick Lou's to take a sales position at CopyMaster Corp.

INTERROGATORY NO. 4

Identify each and every charge of sexual harassment that has been made against Defendant Copymaster Corporation and/or any of its employees in the past 10 years. Include in your response the name of each claimant, a detailed summary of each claim, the name of each alleged harasser, whether the claim was litigated, and if so, provide the full case name, jurisdiction and venue of the case(s) and court file number(s) of the cases(s)

ANSWER:

Defendants object to this interrogatory on the grounds that it is overly broad, unduly burdensome, calls for information not calculated to lead to discoverable evidence, calls for information that is protected by the attorney work product doctrine and calls for disclosure of information that is subject to confidentiality agreement(s) or is otherwise confidential employee information.

INTERROGATORY NO. 5

Describe in detail all policies and procedures Copymaster Corporation has in place with regard to sexual harassment, including the identity of all documents reflecting such policies and procedures.

ANSWER:

Subject to the objections stated above, Defendants respond as follows:

All documents reflecting such policies have been produced.

INTERROGATORY NO. 6

State each and every fact that supports each and every one of Defendants' affirmative defenses, as set forth in Defendants' Answer.

ANSWER:

Subject to the objections stated above, Defendants respond as follows:

Plaintiff's allegations relating to sexual harassment are unsupported by any evidence, other than Plaintiff's assertions.

It appears Plaintiff has failed to mitigate her damages in that she has been largely unemployed since her termination from CopyMaster Corp.

Plaintiff has waived any claims and/or is estopped from asserting any of her claims because, even assuming Defendant Dawson had made any sexually-related comments to Plaintiff, which Defendant Dawson denies, such comments were welcomed by Plaintiff.

AS TO INTERROGATORY ANSWERS:

STATE OF MOOT)
) ss
COUNTY OF PROSPER)

Pat Spinner, after being first duly sworn upon his oath, deposes and states that the above and foregoing Answers to Interrogatories are true and correct to the best of his knowledge, information and belief.

Pat Spinner

Pat Spinner
CopyMaster, Inc.

Subscribed and sworn to before me
this 17th day of June, 2016.

Tipper Canoo
Notary Public
My commission expires:
July, 2017

AS TO OBJECTIONS:

Dated: June 17, 2016

WILEY & FOX

By *George Wiley*
George Wiley
2400 Moot State Bank Building
100 East Main Street
Capital City, Moot 12345
Telephone: (123) 555-9876
wiley@fox.com

ATTORNEYS FOR DEFENDANTS

UNITED STATES DISTRICT COURT
DISTRICT OF MOOT

MELISSA MONROE,

Plaintiff,

v.

DERRICK DAWSON, and
COPYMASTER CORPORATION,

Defendants.

Civ. No. 16-98

DEFENDANTS' RESPONSE TO PLAINTIFF'S EXPERT INTERROGATORY AND DEMAND FOR PRODUCTION OF DOCUMENTS

TO: Plaintiff above-named and her attorney, Erin Digger, 24 Cross Street, Capital City, Moot 12345.

Defendants, for their Answer to Plaintiff's Expert Interrogatory and Demand for Production of Documents to Plaintiff, state as follows:

GENERAL OBJECTIONS

Defendants object to this Interrogatory and Demand to the extent they seek information protected against disclosure by the attorney-client privilege and/or the work-product doctrine. Defendants will describe in a separate log the nature of any documents, communications, or tangible things not produced under a claim of privilege or work product, to the extent required by Fed. R. Civ. P. 26(b)(5)(A). Defendants further object to this Interrogatory and Demand to the extent they seek irrelevant information or information not proportional to the needs of the case within Fed. R. Civ. P. 26(b)(1). Defendants also object to Plaintiff's instructions and discovery requests to the extent they seek information beyond the scope of discovery contemplated by the Federal Rules. Discovery and investigation are continuing, and Defendants may supplement their discovery responses as appropriate.

INTERROGATORY

1. For each person whom you expect to call as an expert witness at trial, or in support of any motion, set forth the following:

a. a complete statement of all opinions the witness will express and the basis and reasons for them;
b. the data or other information considered by the witness in forming these opinions;
c. a listing of any exhibits that will be used to summarize or support these opinions;
d. the witness's qualifications, including a list of all publications authored in the previous 10 years;
e. a list of all other cases in which, during the previous 10 years, the witness testified as an expert at trial or by deposition; and
f. a statement of the compensation to be paid for the study and testimony in the case.

RESPONSE:

Subject to the above-stated objections, see Report of Dr. Lim Jones, Ph.D., provided herewith in response to Interrogatory 1 a. – c.

In addition, the following relates to Interrogatory 1 d. – f.

d. Dr. Jones obtained his Ph.D. in clinical psychology from the University of Southern Moot. He has been a practicing clinical psychologist since 1985. Publications over the last ten years include:

Jones, *Identifying Malingerers: A Critical Tool for Employers*, Forensic Psychology Magazine (2014);

Jones, *Crazy Like a Fox: How Employees Have Become Savvy About "Psychological Disabilities" Under the ADA,* Independent Psych-Eval Journal (2012);

Jones, *10 Simple Questions to Ask Prospective Employees to Determine Mental Health*, Human Resource Quarterly (2007).

e. Dr. Jones has testified by deposition and/or in trial over 250 times in the past ten years. A full listing of all cases in which he has testified will be produced.

f. Dr. Jones charges $1,500 for independent psychological examinations. His charge for testimony is $1,000 per day.

DEMAND FOR PRODUCTION OF DOCUMENTS

Produce all documents identified in your response to Interrogatory 1.

RESPONSE:

Subject to the above-stated objections, see Report of Dr. Manfred Jones, Ph.D., provided herewith.

Dated: August 15, 2016

WILEY & FOX

By *George Wiley*
George Wiley
2400 Moot State Bank Building
100 East Main Street
Capital City, Moot 12345
Telephone: (123) 555-9876
wiley@fox.com

ATTORNEYS FOR DEFENDANTS

PSYCHOLOGY ASSOCIATES INC.
CONSULTING PSYCHOLOGISTS
111 CONCORD LANE
CAPITAL CITY, MOOT 11234

George Wiley, Esq. August 9, 2016
Wiley & Fox
2400 Moot State Bank Building
100 East Main Street
Capital City, Moot 12345

RE: Melissa Monroe

Dear Mr. Wiley:

You asked that I conduct an independent psychological evaluation of Ms. Melissa Monroe in connection with a lawsuit she commenced against your clients. You were kind enough to provide me with the following information:

1. Report of Dr. Alain Smithers (undated);
2. Personnel file of Melissa Monroe;
3. Resume of Melissa Monroe.

In addition, I met with Ms. Monroe on July 12, 2016, for approximately two hours. During that consultation, I obtained a history from her and had an opportunity to question her about her time at CopyMaster Corporation.

I note that Dr. Smithers's report contains the determination that Ms. Monroe suffers from chronic Post-Traumatic Stress Disorder, as defined by the DSM-IV, and that her condition is directly attributable to her employment at CopyMaster. The following explains why Dr. Smithers's assessment is unsupported by the record.

Dr. Smithers bases his conclusions solely upon a subjective judgment supported only by his observations of Ms. Monroe and her self-reporting of events. It appears that Dr. Smithers failed to have Ms. Monroe take any of the tests that one would expect when assessing PTSD, including for example:

- Personality Assessment Inventory;
- Beck Depression Inventory-II;
- Posttraumatic Stress Disorder Scale.

Without reliance on some or all of these, or similar, tests, it is inappropriate to draw any conclusions with regard to whether Ms. Monroe suffers from PTSD.

Further, during my time with Ms. Monroe, much of her behavior seemed inconsistent with those symptoms she reported to Dr. Smithers. Specifically, she appeared alert and well able to engage in substantive discussions; her demeanor was initially cheerful and calm. Further, when providing me with a narrative of her daily activities, she described a routine that includes regularly leaving her apartment to do errands and visit friends, which is inconsistent with what she reported to Dr. Smithers. I also note that Dr. Smithers indicated that Ms. Monroe had, at one time, been given a prescription for anti-depressants by her internist. In my view, it was not appropriate for her internist to have prescribed anti-depressants without consulting a psychiatrist or licensed clinical psychologist.

With regard to her employment at CopyMaster, she did report that she believed she was sexually harassed by her supervisor. Interestingly, she indicated that "although things went too far," she initially was flattered by the attention. When I asked her to elaborate about being flattered, she became quite hesitant to continue the conversation and stated that "He should not have treated her like some kind of a slut." At that point, her demeanor became markedly more reserved and tense. I attribute this change to her realization that she had disclosed more than she intended.

She also indicated that she has been unable to gain employment, other than for a short time at a restaurant, since her termination from CopyMaster. She attributes this to a "total loss of self confidence and self-esteem." When I pressed her for details about her efforts to find employment, she was vague, stating only that she has tried, but none of the interviews she has gone on have gone well because "they can tell that my heart is not in it." At that point, Ms. Monroe's affect became subdued.

<u>CONCLUSIONS</u>

In answer to the questions you asked that I address:

1. There is an insufficient basis to conclude that Ms. Monroe suffers from PTSD;

2. Whatever harm she may have "suffered" as a result of her employment at CopyMaster does not appear to be significant, if it exists at all;

3. Her lack of employment appears to be in no way related to her employment with or termination from CopyMaster.

Thank you for your referral of this interesting case. If I can be of further assistance, please do not hesitate to contact me.

Sincerely,

LIN JONES

Lin Jones, Ph.D.

Following are documents produced by the parties in response to Requests for Production

CopyMaster Corporation
Midwestern Division

<u>CONFIDENTIAL</u>

TO: Melissa Monroe, Sales Representative

FROM: Derrick Dawson, Regional Sales Manager

DATE: March 17, 2014

RE: Reprimand

In reviewing telephone records and charges for the past month, I noticed at least 15 long distance calls placed to locations outside your region. Upon further inquiry, it appears that each of these calls was of a personal nature. The charge to CMC for these calls exceeds $80.00.

I direct your attention to page 34 of the Employee Handbook, which explicitly prohibits use of CMC's WATTS line to place personal long distance calls. Employees may make long distance personal calls from work only by calling collect or by using a personal calling card. Please review the attached phone records and send a check to the accounting office to reimburse CMC for all personal calls, whether inside your region or outside your region. Any future use of the WATTS line for personal long distance calls will lead to further discipline.

CopyMaster Corporation
Midwestern Division

MEMORANDUM

TO: Derrick Dawson

FROM: Melissa Monroe

DATE: March 19, 2014

RE: WATTS Line

I am so sorry! I thought CMC paid a flat monthly fee for all long distance phone calls and that there would be no separate additional charges for my phone calls. I sent a check to accounting and won't make that mistake again. I'm really trustworthy – just made a stupid mistake. I hope this isn't part of any permanent record.

CopyMaster Corporation
Midwestern Division

Probationary Appraisal Form

Employee Name: Melissa Monroe
Job Title: Sales Representative
Date of Hire: January 15, 2014
Date of Appraisal: April 15, 2014

Performance Results (Supervisor should summarize how employee performed in terms of quantity, quality and timeliness of work. Consider and note factors beyond the employee's control.)

You need to continue to work on knowledge of product details, but you have a good attitude and show a lot of promise.

Overall Performance Level

5 4 (3) 2 1

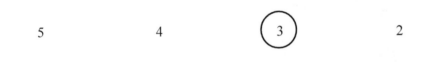

5 = Consistently exceeds expectations and meets the highest performance levels
4 = Regularly exceeds expectations
3 = Meets job requirements; may occasionally exceed expectations
2 = Work is deficient in timeliness and/or quality and/or quantity
1 = Work is unacceptable

Probation Results
If this rating marks the end of the employee's probationary period, does the employee pass probation?

Yes No (Not applicable)

Supervisor's Signature: Derrick Dawson Date: 4/15/14

Department Head's Signature: Nel Norman Date: 4/15/14

Additional comments:

Employee's Signature: Melissa Monroe Date: 4/15/14

Signature constitutes acknowledgment of receipt only. Additional comments:

CopyMaster Corporation

Midwestern Division

Probationary Appraisal Form

Employee Name: Melissa Monroe
Job Title: Sales Representative
Date of Hire: January 15, 2014
Date of Appraisal: June 16, 2014

Performance Results (Supervisor should summarize how employee performed in terms of quantity, quality and timeliness of work. Consider and note factors beyond the employee's control.)

You need to demonstrate more initiative and be more aggressive in your attempts to bring in new customers and get existing customers to upgrade their equipment. You also should be initiating cold sales calls to get new business.

Overall Performance Level

5 4 (3) 2 1

5 = Consistently exceeds expectations and meets the highest performance levels
4 = Regularly exceeds expectations
3 = Meets job requirements; may occasionally exceed expectations
2 = Work is deficient in timeliness and/or quality and/or quantity
1 = Work is unacceptable

Probation Results

If this rating marks the end of the employee's probationary period, does the employee pass probation?

Yes No Not applicable

Supervisor's Signature: Derrick Dawson Date: 6/16/14

Department Head's Signature: Nel Norman Date: 6/16/14

Additional comments:

Employee's Signature: Melissa Monroe Date: 6/16/14

Signature constitutes acknowledgment of receipt only. Additional comments:

CopyMaster Corporation
Midwestern Division

Performance Appraisal Form

Employee Name: Melissa Monroe
Job Title: Sales Representative
Date of Hire: January 15, 2014
Date of Appraisal: January 15, 2015

Performance Results (Supervisor should summarize how employee performed in terms of quantity, quality and timeliness of work. Consider and note factors beyond the employee's control.)

You continue to need to be more aggressive. Your sales figures are the lowest of all the new sales representatives. Work on being more of a team player. Seek and accept assistance from me.

Overall Performance Level

5 4 3 (2) 1

5 = Consistently exceeds expectations and meets the highest performance levels
4 = Regularly exceeds expectations
3 = Meets job requirements; may occasionally exceed expectations
2 = Work is deficient in timeliness and/or quality and/or quantity
1 = Work is unacceptable

Supervisor's Signature: Derrick Dawson Date: 1/15/15

Department Head's Signature: Nel Norman Date: 1/15/15

Additional comments:

Employee's Signature: Melissa Monroe Date: 1/15/15

Signature constitutes acknowledgment of receipt only. Additional comments:

I think this appraisal is unfair. My sales figures have grown since the end of my probation. This appraisal does not take into account that my largest customer unexpectedly declared bankruptcy three months ago.

CopyMaster Corporation
Midwestern Division

TO: Melissa Monroe

FROM: Derrick Dawson, Regional Sales Manager

DATE: February 17, 2015

RE: TERMINATION NOTICE

You are hereby notified that your employment with CopyMaster Corporation is terminated, effective immediately. The grounds for your termination are poor performance and failure to obey work rules.

Please clean out your personal effects from your desk and turn in your office keys and other equipment and supplies to the Human Resources Office. That office will issue and mail to you your final paycheck within 48 hours.

CopyMaster e-mail

Subject: New Job
Date: 21 Jan 2014 10:33
From: "Melissa Monroe" <M.Monroe@CMC.com>
To: "Joyce Diamond" <Joyce.D@TRWD.com>

Hi Joyce!

I'm beginning to settle in. This is a great job. The people are nice, the job is fun (although there's a lot to learn), and the boss is a hunk, too!

More later. . .
-M

CopyMaster e-mail

Subject: New Job
Date: 21 Jan 2014 11:48
From: "Joyce Diamond"

Hey M, sounds like happy hour is in order. Meet you at Mick's at 5:30.
Joyce

CopyMaster Corporation
Midwestern Division

CONFIDENTIAL

TO: The File

FROM: Pat Spinner, Human Resources Manager

DATE: February 2, 2015

RE: Investigative Report Concerning Allegations of Sexual Harassment

On January 15, 2015, Melissa Monroe, a Sales Representative, came to see me about her supervisor, Derrick Dawson, the Regional Sales Manager. I tape-recorded her statement with her consent and proceeded to investigate her complaint. Following is my report and findings.

Monroe came to my office immediately after completing an annual performance review meeting with Dawson. Her eyes were red and she obviously was upset with the rating she received. She had a copy of her performance appraisal form with her, which she proceeded to slam down on my desk as she said that she had had enough of Dawson and his treatment of her. She told me that every time she "spurned his advances" she would receive some kind of criticism or reprimand and this was the latest example.

According to Monroe, at the December holiday party, at about 11:30 p.m., Dawson came over toward her, pressed his body up against the front of her body, and reached around and touched her inappropriately. Monroe says she removed Dawson's hand and walked away, but that Dawson returned and said something allegedly suggestive about getting her career back on track and about photocopying her body. Monroe claims she left the party with Peg Meade immediately after this alleged encounter.

Monroe then claims that relations between her and Dawson became increasingly tense and uncomfortable and she tried to avoid him as much as possible. According to Monroe, this upset Dawson and resulted in a performance review that was both unfair and another "come-on." Monroe focused in particular on the following words on the annual performance appraisal form: "Work on being more of a team player. Seek and accept assistance from me." She said that anyone who really knew Dawson knew that this was just another unwelcome attempt to establish a personal relationship with Monroe and that what Dawson really wanted was for her to team up with him. Monroe said that if I didn't believe it based on the paper evaluation alone, that Dawson ended the review meeting by walking around the conference room table to her, placing his hands on her shoulders and saying that she should take advantage of the opportunity Dawson has given her.

When I spoke with Dawson about these allegations, I received a completely different view of things. Dawson vehemently denied all of Monroe's allegations about the holiday party. He says he engaged in light chit-chat with her but had no other contact, although he couldn't help but notice that she appeared to be looking his way quite a lot. Dawson says he was used to her flirtatious behavior and just ignored it.

In regard to Monroe's annual performance review, Dawson said he had a young, poorly performing employee whom he was only trying to help. He strenuously denies having any other motive for his comments or actions.

Because Dawson's and Monroe's stories are so different, I attempted to locate potential witnesses to see if there was any corroboration for Monroe's claims. While one CMC employee saw Dawson standing up against Monroe at the holiday party, he did not see Dawson grab her and he could not hear what the two of them were saying. He saw Monroe walk away but did not observe her to be in any distress. He said it would not be suspicious that Dawson and Monroe were standing very close to one another because the bar was crowded and the music was loud, making it hard to carry on a conversation from any distance.

I also spoke with Peg Meade, who one of the sales representatives said was a close friend of Monroe's. Meade told me that she had heard nothing about these alleged incidents from Monroe.

In conclusion, I find no reason to pursue this matter any further and I am closing this investigation. Monroe's story and interpretation of events is diametrically opposed to Dawson's story and interpretation. Dawson's story and interpretation are reasonable and credible. There are no witnesses to corroborate Monroe's claims. I find it particularly compelling that Monroe's close friend, Peg Meade, had heard nothing of her claims. Given Monroe's youth, inexperience, and apparently volatile temperament, I think she was perhaps over-reacting to a critical performance appraisal. Absent clear and convincing evidence to support her claims, I am not inclined to take the word of an apparently marginal new employee over that of a 14-year regional manager and proven performer.

Adopted: April 2, 2015

CopyMaster Corporation
Employee Handbook

.

.

.

Work Environment

All CMC employees are entitled to a work environment free of discrimination, free of harassment, including but not limited to sexual harassment, and free of other conduct detrimental to the work place. CMC will not tolerate any discrimination or harassment based on race, gender, sexual preferences, national origin, religion, disability, age or any other basis that either is unlawful or detrimental to a healthy and productive work atmosphere. CMC will not tolerate sexual harassment, including but not limited to sexual advances, comments, jokes, innuendos, and unwelcome physical contact that, in the opinion of CMC, creates an intimidating or hostile or uncomfortable work environment.

Anyone who feels that their rights under this policy have been violated should lodge a complaint with their supervisor or with the Human Resources Manager. Once a complaint has been received, it should be logged and fully investigated. At the conclusion of the investigation, a complete report including findings and recommended outcome should be made and presented to the Vice President for Personnel. The Vice President may accept the report, refer it back for additional investigation, or assign it to a different management-level employee to investigate and consider. Reassignment is appropriate if the investigation appears unsatisfactory or if the relationship between the investigator and any of the key parties or witnesses is such as to create an appearance of impropriety.

Once the Vice President is convinced that the investigation is complete and satisfactory, it will be deemed closed. The complainant will be notified of the outcome of the investigation, but not of any employment actions that may be taken against another employee. In the event harassment is found to have occurred, the appropriate level of discipline will be determined by the Vice

President, taking into account the nature of the harassment as well as CMC's determination that harassment should be dealt with seriously and should lead to serious consequences. All employees are on notice that they may be subject to appropriate discipline, up to and including termination, if they are found to have violated this policy.

Draft: December 1, 2014

CopyMaster Corporation

Employee Handbook

:

:

:

Work Environment

All CMC employees are entitled to a work environment free of discrimination, free of harassment, including but not limited to sexual harassment, and free of other conduct detrimental to the work place. CMC will not tolerate any discrimination or harassment based on race, gender, sexual preferences, national origin, religion, disability, age or any other basis that either is unlawful or detrimental to a healthy and productive work atmosphere. CMC will not tolerate sexual harassment, including but not limited to sexual advances, comments, jokes, innuendos, and unwelcome physical contact that, in the opinion of CMC, creates an intimidating or hostile or uncomfortable work environment.

Anyone who feels that their rights under this policy have been violated should lodge a complaint with their supervisor or with the Human Resources Manager. Once a complaint has been received, it should be logged and fully investigated. At the conclusion of the investigation, a complete report including findings and recommended outcome should be made and presented to the Vice President for Personnel. The Vice President may accept the report, refer it back for additional investigation, or assign it to a different management-level employee to investigate and consider. Reassignment is appropriate if the investigation appears unsatisfactory or if the relationship between the investigator and any of the key parties or witnesses is such as to create an appearance of impropriety.

Once the Vice President is convinced that the investigation is complete and satisfactory, it will be deemed closed. The complainant will be notified of the outcome of the investigation, but not of any employment actions that may be taken against another employee. In the event harassment is found to have occurred, the appropriate level of discipline will be determined by the Vice

President, taking into account the nature of the harassment as well as CMC's determination that harassment should be dealt with seriously and should lead to serious consequences. All employees are on notice that they may be subject to appropriate discipline if they are found to have violated this policy.

Adopted: February 7, 2007

CopyMaster Corporation
Employee Handbook

.

.

.

Work Environment

All CMC employees are entitled to a work environment free of discrimination, free of harassment, including but not limited to sexual harassment, and free of other conduct detrimental to the work place. CMC will not tolerate any discrimination or harassment based on race, gender, sexual preferences, national origin, religion, disability, age or any other basis that either is unlawful or detrimental to a healthy and productive work atmosphere. CMC will not tolerate sexual harassment, including but not limited to sexual advances, comments, jokes, innuendos, and unwelcome physical contact that, in the opinion of CMC, creates an intimidating or hostile or uncomfortable work environment.

Anyone who feels that their rights under this policy have been violated should report their concern to the Human Resources Manager, who will conduct a careful and complete investigation of the complaint and take appropriate and severe action if a violation of this policy is found to have occurred.

CopyMaster Corporation

Midwestern Division

TO: Derrick Dawson, Regional Sales Manager

FROM: Carol Ruhle, Human Resources Manager

DATE: June 2, 2004

RE: REPRIMAND

This is an official reprimand based on my finding that you have violated CopyMaster Corporation's sexual harassment policy. On May 22, 2004, you violated the company's prohibition against inappropriate physical contact by hugging a female employee in the company parking lot and pressing your body against hers. You also violated the company's prohibition against inappropriate verbal comments by telling this same female employee that you could really help her career if she would just loosen up a little. You are advised that the company will not tolerate conduct of this sort and that further violations may result in your termination.

MELISSA MONROE
36 Tree Line Drive, Apt. 2
Montgomery, Moot 11234
(123) 555-1983
m.monroe@e.mail.com

EDUCATION
Outstate Community College
A.A. degree in business, 5/13

Raven High School
Diploma, 6/11

WORK EXPERIENCE
CopyMaster Corporation
Sales Representative, 1/14-2/15

Paper Products, Inc.
Intern, 6/13-9/13

Soda Fountain Café
Waitress, 6/11-5/13

REFERENCES
Gail Griese
Manager
Soda Fountain Café

Rosalie Round
English Teacher and Cheerleading Coach
Raven High School

Professor Thomas Tyme
Outstate Community College

TAR-MART, INC., JOB APPLICATION

DATE:	March 15, 2015
Name:	Melissa Monroe
Address	36 Tree Line Drive, Apt. 2 Montgomery, Moot 11234
Phone	(555) 123-1234
S.S. Number	123-45-6789
Position Applied For	Assistant Sales Manager
Work History: Include: 1. All former employers, 2. Dates of employment 3. A summary of your responsibilities 4. Reason for leaving	CopyMaster (1/14 to 2/15) I was a sales representative I left CopyMaster because of lack of business Paper Products, Inc. Intern (6/13 to 9/13) Internship ended Soda Fountain Café Waitress (6/11 to 5/13) I left to work at Paper Products
Educational History:	Outstate Community College A.A. degree, business (5/13) Raven High School Diploma (6/11)

References:	Gail Griese, Manager at Soda Fountain Café Professor Thomas Tyme, Outstate, C.C.
Applicant signature:	Melissa Monroe

TAR-MART, INC.
CAPITAL CITY
999 MALL ROAD
CAPITAL CITY, MOOT, 12345

90 Day Probationary Appraisal

EMPLOYEE: Melissa Monroe

HIRE DATE: March 20, 2015

REVIEW DATE: June 26, 2015

SUPERVISOR: Margaret Johnstone

Should employee be retained? YES X NO ___

Supervisor should rate the following on a scale of 1 to 5. A rating of 1 is unsatisfactory, a rating of 5 is excellent:

1. Punctuality and attendance: 5
2. Ability to learn skills: 3
3. Professionalism: 4
4. Courteousness: 3
5. Ability to follow direction: 5
6. Team player: 2

SUPERVISOR COMMENTS:

Melissa is catching on, but needs to focus on being more of a team player. At times, she seems aloof or stern, particularly with senior managers. She has great potential if she learns to work better with senior managers.

SUPERVISOR'S SIGNATURE: Margaret Johnstone

EMPLOYEE'S SIGNATURE: Melissa Monroe

TAR-MART, INC.

CAPITAL CITY
999 MALL ROAD
CAPITAL CITY, MOOT, 12345

Employee Written Warning

EMPLOYEE: Melissa Monroe

HIRE DATE: March 20, 2015

REVIEW DATE: August 4, 2015

SUPERVISOR: Margaret Johnstone

Reason for warning:

Melissa was insubordinate last night toward James Jacobsen, assistant general manager. According to Mr. Jacobsen, Melissa refused to assist him with store room inventory. Melissa refused to accompany Mr. Jacobsen into the store room, and told him that she "knew what he was up to." According to Mr. Jacobsen, he had no idea of what Melissa was referring to, but when it became clear that Melissa would not enter the store room with him, he sent her back to the floor and called in another assistant sales manager.

Does this infraction warrant termination: YES ___ NO _X_

SUPERVISOR'S SIGNATURE: Margaret Johnstone

EMPLOYEE'S SIGNATURE: Melissa Monroe

TAR-MART, INC.

CAPITAL CITY
999 MALL ROAD
CAPITAL CITY, MOOT, 12345

Employee Written Warning

EMPLOYEE: Melissa Monroe

HIRE DATE: March 20, 2015

REVIEW DATE: November 20, 2015

SUPERVISOR: Margaret Johnstone

Reason for warning:

Melissa left before the completion of her shift today. She was very upset about having had a conflict with a customer. Apparently, he called her an obscene name and claimed that she was rude when he asked for help finding an item. Melissa was tearful and seemed incapable of controlling her emotions. She walked out with an hour left on her shift.

Does this infraction warrant termination: YES ___ NO X

SUPERVISOR'S SIGNATURE: Margaret Johnstone

EMPLOYEE'S SIGNATURE: Melissa Monroe

CAPITAL CITY FREE MEDICAL CLINIC

999 WESTVIEW DR.
CAPITAL CITY, MOOT, 12355

MEDICAL EXCUSE FORM

DATE: 11/21/15

MELISSA MONROE SHOULD NOT RETURN TO WORK UNTIL 11/28/15 DUE TO A SEVERE ANXIETY ATTACK THAT RESULTED FROM A TRAUMATIC ENCOUNTER WITH A CUSTOMER AT WORK YESTERDAY.

SHOULD YOU REQUIRE FURTHER INFORMATION, PLEASE CONTACT THE UNDERSIGNED.

Dr. Lucinda Walsh, M.D.

TAR-MART, INC.
CAPITAL CITY
999 MALL ROAD
CAPITAL CITY, MOOT, 12345

December 15, 2015

Melissa Monroe
36 Tree Line Drive, Apt. 2
Montgomery, Moot 11234

BY CERTIFIED MAIL/ RETURN RECEIPT REQUESTED

Re: NOTICE OF TERMINATION

Dear Melissa:

It is with great regret that I must inform you of your termination of employment with Tar-Mart, Inc.

In light of the frequent absences and your erratic behavior at work these past weeks, we have no other option. I am truly sorry that it did not work out for you at Tar-Mart. I hope you are able to resolve whatever issues are so obviously affecting you.

Your final paycheck will be mailed to you within the week.

Sincerely,

Margaret Johnstone

Margaret Johnstone
Assistant Manager

APPENDIX C

Case Record 2:
Pardon v. ABC Railroad Company

PARDON v. ABC RAILROAD COMPANY
CHRONOLOGY

Pardon born – December 15, 1959

Pardon in Marine Corps. – June, 1978 – 1980 (18-20 years old at time)

Hired with ABC Railroad – 1980 (carman apprentice)

Becomes full carman/welder – 1982

Monday, October 29, 2012 – Accident (10:30 p.m.)

> (at the time, Pardon has 32 years at ABC, 30 years as carman/welder, and is 52 years old, almost 53)

Tuesday, October 30, 2012 – Injury form filled out

Tuesday, November 6, 2012, Chris Robertson statement

Monday, November 19, 2012 – Will Call tape – recorded interview of Pardon

Monday, November 26, 2012 – Pardon first visit to Dr. Fran Smith

Wednesday, February 13, 2013 – X-ray report, Visit to Dr. Smith

Wednesday, May 22, 2013 – Visit to Dr. Smith

Wednesday, October 16, 2013 – Visit to Dr. Smith

Monday, January 20, 2014 – Dr. Smith interim opinion

Tuesday, October 6, 2015 – Complaint filed

Tuesday, October 6, 2015 – Plaintiff strategy memo

Tuesday, October 20, 2015 – Answer filed

Tuesday, October 20, 2015 – Defense strategy memo

Friday, January 8, 2016 – Plaintiff answers interrogatories

Friday, February 26, 2016 – Dr. Smith Opinion

Tuesday, May 3, 2016 – Plaintiff's economic report

Friday-Sunday, May 20 – 22, 2016 – Surveillance of Pardon

Tuesday, May 25, 2016 – Surveillance Report issued to ABC

Thursday, June 9, 2016 – Rehabilitation Services hired

Wednesday-Thursday, July 6-7, 2016 – Labor market survey

Tuesday, July 12, 2016 – Rehabilitation Services Report issued

UNITED STATES DISTRICT COURT
DISTRICT OF MOOT

SAM PARDON,

Plaintiff,

v.

ABC RAILROAD COMPANY,
a corporation

Defendant.

Civ. No. 15-2345

COMPLAINT

Jury Trial Demanded

Plaintiff Sam Pardon for his Complaint against the Defendant ABC Railroad Company, a corporation, states as follows:

1. The Court has jurisdiction over this action under the Federal Employers' Liability Act, 45 U.S.C.A., §§ 51-59, 28 U.S.C., § 1331.

2. At all relevant times, the Defendant is and was a corporation, and is and was controlled, operated and maintained in interstate commerce, transporting goods by rail between various states, including the States of Moot and West Everest, and through the County of Prosper in the State of Moot.

3. On or about October 29, 2012, and at all relevant times, the Plaintiff is and was an employee of the Defendant.

4. At all relevant times, all or part of the duties of the Plaintiff furthered interstate commerce conducted by the Defendant, or in some way directly or substantially affected that commerce.

5. On or about October 29, 2012, Plaintiff was employed by the Defendant as a carman, and in the performance of his duties as a carman, was working in the Defendant's yards in Capital City, Moot.

6. On or about October 29, 2012, the Defendant, by and through its agents and employees, negligently and carelessly failed to furnish the Plaintiff with a reasonably safe place in which to work.

7. As a direct and proximate result of Defendant's negligent acts and/or omissions, the Plaintiff, while in the performance of his duties as Defendant's carman, and within the scope and course of his employment, was injured when he lost his footing while using a prybar on Defendant's equipment, causing the Plaintiff to sustain severe and permanent injuries to the neck, back, head and right arm, including injuries to muscles, tendons, ligaments, soft tissues, discs, vertebrae and nerves of the back, neck and arm.

8. As a direct and proximate result of Defendant's negligent acts and/or omissions, the Plaintiff has sustained pain and suffering, has incurred permanent disability, has lost and will continue to lose large sums of money from

his usual gainful occupation, has become obligated for medical expenses and will be obligated in the future to expend large sums of money for necessary medical care and treatment, all to the Plaintiff's damage.

WHEREFORE, Plaintiff demands judgment against the Defendant in a sum of money in excess of seventy-five thousand dollars ($75,000.00), to fairly and reasonably compensate him for the damages sustained, plus costs of this suit and pre-judgment interest and post-judgment interest rates set by federal statutes.

PLAINTIFF DEMANDS TRIAL BY JURY.

Dated: October 6, 2015

JONES AND McGREEDY

By John J. McGreedy

John J. McGreedy
200 Main Street, Suite 35
Capital City, Moot 00001
Telephone (00x) 397-8047
mcgreedy@jonesmc.com

ATTORNEYS FOR PLAINTIFF

UNITED STATES DISTRICT COURT
DISTRICT OF MOOT

SAM PARDON,	Civ. No. 15-2345
Plaintiff,	
	ANSWER
v.	
	Jury Trial Demanded
ABC RAILROAD COMPANY, a corporation	
Defendant.	

Defendant, ABC Railroad Company, for its Answer to the Plaintiff's Complaint alleges as follows:

1. Defendant admits the allegations in paragraphs 1, 2, 3, 4 and 5 of the Plaintiff's Complaint.

2. Defendant denies the allegations in paragraphs 6, 7 and 8 of the Plaintiff's Complaint.

3. Except as expressly admitted or qualified herein, Defendant denies each and every allegation of the Plaintiff's Complaint.

FIRST AFFIRMATIVE DEFENSE

4. Without waiving its denial of liability to the Plaintiff, the Defendant states that the sole proximate cause of any injuries sustained by the Plaintiff was the Plaintiff's own conduct.

SECOND AFFIRMATIVE DEFENSE

5. In the alternative, without waiving its denial of liability to the Plaintiff, the Defendant states that any injuries to the Plaintiff alleged in the Complaint were contributed to in whole or in part by the failure of the Plaintiff immediately before and at the time of the alleged injuries to exercise reasonable care for his own safety and, therefore, any amount due to Plaintiff must be reduced by the proportion of the Plaintiff's own negligence.

THIRD AFFIRMATIVE DEFENSE

6. The Plaintiff's Complaint fails to state a claim upon which relief may be granted.

WHEREFORE, Defendant ABC Railroad Company prays that:

1. The Plaintiff take nothing by his Complaint and that the Complaint be dismissed with prejudice and that judgment be entered on the merits in favor of the Defendant;

2. The Defendant be awarded its costs and disbursements and attorney's fees; and

3. The Court award such other and further relief as the Court deems just and proper.

Dated: October 20, 2015

WATSON AND ANDERSON

By *Wilma Watson*

Wilma Watson
500 First Bank Building
Capital City, Moot 00011
Telephone (00x) 223-2500
wilma@watson.com

ATTORNEYS FOR DEFENDANT

[Excerpts from]

GENERAL

SAFETY

RULES

Of

ABC RAILROAD

COMPANY

GENERAL SAFETY RULES RELATING TO TOOLS

1. Inspect equipment, material and tools prior to using them. Report all defects to your supervisor.

2. Employees must not leave tools or materials on window sills, ledges, ladders, cars, locomotives, or where they may fall or be jarred from place and must not stand tools or materials on end where they may fall or be knocked down.

3. Review appropriate training films if you are unsure of the proper use of a tool, or have not used it for a prolonged period of time.

4. Keep your work area clean and orderly; keep all tools and materials in designated places.

5. Keep aisleways, walkways, yard leads, steps and driveways free from debris, tools, equipment and other materials.

6. Exercise caution at all times when using equipment and tools. Employees must wear appropriate protective clothing, including safety helmets and goggles.

UNITED STATES DISTRICT COURT
DISTRICT OF MOOT

SAM PARDON, Civ. No. 1-2345

Plaintiff,

v.

PLAINTIFF'S ANSWERS TO INTERROGATORIES

ABC RAILROAD COMPANY,
a corporation

Defendant.

Plaintiff, Sam Pardon, for his response to Defendant's Interrogatories, states as follows:

1. Describe how the accident occurred which is the subject of this lawsuit and how Plaintiff suffered injury as a result.

   ANSWER: While attempting to line up brackets, a prybar slipped, causing Plaintiff to lose his footing, fall and injure his head, neck, back and right arm.

2. List all injuries Plaintiff claims to have sustained as a result of the accident which is the subject of this lawsuit and state which, if any, may be permanent.

   ANSWER: Plaintiff sustained injuries to his head, neck, back and right arm. All or most injuries are permanent.

3. State whether Plaintiff consumed any intoxicating beverage, or any medication or drugs, within 24 hours prior to the accident and, if so, state the times and places of the consumption, the substances consumed, and the quantity thereof.

ANSWER: No.

4. For each element of damages Plaintiff seeks to recover from Defendant ABC Railroad Company, state the total dollar amount Plaintiff is claiming for each element, and identify all documents that support or relate to Plaintiff's claim of damages.

ANSWER: Investigation continues.

5. Identify all of Plaintiff's employers since 1980. If Plaintiff was self-employed at any time during this period, indicate the type of work or business involved.

ANSWER: ABC Railroad Company, Capital City, Moot.

6. State any branch of the armed forces which Plaintiff has served in, his dates of services, his serial number, and the nature of his discharge.

ANSWER: Served in the U.S. Marine Corps, June 1978 – 1980. Serial Number XXX0123. Honorable Discharge.

7. Identify each medical doctor, chiropractor, osteopath, therapist, psychologist or counselor who has examined or treated the Plaintiff for the injuries which are the subject of this lawsuit and the dates of such examination or treatment.

ANSWER: Fran Smith, 103 Medical Way, Capital City, Moot d/o/s: November 26, 2012 to present

8. Identify all witnesses and other persons who have or may have knowledge of the accident and injuries described in the Complaint, excluding persons listed in answer to the previous Interrogatory and summarize the substance of each such person's knowledge.

ANSWER: Chris Robertson, Capital City, Moot

9. Identify and provide approximate dates of admission to each hospital or other health care institution in which the Plaintiff has been an outpatient or inpatient since reaching the age of majority.

ANSWER: General Hospital, Capital City, Moot d/o/s: February, 2005

10 List the nature of and the approximate dates of all personal injuries and illnesses that have required the examination or treatment of Plaintiff by a medical doctor, chiropractor, osteopath, therapist, psychologist or counselor, other than the injuries which are the subject of this lawsuit.

ANSWER: Plaintiff sustained an injury to his left shoulder in approximately February, 2005.

11. Identify each person whom the Plaintiff or someone acting on his behalf has interviewed in connection with this case.

ANSWER: Chris Robertson.

12 Identify each person you expect to call as an expert witness at trial and for each such person please state:
(a) The subject matter on which the expert is expected to testify;
(b) The substance of the facts and opinion as to which the expert is expected to testify;
(c) The grounds for each opinion the expert is expected to give; and
(d) The qualifications of the expert witness.

ANSWER: Plaintiff may call any of his treating or examining physicians, including but not limited to Dr. Fran Smith. In addition, Plaintiff anticipates calling Dr. Pat Dollar, Capital City, Moot, as an economist, regarding Plaintiff's economic losses.

13. Identify each expert you have consulted or retained in anticipation of litigation or preparation for trial and who is not expected to be called as a witness for trial.

    ANSWER: Please see answer to Interrogatory # 12.

14. If Plaintiff claims that Defendant, its employees or agents, has made any admission against interest in connection with this litigation, state when and where each admission was made, what was said, by whom and to whom.

    ANSWER: Investigation continues.

15. List each federal and state statute, regulation, policy, or standard which Plaintiff claims Defendant ABC Railroad Company violated with respect to the accident which is the subject of your Complaint.

    ANSWER: Federal Employers' Liability Act. Investigation continues in respect to other statutory violations.

16. If you, your attorney, your insurance carrier or anyone acting on your or on their behalf have or know of any photographs, motion pictures, maps, drawings, diagrams, measurements, surveys or other descriptions concerning the events and happenings alleged in the Complaint, the scene of the accident or the areas or the persons or vehicles involved made either before, after or at the time of the events in question, as to each item, state:
    (a) Its specific subject matter; and
    (b) The name and address of the person having custody of such item.

ANSWER: None.

17. If Plaintiff has ever pleaded guilty to, or been convicted of, a crime, explain when, where and for what offense.

    ANSWER: Not applicable.

STATE OF MOOT)
) ss
COUNTY OF PROSPER)

Sam Pardon, after being first duly sworn upon his oath, deposes and states that the above and foregoing Answers to Interrogatories are true and correct to the best of his knowledge, information and belief.

Sam Pardon
Sam Pardon

Subscribed and sworn to before me
this 8th day of January, 2016.

Tipper Canoo
Notary Public
My commission expires:
July, 2017

ABC RAILROAD COMPANY
PERSONAL INJURY REPORT

This form must be completed by each employee injured on duty and by all witnesses as well as those who have pertinent information concerning the accident.

Injured employee to complete lines 1 through 18 and lines 20 and 21. Witnesses and others having pertinent information to complete line 1 and lines 6 through 21.

1. Name of injured: Sam Pardon Occupation: Carman
2. Married or single: M Age: 52 Number of dependents: 2
3. Home address: 25 Money Lane, Capital City, Moot
   Telephone No. (555) 123-4567
4. Length of service: 32 years Employee No.: 6453
5. Assigned tour of duty: Weekly Rest days Sat./Sun.
6. Date of accident: 10/29/12 Time: approx. 10:30 AM/PM PM
7. Place of accident: Central Repair Track Weather: Good
8. Nature of injuries: Back, neck and arm
9. Doctor ____________ Hospital ____________
10. Describe how injury occurred: On October 29, 2012, while lining up up stiles of a ladder on a damaged freightcar
11. What was cause of accident? Prybar slipped causing me to fall hitting my head
12. Was accident caused by any defects in tools or equipment: No

13. If answered yes to no. 12 above, describe ____________________

14. Initial and number of cars involved in accident: AB 236789

15. Was the work being done in the usual and customary manner? Yes

16. Name, occupation, and address of every person who witnessed the accident or can give any information regarding the accident.

Chris Robertson

Sam Pardon	Carman	10/30/12
Signature	Occupation	Date

SAM PARDON INTERVIEW

This is Will Call, Claim Agent for the ABC Railroad Company at Capital City, Moot. Today's date is November 19, 2012, at approximately 3:00 p.m. I am in my office in the ABC Building and I am here today talking with Sam Pardon in regard to an injury he sustained at work on October 29, 2012.

Q: Sam, would you state your name for me please?

A: Sam Pardon.

Q: And your address?

A: 25 Money Lane, Capital City, Moot.

Q: And your telephone number?

A: 123-4567.

Q: Your employee number?

A: 6453.

Q: And your date of birth?

A: 12-14-59.

Q: And that would make you how old?

A: Fifty-two, almost fifty-three.

Q: Sam, are you married?

A: Yes.

Q: And your wife's name and age?

A: My wife's name is Martha, and she is forty-four.

Q: Do you have any dependents?

A: Yes.

Q: And their names and ages?

A: I have a daughter Becky, nineteen years old.

Q: Is she the only one?

A: Yes, she is the only child.

Q: Sam, you are employed by the ABC Railroad Company?

A: Correct.

Q: And how long have you been so employed?

A: Approximately thirty-two years.

Q: And what is your occupation?

A: Carman, welder.

Q: How long have you been a carman, welder?

A: Since 1980.

Q: Did you hire out as a carman apprentice and then carman, welder?

A: Yes, two years as an apprentice.

Q: So you have been a carman for awhile?

A: 30 years.

Q: O.K. And has all your time been spent around the Capital City area?

A: You mean, all my life or . . .?

Q: All your working time with ABC Railroad.

A: Yes.

Q: Sam, October 29th of this year you sustained an injury, is that correct?

A: Yes.

Q: About what time of the day was that?

A: Well, I'd say it was around approximately 10:30 at night.

Q: And where were you working at that time?

A: Two track. Known as a rip track.

Q: O.K. and that is underneath the shed?

A: Under the shed, central repair.

Q: O.K., and who was working with you?

A: Chris Robertson.

Q: Was there anybody else around or working with you?

A: Just, just the two of us.

Q: Just the two of you. What were you all doing?

A: We were attempting to, I was trying to use a prybar to get a ladder stile lined up, the hole in the ladder stile lined up with the bracket, so Robertson could put a huck bolt in it. The prybar slipped and the pressure of it, it just kind of threw me off my feet and I spun when I fell down. I hit just more or less landed in a sit down position. Hit the back of my neck on the way down, and knocked my helmet off.

Q: Now the ladder stile, that's s-t-i-l-e?

A: Yes.

Q: And that's basically one side of the ladder?

A: Yes.

Q: O.K., and a stile would be a vertical piece that holds your steps?

A: Holds the steps, yes.

Q: What end of the car were you working on, do you remember?

A: I'm not sure but I believe it was the A end of the car.

Q: Now, that's a gondola car . . .

A: Yes, that's right.

Q: That you were working on? Do you know, was that an ABC car?

A: Yes.

Q: Are there ladders on both sides of both ends on the gons?

A: I believe there are ladders on all four corners of that car.

Q: Where was the ladder you were working on?

A: It would have been AR, the AR end.

Q: AR. And that's the A end, right side?

A: Yes.

Q: Was this car in, Sam, because of the ladder?

A: No, this car had been damaged in a derailment. Been wrecked.

Q: O.K., so it was just generally in because it had been torn up, and your job was to fix whatever was broken?

A: Yes.

Q: Now, the ladder is held onto the car with huck bolts, did you tell me?

A: Yes.

Q: All right. And I assume that you were trying to bring the ladder straight up against the car, and Robertson would have put a huck through it then?

A: Yes, I was trying to line the holes up in the stile with the bracket on the car.

Q: Were there up and down movements needed to line it up, or could you just pull it straight in?

A: Just pull it straight in.

Q: What kind of bar were you using?

A: I think they call it a prybar. Big long heavy bar.

Q: Got any idea how long, how heavy?

A: I'd say it's probably at least five feet long, and probably weighs about fifty pounds.

Q: Is there a hook on the end of that one?

A: No, it's just got a little curve on the end of it.

Q: Just a one end kind?

A: One end just kind of turns up. They used to use them a lot to roll cars down there. They had a little flange underneath them. You could put them underneath wheels and move the cars.

Q: And to fix the stile you'd hook that little flange or whatever underneath the ladder somewhere and . . .

A: Well I had it hooked under the ladder and I was pushing on the other end of it.

Q: Was there anything wrong with the bar? Was it . . .

A: No, the bar wasn't defective.

Q: O.K. Would you say this was normal procedure for doing that? Any other way you could have done it that would have been better?

A: Well we could probably hook the pole jack up to the, you know, find a place to hook it which would have been kind of hard to do, but we do it a lot. It's done a lot.

Q: Depends on how hard they are? To move and stuff? But usually if it can be done this way, it's done this way and then if it's . . .

A: It's a lot faster to use the prybar.

Q: All right. Now you're standing on the floor? How was your footing? Pretty good?

A: I don't remember.

Q: Nothing to trip you up or anything?

A: Well we had hoses and everything lying around there. We had a lead torch and hoses of all kinds lying on the ground. We just let them lie there because, you know, we couldn't help it.

Q: But in that area is the concrete pretty much level with the top of the rail? Or is there . . .

A: No, the rail sits up above the concrete.

Q: Does it?

A: Yes.

Q: So would you have probably had one foot outside the rail and one foot inside?

A: I probably did.

Q: Do you recall?

A: I might have possibly had both feet inside the rail.

Q: And you were pushing straight out, you weren't pulling back on the bar were you?

A: I was pushing straight in to the end of the bar. I take that back. I believe I was outside of the rail. In fact the pressure I was using, I was trying to get the outside stile lined up.

Q: O.K., then that would have been the one right at the corner of the car basically?

A: Yes, the corner of the car.

Q: O.K., and you were pushing on it? What happened, the bar slipped out?

A: The bar slipped out. I must not have had a good grip on it. I had the flange of the bar in there pushing on it, and it slipped out. And when it slipped then my feet went out from underneath me and I had quite a bit of force on it, you know. Quite a bit of spring in that metal.

Q: O.K., now . . .

A: I dropped the bar; it fell on me but I don't know . . .

Q: O.K., now, when the bar slipped I assume you lost your balance going forward type of thing?

A: Well I don't know exactly how it happened but by the time I got turned around I was pointed away from the car and I hit my neck, the back of my neck on a pin lifter and I was facing it when I started out. But I completely spun around before I fell. And then I fell down and I hit my head on a pin lifter, the uncoupling device, and knocked my helmet off. Then I went on down and went under the pin lifter and hit the ground and the rail.

Q: O.K., so you must have been turning or something as you fell?

A: Well, probably when the bar slipped it caused me to turn because of the position I was standing in.

Q: O.K., now you say you dropped the bar; where did that strike you?

A: I don't even remember whether the bar hit me or not. It hit the rail I know, but I don't know whether it might have hit me.

Q: O.K., now you hit the back of your neck on the pin lifter?

A: Yes.

Q: O.K., and that would have been where, maybe two inches above the collar approximately?

A: No, probably farther than that. It was up in here.

Q: Even higher on the back of the head?

A: Yes

Q: So you were actually hit on the back of the head, and not really on the neck?

A: Well, it's hard for me to tell the difference exactly.

Q: What else did you hurt Sam?

A: Well I had some back pain too. I still have some pain in my shoulder. Now I don't know if that was from the sudden hitting of it and jerking my neck, maybe a whiplash or whatever, but I still have some pain in my shoulder blade too.

Q: Did you strike any other part of your body when you fell, that you can recall?

A: Just my back when I hit the ground, that's all I know.

Q: You hit your back on the ground?

A: Yes, I hit the rail or something. I hit it on something, I don't know.

Q: So basically you're having pain in your back, your neck and your . . .

A: I'm having pain in my leg and my back because my right side was sore, near the shoulder blade area.

Q: And that's around on the shoulder right there? Were you able to get up under your own power then?

A: Got up under my own power.

Q: O.K., you finished working that day then?

A: I kept working that day, but went home early. We weren't that busy, and I was hurting.

Q: Were you able to get the ladder, the huck bolt in the ladder? Did you go ahead and finish that?

A: Yes, Robertson finally got it in there.

Q: Did you go back and use the bar again?

A: No, Robertson used the pole jack on it.

Q: He went and got a pole jack then, and set it up to pull the stile in?

A: Yes.

Q: Did Robertson make any comment to you?

A: No, I don't think that he said a thing. You understand, Robertson and I are not the best of friends? We very seldom speak. The only time we speak is when we have to. -----. Really, this goes back quite a ways, so no sense in discussing that.

Q: That'll be fine. Now did you go to the doctor right away?

A: No, if I don't feel better, I'm supposed to see Dr. Fran Smith on November 26.

Q: Now, Sam, we have a record of another occurrence in February, 2005. You want to tell me about that?

A: That's when I was using a car puller to pull cars out on two track. This is one of these lifter car pullers they use to pull a whole string of cars.

Q: O.K., it's got a big long cable to it, is that it? And you were pulling the cable out to hook on to the car?

A: Yes.

Q: And what track was that on?

A: It's on two track two. Between two and three track.

Q: O.K., and that's pulling north or south?

A: Well that's to pull the car south. Pull the cable north.

Q: So you were pulling it north to hook up? How far north did you have to pull it?

A: Approximately six or seven car lengths, maybe eight.

Q: Would you have had to pull it to the center avenue?

A: Oh no, not near that far.

Q: All right, and while you were pulling it you felt the pain in your shoulder?

A: Yes.

Q: Were you able to go ahead and get it pulled out then and hook it up to the car?

A: Yes, I eventually got it all pulled out.

Q: And you were doing that without assistance?

A: Yes.

Q: O.K., Sam, how did that shoulder feel before October 29?

A: I still had pain every once in awhile, but mostly it felt fine.

Q: The pain you're feeling, you feel is more from the incident on October the 29th?

A: Oh, definitely, I don't think that there's any fault or anything with the 2005 deal.

Q: Sam, I believe that's all I've got. Are you aware this is being recorded?

A: Yes.

Q: And is that done with your permission?

A: Yes.

Q: And have all of the answers been true and correct to the best of your knowledge?

A: Yes.

Q: O.K., and would you state your name for me again please?

A: Sam Pardon.

Q: O.K., thank you.

STATEMENT OF CHRIS ROBERTSON

I am a carman employed by ABC Railroad Company for 10 years.

On October 29, 2012, I was working the night shift with Sam Pardon. We were fixing damaged rail cars at the central repair track in Capital City.

At about 10:30, Sam Pardon and I were working on a damaged ABC gondola. We were fixing a ladder on one end of the car.

Sam was working with a prybar to try to set one damaged stile in position for rebolting. I was looking at our repair checklist for the evening.

I heard a yell. When I looked up, Sam was sitting on the railroad tracks. He was holding the back of his neck, and rubbing his right shoulder. The prybar was on the ground a couple of feet away from Sam. He was clearly hurting from the grimace on his face.

Sam got up slowly and sat down on the steps of a nearby rail car. I asked if he needed a doctor. He said no.

I finished the work on the gondola ladder by myself. Since we weren't too busy that night, Sam quit early and went home.

As I recall, the overhead lights at the repair track were on and working. I don't remember any slippery spots in that area. Sam and I both were wearing work gloves and helmets. We did have tools around in the area. I don't remember if there were any where Sam was working.

There was a come-along nearby. This is a tool with a chain and a hatchet handle, and you loop two pieces together to use it. We could have selected that instead of the prybar to try to straighten out the ladder stile if we wanted. Sam asked me for the prybar to use right before the accident.

Dated: November 6, 2012

Chris Robertson

Chris Robertson

Brine & Associates
Professional Investigations
200 Exchange Building
Capital City, Moot 00011

May 25, 2016

Will Call
ABC Railroad Company
ABC Building
Capital City, Moot 00011

Re: Sam Pardon

Dear Will:

Enclosed please find the reports regarding Sam Pardon.

We were able to obtain surveillance of Pardon playing golf. He played golf for at least three hours in 95 degree heat while he walked the entire course and carried his bag on his shoulder. It should be noted that this golf course is 6491 yards long or 3.7 miles.

If you have any questions regarding this case, please give me a call.

Sincerely,

Jan Walsh
Operations Manager

Case No. 175-01
Re: Sam Pardon
Friday, May 20, 2016

Surveillance:
Page One of Two

6:30 a.m.	Investigator Alex Jones established a surveillance position overlooking the Pardon residence at 25 Money Lane in Capital City, Moot. It was determined that Pardon was home at this time.
7:44 a.m.	Pardon was observed walking from his residence into the garage located behind the residence.
	Pardon entered the garage and then entered a blue and tan pick-up truck, Moot license plate number 123JKL. Pardon then departed the area driving the vehicle. His actions inside the garage were not visible due to poor light conditions.
7:50 a.m.	Pardon arrived at the Hardee's Restaurant parking lot located on Wilson Street in Capital City. Pardon exited the vehicle in one fluid motion and walked across the parking lot and entered the restaurant. Pardon displayed no visible signs of pain or discomfort exiting the vehicle.
8:20 a.m.	Pardon exited the restaurant, walked to his vehicle and entered it without any apparent difficulty.
8:58 a.m.	Pardon arrived at the "Capital City Golf Club" located off of Highway 100 South.
9:15 a.m.	For the next two hours, Pardon was observed golfing. He golfed the back nine, including holes 10 through 18.

Case No. 175-01
Re: Sam Pardon
Friday, May 20,
2016

Surveillance:
Page Two of Two

While hitting the golf ball, Pardon bent forward slightly at the waist and twisted his upper torso. Then, in one rapid fluid motion twisted and straightened up as he struck the ball with the club, ending up with his upper torso twisted to the left. This action was repeated numerous times on each "hole." Pardon showed no signs of pain or discomfort during any of his swings. Pardon walked the entire nine holes, a total of approximately 3350 yards or approximately 2 miles. He pulled his golf clubs behind him on a golf cart, using his right arm, as he walked the golf course.

During the entire period of observation, Pardon did not display any visible signs of pain or discomfort while hitting the ball.

11:10 a.m. After departing the 18th green, Pardon walked to his vehicle and was observed lifting his golf bag with clubs into the rear of his pick-up truck. He lifted the clubs with his right hand and swung them into the truck. He then entered his vehicle without apparent difficulty, and departed the area.

11:30 a.m. Pardon arrived at his residence. His actions exiting the vehicle and entering the residence were not observable.

12:00 Noon No further activity was observed, and the surveillance was discontinued.

Case No. 175-01
Re: Sam Pardon
Saturday, May 21, 2016

Surveillance:
Page One of Two

7:00 a.m.	Investigator Alex Jones established a surveillance position in the vicinity of the Pardon residence located at 25 Money Lane, Capital City, Moot. Pardon's Ford pick-up truck was not observed in the area and it was determined that he was not at home at this time.
7:30 a.m.	A spot check was made at the Capital City Golf Club. Pardon's truck was observed parked in the parking lot. It was determined that he was inside the clubhouse at this time.
9:02 a.m.	Pardon and three unidentified W/M's were observed on the first tee of the golf course. It was determined that Pardon was involved in an eighteen hole golf outing. Pardon then proceeded to play eighteen holes of golf. It should be noted that Pardon traveled the course in a motorized golf cart. Various surveillance positions were established at the golf course. During this time, Pardon was observed bending forward at the waist at an approximate 90 degree angle and picking up his golf ball with his right hand.
1:13 p.m.	Pardon was observed driving his golf cart from the 18th green to his truck. He placed his clubs in the bed of the truck without apparent difficulty and returned to the clubhouse.
2:49 p.m.	Pardon was observed departing the area driving his truck.

Case No. 175-01
Re: Sam Pardon
Saturday, May 21, 2016

Surveillance:
Page Two of Two

3:08 p.m.	Pardon arrived at his residence. He parked his truck in the garage and entered the residence where his actions were not observable.
4:00 p.m.	No further activity was observed and the surveillance was discontinued.

Case No. 175-01
Re: Sam Pardon
Sunday, May 22, 2016

Surveillance:
Page One of Two

7:30 a.m.	Investigator Alex Jones established a surveillance position in the vicinity of the Pardon residence located at 25 Money Lane, Capital City, Moot It was determined that Pardon was at home at this time.
8:17 a.m.	Pardon was observed departing the area driving his Ford truck.
8:40 a.m.	Pardon arrived at the Capital City Golf Club. He exited his vehicle in one fluid motion and walked to the clubhouse where his actions were not observable.
10:21 a.m.	Pardon was observed on the first tee of the golf course with three unidentified W/Ms. Pardon was observed sitting in a motorized golf cart. It was determined that he was playing golf this day. Several surveillance positions were established at the golf course. During this time Pardon's actions included golf swings and picking up his golf clubs and balls off the ground. Pardon performed each of these tasks repeatedly and at no time did he show any signs of pain, discomfort or restricted movement.
12:29 p.m.	Pardon was observed driving his golf cart from the ninth green to his truck. He placed his clubs in the bed of the truck with his right arm, and walked to the clubhouse where his actions were not observable.

Case No. 175-01
Re: Sam Pardon
Sunday, May 22, 2016

Surveillance:
Page Two of Two

1:38 p.m.	Pardon was observed departing the area driving his truck.
2:00 p.m.	Pardon arrived at his residence. He parked his truck in the garage and entered the residence where his actions were not observable.
3:00 p.m.	No further activity was observed and the surveillance was discontinued.

REHABILITATION SERVICES

25 Center Street
Capital City, Moot 00011

July 12, 2016

Wilma Watson
500 First Bank Building
Capital City, Moot 00011

Re: Sam Pardon/ABC Railroad

VOCATIONAL REHABILITATION EVALUATION

This case was referred to RS on 6-09-16, and we were asked to evaluate Sam Pardon's ability to perform his regular work with the railroad and to determine what other vocational alternatives might be available for him in his area of residence.

Background information, including Dr. Fran Smith's findings were provided for my review. My findings regarding employability are as follows:

PHYSICAL/MEDICAL UPDATE

Dr. Smith indicates that Pardon should limit himself to 15 pounds of any force exertion, with his right arm. Dr. Smith also feels that Pardon would need a job which would enable him to move around as needed, and to rest as needed. Furthermore, Dr. Smith states that the job would need to let Pardon take his prescribed medicine.

I have also seen a surveillance report, apparently made on several different days, describing Pardon getting in and out of a truck and playing golf. Even though I am not a physician, I would say as a rehabilitation counselor that Pardon seems to be capable of a great deal more physical capacity than described by Dr. Smith.

FAMILY AND SOCIAL BACKGROUND

Pardon and his spouse live in Capital City, Moot. They have one daughter residing at home.

Pardon's spouse is employed by Moot Regional Telephone Company in Capital City.

In addition to her income, they are living on Pardon's railroad retirement disability of around $1300.00 per month, I understand.

EDUCATIONAL BACKGROUND

I understand Pardon graduated from high school in Capital City.

I gather he has learned a great deal about welding in on-the-job training with ABC Railroad. In addition, he has functioned as a union rep. Functioning as a rep would give him added experience in a managerial or supervisory type role, and certainly would give him experience in handling and dealing with financial matters.

VOCATIONAL HISTORY

Pardon has worked for the ABC Railroad since 1980.

While working for the railroad he worked his way up from carman apprentice to journeyman carman-welder. This is the position he has worked through his entire career.

By performing his past work, Pardon has proven that he is capable of applying principles of a rational system to solve practical problems and deal with a variety of concrete variables in situations where only limited standardization exists. He is able to interpret a variety of instructions, furnished in written, oral, diagrammatic, or schedule form.

His mathematics ability should enable him to make arithmetic calculations, involving fractions, decimals, and percentages. His language development should enable him to interpret technical manuals, as well as drawings and specifications, such as lay-outs or blueprints. He would also be capable of filing, posting, and mailing such materials as forms, checks, receipts, and bills.

His past work performance has shown that he has at least average intelligence, verbal ability, numerical ability, spatial perception, motor coordination, and manual dexterity.

He has shown in past work activities that he can enjoy working in both a non-social atmosphere with things and machines, as well as dealing with people influencing them, etc. He is used to being objectively evaluated and to meeting precise standards.

FUNCTIONAL RESTRICTIONS/LIMITATATIONS

If one assumes Dr. Smith's limitations, then Pardon would be capable of light work, which did not require force of more than 15 pounds with his right arm, which would allow some alternate sitting and standing through the work day.

On the other hand, if the surveillance report is accurate, then Pardon may very well have virtually no limitations.

SUMMARY AND CONCLUSION

Even with Dr. Smith's limitations there are a number of jobs that Pardon could perform. I have proceeded to do a labor market survey in Pardon's residential area, to determine appropriate job openings that exist now, have existed in the recent past or are likely to exist in the future. These will be explained in more detail, in the attached labor market survey.

I would be more than happy to assist Pardon in locating one of these positions, if he has an interest in them. Also, if you can arrange for us to meet with Pardon, and to provide rehabilitation services, we are ready to begin so, at once.

If you have any questions, please feel free to give me a call.

Sincerely,

Bert Martin
Bert Martin, M.Ed., C.R.C.
Rehabilitation Counselor

LABOR MARKET SURVEY

This labor market survey was conducted on 7/06/16 and 7/07/16. Calls were made in the Capital City area. Thirty calls were made, and 3 openings were located. This is very encouraging to find almost a 10% positive response, just to calls made within a 2-day period.

We checked for a number of different positions. These include: driver for a limo service, driver for shipping services, tech position within small engine repair companies, applicator for lawn maintenance, store manager/trainee position (convenience stores), hotel/motel clerk/manager-trainee, department store clerk, hospital non-professional position, service station attendant, taxi cab driver, delivery service driver, screen printing trainee, and fast food management trainee. We also checked on openings for production/assembly workers and machine operators. We tried to find salaries out from all employers, and were successful with a number of these.

Listed below are the three **positive** responses from various employers contacted.

LIMO DRIVER
Super Duper Limo
212 S. University
Capital City, Moot

This is a limo company listed within the Capital City phone book. Contact with the manager indicated that they had a position open for a driver. The salary was $8.00/hr. plus tips. They would like for our person to come in to apply for the position if he is interested.

SMALL ENGINE REPAIR

Roger's Engine Service
501 N. Poplar
Capital City, Moot

They would be interested in training a new employee. Work is bench work, and is year-round. A person could do this with lifting limitations and even with a bad back, especially if modifications were provided (lifting device, stool). Salary is paid on a commission basis, 50% of the work completed. This would average out to pay around $250-350 per week, and sometimes more with Spring and Summer overtime work.

LAWN MAINTENANCE

The Green Lawn Shop
Rt. 15 West
Capital City, Moot

Asked that we have an interested person apply in late July for a lawn care tech position. They expect more than one full-time opening at that time, which would be permanent for good employees. Salary is $6.00/ph to start.

CURRICULUM VITAE

NAME: Fran Smith, M.D.

ADDRESS: 2300 Central Medical Building, Capital City, Moot

DATE OF BIRTH: November 3, 1952

PLACE OF BIRTH: Sacramento, California

MARITAL STATUS: Married – Three Children

SELECTIVE SERVICE CLASSIFICATION: 1-D (U.S. Army Reserve)

PRE-MED EDUCATION: Moot State University
Capital City, Moot
B.S. – 1974

MEDICAL EDUCATION: Moot State University School of Medicine
Capital City, Moot
M.D. – 1978

PROFESSIONAL TRAINING:

Internship
Type: Surgical
General Hospital
Capital City, Moot
July 1978 through June 1979

Residencies
Type: Internal Medicine
General Hospital
Capital City, Moot
June 1979 through June 1981

Type: Neurology
Moot State University Hospital
Capital City, Moot
July 1981 through June 1984

ACADEMIC APPOINTMENTS:

Ass't Clinical Prof. Of Neurology – Moot State University
School of Medicine
July 1984 –

MILITARY SERVICE:

Captain
U.S. Army Reserve and
National Guard of Moot
1980 - Present

POST GRADUATE EDUCATION:

National Academy of Neurology Meeting
Saint Louis, Missouri
April, 1981

Neuroradiology Course
West Nordeast University, Boston, Massachusetts
September, 1981

Course on Neurobiology of Aging
Hampton University, New York City, New York
June, 1984

HONORS AND AWARDS:

Awarded full tuition scholarship at Moot State University School of Medicine for year July, 1976 – June, 1977

SOCIETY AFFILIATIONS:

The Moot Academy of Sciences
National Academy of Neurology (Assoc.)
Capital City Medical Society

HOSPITAL APPOINTMENTS:

General Hospital, Capital City
Moot State University Hospital, Capital City

STATE LICENSES AND CERTIFICATES:

Moot State
Moot Board of Medical Examiners
Certified Moot Board of Neurology, 1984
Certificate No. 11673

PUBLICATIONS:

Smith, Fran. "Neurology for Beginners," Moot Neurology Journal, Vol. 6, No. 2 (September, 2006).

SMITH NEUROLOGICAL INSTITUTE, LTD.
2300 Central Medical Building
Capital City, Moot 00011

January 20, 2014

Re: Sam Pardon

To Whom It May Concern:

Sam Pardon initially came under my care on November 26, 2012, for neurological care as a result of injuries sustained at work on about October 29, 2012. His difficulties involve neck pain, headaches, right arm and shoulder weakness and right-sided numbness.

On his examination both initially and on follow-up examinations on February 13, 2013, May 22, 2013 and October 16, 2013, there continued to be prominent cervical spasm, limited neck motion, weakness in the right arm involving the triceps, wrist extensors, thenar and hypthenar muscles as well as decreased sensation in the right C7 and C8 dermatomal distribution and decrease in the right triceps reflex.

Testing was done including EMG studies which confirm the right C7 and C8 radiculopathies. Skull x-rays showed no recent traumatic abnormality but there was evidence of some arthritic changes in the neck.

At my direction the patient was placed on medication for muscle spasm and pain. He has had limited activity with a force limitation of fifteen pounds.

The patient's condition has remained relatively stable with some modification of spasm related to decreased activity. At this time, however, he continues to have the radicular abnormalities with sensory loss, motor deficit and reflex changes as noted above.

At my direction the patient will continue to remain on a limited force exertion of fifteen pounds with changing posture and resting as needed and using heat and massage as necessary.

At this time the patient's condition still remains quite guarded and full prognosis cannot be forthcoming at this time.

Should any other information be required, please feel free to contact me.

Sincerely yours,

Fran Smith, M.D.

SMITH NEUROLOGICAL INSTITUTE, LTD.
2300 Central Medical Building
Capital City, Moot 00011

February 26, 2016

Re: Sam Pardon

To Whom It May Concern:

Sam Pardon returned today for follow-up. His condition remains relatively unchanged. He continues to have persistent neck pain to a moderate severe degree, although at times it is even worse. He notes this with almost any slight increase in activity or even changes in the weather. He denied any other changes and stated that his arm problems persist.

On examination today he continues to have the moderate neck spasm and limited neck motion. Forward motion of the neck was limited to sixty degrees, extension to twenty degrees and lateral flexion to thirty degrees bilaterally.

He still evidences the arm weakness which was defined earlier especially in the triceps, wrist extensors, thenar and hypothenar muscles on the right. Sensation was decreased in the right C7 and C8 distributions and there continued to be marked depression of the right triceps reflex which was now almost absent.

Accordingly, it is now my opinion that Sam Pardon's condition will remain permanent.

Sincerely yours,

Fran Smith, M.D.

Patient Name: Pardon, Sam
Physician: Dr. Fran Smith

Date of EMG: 2-13-13
Room Number: OP

An EMG was performed in both arms and shoulders using a concentric coaxial needle. Muscles tested included the right and left supraspinatus, right and left deltoid, right and left biceps, right and left triceps, right and left wrist extensors, right and left thenar and right and left hypothenar muscles. There was no abnormal insertional activity. At rest there were rare fasciculations and fibrillations appreciated. On minimal and maximal effort however denervation was evident in the right triceps, right wrist extensor, right thenar and right hypothenar muscles.

NERVE	DISTAL LATENCY	NERVE CONDUCTION VELOCITY
Right median	4.2	47
Right ulnar	2.8	50
Left median	4.0	55
Left ulnar	2.7	54

<u>IMPRESSION:</u>
Therefore with the findings above this patient evidences right C7 and C8 radiculopathies.

____
Fran Smith, M.D.

GENERAL HOSPITAL
CAPITAL CITY, MOOT

NAME:	Sam Pardon	X-RAY NO. 99-2004
ADDRESS:	25 Money Lane, Capital City, Moot	ROOM: OP DELIVERED TO CHART: 2-13-13
DOCTOR:	Dr. Fran Smith	AGE: 53 SEX: Male
DATE OF EXAM:	2-13-13	
DICTATED ON:	2-13-13	

Cervical Spine:
Examination failed to demonstrate evidence of fracture or subluxation. There is mild narrowing of the disc space between C7 and C6 and anterior degenerative osteophytes are noted adjacent to this disc level. There is very mild narrowing of intervertebral foramina corresponding to the right and left 5th cervical nerve roots. The foramina corresponding to the 7th and 8th nerve roots appear normal bilaterally.

Conclusion:
1. Minimal degenerative changes as described above.

Skull Series:
There is no evidence of fracture or bony destruction. The sella turcica appears normal. The paranasal sinuses are well aerated. There is a thin curvilinear rim of calcification directly superior to the anterior clinoid processes on the lateral views. I do not appreciate this density distinctly on the Townes or AP views. This may represent some calcification within the supraclinoid internal carotid artery.

Summary:
1. No fracture evidence.

Radiologist: *Alice Langer, M.D.*

IN THE UNITED STATES DISTRICT COURT
FOR THE DISTRICT OF MOOT

SAM PARDON, Civ. No. 15-2345

Plaintiff,

v.

ABC RAILROAD COMPANY
a corporation,

Defendant.

RULE 26(a)(2)(B) REPORT OF PAT DOLLAR

Pat Dollar has been retained by Jones and McGreedy to assist with its representation of Plaintiff in the above matter. I have estimated the present value of Sam Pardon's economic losses range from $311,324 to $513,047.

OPINIONS TO BE EXPRESSED AND
THE BASIS AND REASONS THEREFOR

BACKGROUND

Sam Pardon was employed by the ABC Railroad Company as carman until October 29, 2012, when Sam Pardon sustained severe and permanent injuries. These injuries caused the loss of compensation and benefits from Pardon's usual gainful occupation and costs of medical care.

Pardon was born on December 14, 1959 and was 52 years old at the time of his injuries. Pardon has a high school diploma and attended college. Pardon was employed by ABC Railroad from 1980 until the injury, working up from carman apprentice to journeyman carman-welder. Pardon's 2011 schedule W-2 reported earnings of $46,986. Pardon was expected to retire in December 2024, at age 65.

ANALYSIS

I have estimated Pardon's past economic losses (from October 29, 2012 to May 2, 2016) and the present value of future economic losses (from May 3, 2016 through retirement at age 65 on December 14, 2024 and, alternatively through retirement at age 62 on December 14, 2021).

Past Compensation Losses

I have assumed Pardon would have continued to be compensated $46,986 per year from October 29, 2012 to May 2, 2016, based on his 2011 annual compensation, to total $164,457 summarized as follows:

Annual Compensation	Years	Lost Earnings
$46,986	3.5	$164,451

Future Compensation Losses

I have estimated the present value of Pardon's future compensation losses (from May 3, 2016 through retirement at age 65 on December 14, 2024 and, alternatively through retirement at age 62 on December 14, 2021), based on his 2011 annual compensation.

Pardon's annual compensation would increase each year and Pardon's future economic losses would be discounted to present value to reflect investment interest. To reflect annual compensation increases and investment interest, a net real discount rate of 1.5 percent (interest would exceed compensation increases) has been used to calculate the present value of future economic losses.

Future compensation has been calculated based on Pardon having complete inability to work until retirement and, alternatively based on Pardon having the ability to earn $16,000 annually ($8.00 x 2,000 annual hours) until retirement. Future compensation is summarized as follows:

	Inability to Work		Minimal Work	
	Retirement At 62	Retirement At 65	Retirement At 62	Retirement At 65
Years	5.6	8.6	5.6	8.6
Annual Compensation	$ 46,986	46,986	30,986	30,986
Total	$ 263,122	404,080	173,522	266,480
Net Real Discount Rate	1.5%	1.5%	1.5%	1.5%
Present Value	$ 222,713	348,596	146,873	229,890

Fringe Benefit Losses

In accordance with the ABC Railroad Company labor contract, Pardon's fringe benefits (including retirement, supplemental pension, health plan and dental plan) have continued. Therefore, no economic loss related to lost fringe benefits has been estimated.

Total Economic Losses

Pardon's total economic losses are estimated as follows:

	Inability to Work		Minimal Work	
	Retirement At 62	Retirement At 65	Retirement At 62	Retirement At 65
Past Losses	$ 164,451	164,451	164,451	164,451
Future Losses	$ 222,713	348,596	146,873	229,890
Total Economic Loss	$ 387,164	513,047	311,324	394,341

The present value of Sam Pardon's economic losses range from $311,324 to $513,047.

My analysis is ongoing and may include consideration of additional documents and information.

DATA OR OTHER INFORMATION CONSIDERED

The data or other information considered to date include my educational and professional experience and reading and analysis of certain documents and information, including, but not limited to:

- Complaint;
- Answer;
- Plaintiff's Answers to Interrogatories;
- 2011 W-2 for Sam Pardon;
- Summary of Fringe Benefits Paid by Carrier; and
- Economic Report of the President, February 2015-Changes in Consumer Price Indexes 1946-2014, Table B-10, and Bond Yields and Interest Rates, 1945-2014, Table B-17.

QUALIFICATIONS

Pat Dollar

I am Associate Dean and Professor of Economics at Moot State University. I have authored and coauthored publications and scholarly material, including regarding labor markets and economic damages. I am a member of the National Economics Association and the National Statistical Association. I received Bachelor of Science (Business Administration) and Ph.D. (Economics) degrees from Moot State University. (A copy of my resume is attached hereto.)

I have been engaged in providing professional economic services in the area of litigation support. I have been retained to assist representation of plaintiffs and defendants in a number of litigated matters, and have offered testimony in five court proceedings. I have conducted engagements regarding personal injury losses and employment.

LISTING OF PUBLICATIONS AUTHORED IN THE PRECEDING TEN YEARS

Monographs published by the Moot Regional Industrial Development Corporation, 2004-2006

"Regional Labor Market: A Skill and Availability Survey," June, 2006 (with Dr. Sam Burns)

"Labor Market Survey for Prosper and Farwell Counties, State of Moot," October, 2006

"Computer Technology in the Capital City Region," February, 2007 (with Boswell White)

"Opportunities for Tourism in the Capital City Region," October, 2007 (with Barbara Whiting)

"Winning Settlements," paper presented at the National Trial Lawyers Association Meeting in San Diego, 2009

"Economic Damages," paper presented at the Moot Trial Lawyers Association meeting, 2010

"The Use of an Economist in Personal Injury Litigation," paper presented at the Moot State Bar Association meeting, 2011

Editor – Journal of Litigation Economics, 2010-Present

LISTING OF CASES IN WHICH TRIAL OR DEPOSITION TESTIMONY WAS PROVIDED WITHIN THE PRECEDING FOUR YEARS

Trial Testimony

In Re: The Marriage of Mrs. Regretful and Mr. Regretful

Able Carpenter v. Capital Construction Company

L.Z. Worker v. Termination Corporation

Deposition Testimony

Able Carpenter v. Capital Construction Company

I. Washurt v. Capital City Insurance Company

Nomo Ney v. Moot Investment Advisors

Victor Timothy v. Automobile Insurers of Moot

Local 1234 v. Moot Publishing Company

In Re: The Marriage of Mr. Courageous and Mrs. Courageous

A.L. Pawn, and all others similarly situated, v. Product Manufacturing, Inc.

Contented Cattle Company v. Farmer Pharmaceutical, Inc.

Medtech Circuits, Inc. v. Techmed Circuits, Inc.

COMPENSATION

Pat Dollar is compensated for professional fees and expenses based on standard rates. The current standard rate for Pat Dollar is $180 per hour.

May 3, 2016

Pat Dollar

Pat Dollar

RESUME

Pat Dollar
116 Cash Street
Capital City, Moot

Date of Birth: December 10, 1969 Married – 3 children
Place of Birth: New York, New York

EDUCATION

Moot State University, Capital City, Moot 1987-1991, B.S. (Business Administration)
Moot State University, Capital City, Moot 1991-2004, Ph.D. (Economics)

ACADEMIC HONORS: Economic Honorary Fraternity, Moot State University
Graduated with Final Honors, Moot State University

EMPLOYMENT

1994-1999	Economist	National Reserve Bank of Capital City
1999-2004	Associate Professor	Moot State University
2004-2006	Director of Econ. Research	Regional Industrial Development Corporation
2006-2008	President	Dollar & Associates
2008-2013	Professor	Moot State University
2013-Present	Associate Dean and Professor	Moot State University, School of Business Administration

PUBLICATIONS AND OTHER SCHOLARLY MATERIALS:

Monographs published by the Moot Regional Industrial Development Corporation, 2004-2006

"Regional Labor Market: A Skill and Availability Survey," June, 2006 (with Dr. Sam Burns)

"Labor Market Survey for Prosper and Farwell Counties, State of Moot," October, 2006

"Computer Technology in the Capital City Region," February, 2007 (with Boswell White).

"Opportunities for Tourism in the Capital City Region," October, 2007 (with Barbara Whiting).

"Winning Settlements," paper presented at the National Trial Lawyers Association Meeting in San Diego, 2009.

"Economic Damages," paper presented at the Moot Trial Lawyers Association meeting, 2010.

"The Use of an Economist in Personal Injury Litigation," paper presented at the Moot State Bar Association meeting, 2011.

Editor – Journal of Litigation Economics, 2010-Present.

COMMUNITY PARTICIPATION

Member of the nonpartisan Ad Hoc Committee appointed by Governor Shake N. Notstirred to establish the Department of Community Affairs, 2007-2009.

Member of the Capital City Planning and Zoning Commission, 2013.

PROFESSIONAL ASSOCIATIONS

National Economics Association

National Statistical Association (Capital City Chapter)

PRIOR TESTIMONY

Approximately 35 depositions and five trial appearances. A list of these is available on request.

The following breakdown represents the estimated value of so-called fringe benefits accruing to operating employees with annual wages of $43,800* or more during the calendar year of 2011.

PAID BY THE CARRIER	PER YEAR	# DURING MONTH
Railroad Retirement	$ 7,954.95	$ 662.91
Supplemental Pension	533.28	44.44
Unemployment	905.00	75.42
Health Plan	3,077.64	256.47
Health Plan (Retiree)	157.20	13.10
Dental Plan	177.36	14.78
1/ Vacations	3,008.00	250.67
1/ Holidays	1,569.52	130.79
2/ Other	662.55	55.21
	$ 18,045.50	$ 1,503.79
RAILROAD RETIREMENT TAX PAID BY EMPLOYEE	4,521.45	376.78

*$43,800 represents the minimum annual wage subject to a maximum railroad retirement tax.

#Per year total divided on a pro-rata basis per calendar month and rounded to the next nearest one cent equivalent.

1/ Taxable to employee as income.

2/ Includes jury duty pay, bereavement pay, AD&D and liability insurance, along with other miscellaneous items attributable to fringe benefits.

RE: SAM PARDON VS. ABC RAILROAD

U.S. DISTRICT COURT, CAUSE NO. 15-2345

Name:	Sam Pardon
Race:	Caucasian
Sex:	Male
Date of Birth:	12/14/59
Education:	High school (couple of months of college)
Employer:	ABC Railroad
Union:	Union Rep
Position:	Carman/welder
Location:	Capital City
Date/Service:	1980 to 2012
Date/Injury:	10/29/12
Nature/Injury:	Neck, back, shoulder, right arm
Employment of Spouse:	Telephone operator (Laid-off?)

APPENDIX D

Case Record 3:
Big River Consulting Company v. Jamie Anderson

UNITED STATES DISTRICT COURT
DISTRICT OF MINNESOTA

BIG RIVER CONSULTING COMPANY,
a corporation

Plaintiff,

v.

JAMIE ANDERSEN,

Defendant.

Civ. No. 00X-1357

COMPLAINT

For its Complaint against Jamie Andersen (Andersen), Big River Consulting Company (Big River) alleges as follows:

JURISDICTION

1. Big River Consulting Company is incorporated in the state of Minnesota, and has its principal place of business in Capital City, Minnesota.

2. Jamie Andersen is a citizen of South Moot, and resides in Main Ville, South Moot, across the river from Capital City.

3. This court has jurisdiction over this action under 28 U.S.C. § 1332, in that the action involves citizens of different states, and there is more than $75,000 in controversy, exclusive of interest and costs.

PARTIES

4. Big River is a financial consulting firm. Its account managers give business and financial advice to clients located in the Capital City and Main Ville greater metropolitan area.

5. Andersen is a former senior account manager for Big River. Andersen worked for Big River for just under two years.

FACTUAL BACKGROUND

6. Big River is one of the premier business and financial consulting firms in Capital City. It gives advice to individuals, and to small and large businesses, regarding such matters as financial planning, strategic vision, marketing strategy, technical support, and forecasting.

7. Approximately twenty-one months ago, on or about January 7, 200X, Big River hired Andersen as a senior account manager. Andersen came highly recommended by several of Big River's clients, who had worked with

Andersen on selected projects while he was a consultant at one of Big River's competitors, Acme Consulting.

8. Andersen's particular expertise is in information systems. While at Acme Consulting, and then while at Big River, Andersen's primary role with clients was to analyze their technology and information management systems and to make recommendations regarding the structure and development of those systems to improve business efficiency.

9. Upon joining Big River, Andersen signed the following covenant not to compete. "While at Big River, and for a period of one year after leaving Big River, [Andersen] will not provide consulting services for any individuals or businesses located within the greater metropolitan area of Capital City, Minnesota, and Main Ville, South Moot."

10. If Andersen had not signed this covenant, Big River would not have employed Andersen, and would not have given Andersen access to Big River clients and data regarding the information systems needs of those clients.

11. Over the last twenty-one months, Andersen had access (a) to the client list of Big River, (b) to the checklists that Big River uses to assess the technology needs of clients seeking information systems advice, (c) to the details of the answers on those checklists relating to specific clients, and (d) to Big

River's internal brainstorming workshops regarding the future direction of information systems developments in the United States.

12. The Big River client list, checklists, checklist answers, and workshops are proprietary and confidential, and are so maintained.

13. Approximately one week ago, Andersen abruptly and without advance notice left Big River and returned to Acme Consulting, where Andersen will have the title of executive account manager.

14. On information and belief, Andersen's duties at Acme will require Andersen to provide consulting services for individuals and businesses located within the greater metropolitan area of Capital City and Main Ville.

15. On information and belief, Andersen's duties at Acme are now requiring Andersen and will continue to require Andersen to violate the covenant not to compete with Big River.

16. Big River has met all conditions precedent to the enforcement of Andersen's covenant not to compete.

CAUSE OF ACTION

17. Andersen is now or is about to be in breach of Andersen's covenant not to compete.

18. Unless the covenant not to compete is enforced, Big River will suffer immediate and irreparable harm, the value of which will exceed $75,000 exclusive of interest and costs.

WHEREFORE, Big River requests that:

1. Andersen's covenant not to compete be enforced;
2. A preliminary and then permanent injunction be entered precluding Andersen from rendering prohibited consulting services.
3. Such other and further relief be granted as the Court may deem just and equitable.

Dated: November 1, 20XX+1

JONES AND McGREEDY

By John McGreedy

John J. McGreedy
Atty No. 1234
123 Central Street, Suite 15
Capital City, MN 55000
Telephone (612) 987-6543
mcgreedy@jonesmc.com

ATTORNEYS FOR PLAINTIFF

UNITED STATES DISTRICT COURT
DISTRICT OF MINNESOTA

BIG RIVER CONSULTING COMPANY, a corporation	Civ. No. 00X-1357
Plaintiff,	**ANSWER**
v.	
JAMIE ANDERSEN,	
Defendant.	

For Andersen's Answer to the Complaint of Plaintiff Big River Consulting Co., Defendant Jamie Andersen alleges as follows:

1. Defendant admits the allegations of paragraphs 1 through 3 of the Complaint.

2. Defendant admits the allegations of paragraphs 4 and 5 of the Complaint.

3. Defendant admits the allegations of paragraphs 6 through 16 of the Complaint, except that Defendant denies the allegations of paragraphs 9, 10, 12, 14, 15, and 16, and alleges (a) that Big River initially employed Defendant without the covenant not to compete, (b) that the information in Defendant's

possession is not proprietary or confidential, and (c) that Defendant's duties for Acme Consulting do not involve direct contact with clients but rather supervision of Acme's managers for the next eighteen months.

4. Defendant denies the allegations of paragraphs 17 and 18 of the Complaint.

AFFIRMATIVE AND OTHER DEFENSES

5. Plaintiff's Complaint fails to state a claim upon which relief may be granted.

6. Plaintiff's Complaint is barred by lack of consideration for the covenant not to compete.

7. Plaintiff's Complaint is barred in whole or in part by the unreasonableness of the covenant that Plaintiff seeks to enforce.

8. Plaintiff's request for injunctive relief should be denied because Plaintiff has not suffered and is not about to suffer immediate and irreparable harm from any conduct of Defendant.

WHEREFORE, Defendant Andersen requests that:

1. Plaintiff's Complaint be dismissed with prejudice;

2. The Defendant be granted such relief as the Court may deem just and equitable including reimbursement for costs.

Dated: November 8, 20XX+1

MCDONALD AND SWIFT

By *Wilma Rogers*

Wilma Rogers
Atty No. 5432
432 First Street
Main Ville, South Moot 00123
Telephone (555) 321-6543
wrogers@mcswift.com

ATTORNEYS FOR DEFENDANT

Big River Consulting Company

January 10, 20XX

Jamie Anderson
123 Little Lane
Main Ville, South Moot 00123

Re: Employment at Big River Consulting Co.

Dear Jamie:

We are very pleased to have you join us at Big River. The following are the terms of your employment:

1. You will join us as a senior account manager.
2. You have represented that your employment with us does not violate any terms and conditions of your current employment with Acme Consulting. Based on that representation, we will indemnify you against any claims to the contrary by Acme.
3. You will be paid a salary of $85,000 per year, with the usual and customary benefits given to all employees of Big River. The salary will be payable twice per calendar month, on the 15th and the last day of the month.
4. Your starting date with Big River will be January 15. You will receive a signing bonus equivalent to that portion of $85,000 which you would have been paid in normal salary on January 15 had you joined us effective January 1. (The signing bonus does not include any benefits, which begin accruing effective your actual starting date of January 15.)
5. You will use your best efforts to assist clients of Big River with their technology and information systems needs.
6. Your employment is terminable at will by either you or by Big River at any time for any reason, upon two weeks notice.

If these terms accurately reflect our agreement, please sign this letter in the space indicated. You may keep the duplicate copy. Please return the signed original to me for our file. We look forward to having you on the team.

Sincerely,

Erin Williams

Erin Williams
Senior Vice President for Human Resources

Agreed:

Jamie Andersen

ADDENDUM TO EMPLOYMENT LETTER

While at Big River, and for a period of one year after leaving Big River, I will not provide consulting services for any individuals or businesses located within the greater metropolitan area of Capital City, Minnesota, and Main Ville, South Moot.

Jamie Andersen

STATE OF MINNESOTA)
)
COUNTY OF KEY)

I, Erin Williams, after being first duly sworn, depose and state as follows:

1. I am a Senior Vice President of Big River Consulting Company. I am responsible for the human resources function.
2. I negotiated the terms of the employment agreement with Jamie Andersen.
3. The agreement was entered into by me and Jamie Andersen on January 10, 200X.
4. Attached to the agreement was an ADDENDUM, containing the terms of our standard covenant-not-to-compete provision with our account managers.
5. We insist that all account managers sign such a covenant. Otherwise, they cannot receive access to our list of clients, information checklists and answers, and training and brain storming workshops.
6. Jamie Andersen had access to all of the items identified in paragraph 5, while employed at Big River.
7. Our client list is maintained in a password-protected database at Big River. Only personnel at the senior account manager level or above have access to the particular database that contains the list. The list is in a separate file which itself requires a separate password for entry. The file is marked "confidential and proprietary." It is a read-only file, which cannot be downloaded or printed except by the President, the Vice President of Marketing, and the Vice President of Information Systems.
8. Our information checklists are proprietary. We maintain checklists in a variety of subject categories as to each Big River client. The checklist in a specific subject category, such as the category for technology and information system needs, is available for a specific client to the account manager or senior account manager working on that category for that client. Whenever an account manager or senior account manager accesses the checklist online in a particular category for a particular client, there is a prompt on the computer requiring the manager to click that he or she

"agrees" to maintain the checklist and answers as proprietary and confidential. Otherwise, the data is not revealed to the manager.

9. Our training and brainstorming workshops for our personnel are proprietary. We discuss specific clients at these workshops. We forecast likely developments in various areas such as technology and information systems in an effort to predict future client needs. Attendance is taken at the workshops, and the attendance sheet which participants must sign contains a reminder of the confidential nature of the discussions.

10. Over the last ten years, two account managers have been terminated for discussing information from our workshops outside of the office with friends who worked at other consulting firms in town. One manager received a formal reprimand for identifying a number of our clients over drinks with an acquaintance at an industry function in Chicago.

11. If Jamie Andersen uses our confidential information at Acme Consulting, Big River will suffer immediate and irreparable harm.

Erin Williams

Erin Williams

Signed and sworn to before
me this 1st day of November, 20XX + 1

Gloria Jones

Notary Public
My commission expires:
February, 20XX + 2

Statement of Jamie Andersen

1. I am currently an executive account manager for Acme Consulting.

2. I was previously a senior account manager for Big River Consulting.

3. I am knowledgeable in the field of technology and information systems.

4. I have a bachelor's degree in business administration from Moot State University. I am working on an M.B.A. degree from the Moot State University Graduate School of Business, with a concentration in information systems management.

5. On January 10, 200X, I signed an employment agreement with Big River. After Erin Williams and I signed the letter agreement in Williams' office, and shook hands, Williams suddenly said as I was leaving the office, "Wait! I didn't give you the covenant not to compete form." Williams left the office and returned a few moments later with a one paragraph page labeled Addendum. Williams had me sign it, and then stapled the Addendum to the Big River copy of the employment agreement. It is not attached to the copy I took with me that I have found in my employment folder at home.

6. Everybody in the business in Capital City and Main Ville has a pretty good idea who Big River's clients are, just as everybody also has a good idea who Acme's clients are. The clients are not especially bashful about playing off one consulting firm against another for better deals on packages of service. When Big River hired me, it already knew about me from Big River clients who happened to be using me for information systems work for which they contracted at the time with Acme. They all figure that if they use different consulting firms for discrete projects, no firm will get complacent with the business.

7. Big River has various information checklists to use with clients to maintain data and to assist account managers in their consulting duties. These forms resemble the kinds of checklists that I have used at Acme. I actually modified the standard forms at both Acme and Big River to suit my own needs.

8. Big River conducts training and brain storming workshops. Mostly these are discussions of industry literature, predicting trends. Acme conducts similar workshops.

9. My current job as executive account manager at Acme is to help train in new account managers who have not completed M.B.A. degrees. My job will not for the foreseeable future involve direct contact with clients.

Dated: November 8, 20XX + 1

Jamie Andersen

Statement of Sloane Fitzgerald

1. I am the administrative assistant to Erin Williams at Big River Consulting.

2. I have been the administrative assistant for the last four years.

3. I was at Big River Consulting on January 10, 200X. My desk is located immediately outside the office of Williams.

4. At approximately 3:30 p.m. on the afternoon of January 10, Williams rushed out of the office and asked me to type our standard covenant not to compete clause that goes with our employment letters. Williams asked me to type the covenant in addendum form to attach to a letter I had prepared earlier in the afternoon for signature by Jamie Andersen.

5. The covenant is in a standard format on our word processing system. As a result, I was able to prepare the addendum in less than five minutes. After preparing the document, I knocked on the door to Williams' office. When Williams opened the door, I handed over the addendum and then went back to my desk.

6. Within a couple of minutes, Jamie Andersen, who had been meeting with Williams since about 3:00, emerged. Andersen and Williams shook hands and said goodbye.

7. Andersen began work with Big River a few days later.

Dated: November 14, 20XX + 1

Sloane Fitzgerald